LOOKING BACK

… the studying of this important moment in our history and its ongoing repercussions moves beyond being the preserve of academics and takes in artists, singers, food enthusiasts, writers, graphic novelists and so many others. Thus, in many ways, this volume too is evidence of the opening up, or…the democratizing, of the study of Partition. But unlike some recent work that tends to focus on Partition histories and stories shorn of their politics, and… historical contexts, this one thankfully retains that anchoring…. the overlaps and resonances between the different contributions are often so rich that they invite an exploration of the parallels—and their contradictions, complexities and nuances—in their own right.

—Urvashi Butalia, *LiveMint*

… a multi-genre and cross-subcontinental volume on Partition. It includes some brilliant short stories translated from Bangla, hitherto unavailable to the English-speaking world.

—Neeti Nair, *The Print*

The anthology…assembles diverse genres from Punjab, West Pakistan and East Pakistan…restoring a sense of plurality and responsibility to reactions to the events.

—Kuldip Singh Dhir, *The Tribune*

… a rich and varied account of a traumatic past. It addresses the experiences of Dalits and Adivasis and explores the ways in which third- and fourth-generation descendants of Partition refugees are developing new ways to tell stories that have been repressed.

—*The Caravan*

LOOKING BACK
The 1947 Partition of India, 70 Years On

Edited by

Rakhshanda Jalil, Tarun K. Saint
and
Debjani Sengupta

Orient BlackSwan

LOOKING BACK: THE 1947 PARTITION OF INDIA, 70 YEARS ON

ORIENT BLACKSWAN PRIVATE LIMITED

Registered Office
3-6-752 Himayatnagar, Hyderabad 500 029, Telangana, India
e-mail: centraloffice@orientblackswan.com

Other Offices
Bengaluru, Bhopal, Chennai, Guwahati, Hyderabad, Jaipur, Kolkata,
Lucknow, Mumbai, New Delhi, Noida, Patna, Visakhapatnam

029628

ISBN 978-93-5287-620-4

Typeset in
Adobe Jenson Pro 11.5/13.4
by Le Studio Graphique, Gurgaon 122 001

Printed in India at
Glorious Printers, Delhi

Published by
Orient Blackswan Private Limited
3-6-752, Himayatnagar, Hyderabad 500 029, Telangana, India
e-mail: info@orientblackswan.com

Contents

POETRY

DRAMA

INTERVIEW

Publisher's Acknowledgements

For granting permission to reproduce copyrighted material used in this volume, the publisher would like to thank the following individuals and organisations.

Usha Chaudhary, for the photograph [4.1] in 'A Sepia-Toned Past: A Photo Album Travels from Maghiana to Delhi' by Aanchal Malhotra.

Pramilla Chhabra and Om Prakash, for the still [7.1] from the film *Chacha Zindabad* (1959) in 'Undoing Partition: Flight of Utopian Fantasies across Borders' by Ravikant.

Debjani Sengupta, for her essay 'Scripting an Enclave's Marginal Lives: Selina Hossain's *Bhumi O Kusum*,' partly based on material from *The Partition of Bengal: Fragile Borders and New Identities*, by Debjani Sengupta (New Delhi: Cambridge University Press, 2016).

Unum Babar, for images [11.1–11.4] of four of her artworks from the series *Thin Cities*, 2013 and 2016, in 'Spaced: Notes Towards An Exhibition' by Salima Hashmi.

Zarina Hashmi, for the image [11.5] of her artwork *Letters from Home*, 2004, in 'Spaced: Notes Towards An Exhibition' by Salima Hashmi.

Salima Hashmi, daughter of Faiz Ahmad Faiz and Alys Faiz, for the letter [11.6] written by Faiz to his wife Alys in 'Spaced: Notes Towards An Exhibition' by Salima Hashmi.

Maya Mirchandani, for the photograph [12.1] in 'Inheriting the Hamam-Dasta and Its Stories' by Maya Mirchandani.

Phool Kumar Bhatia, for permission to translate an extract of *Chhata Dariya* by Fikr Taunsvi (pen name of Ram Lal Bhatia), included here as 'The Sixth River: A Journal from the Time of the Partition of India.'

Narayani Gupta, for 'Dandakaranya: Some Memories in Words' by Saibal Kumar Gupta.

Manas Ray, for 'Orality of Silence.'

Inder Dev Singh Musafir, for permission to translate Gurmukh Singh Musafir's story 'Allah Wale,' included here as 'People of God.'

Meera Sikri, for permission to translate her story 'Saccho Sach,' included here as 'Nothing but the Truth.'

Syed Muhammad Ashraf, for permission to translate his story 'Doosra Kinara,' included here as 'The Other Shore.'

Zakia Mashhadi, for her story 'Sada-e Baazgasht,' included here as 'The Echo.'

Joya Mitra, for her story 'Ghrinar Samasya,' included here as 'A Face to Hate.'

Sunanda Bhattacharya, for permission to translate her story 'Borderer Golpo,' included here as 'Border Stories.'

Jhumur Pandey, for permission to translate her story 'Mokkhodasundorir Haranoprapti,' included here as 'Lost and Found.'

Selina Hossain, for permission to translate her story 'Meyetir Bari Phera,' included here as 'The Return.'

Anil Acharya and Sandipan Sen of *Anustup*, for permission to translate the poem 'Mrityur Por: Kuri Bochhor' by Birendra Chattopadhyay, included here as 'After Death: Twenty Years.'

Sankha Ghosh, for his poem 'Punorbashon,' included here as 'Rehabilitation.'

Javed Akhtar, for permission to translate his poem 'Fasaad ke Baad,' included here as 'After the Riot.'

The University Press Limited, for 'Six Shared Seasons' by Kaiser Haq. This poem first appeared as 'Grishma, Barsha' in *Published in the Streets of Dhaka: Collected Poems*, by Kaiser Haq (Dhaka, 2012), pp. 12–13. Published here with permission from The University Press Limited, Dhaka, Bangladesh.

Sukrita Paul Kumar, for the poem 'Cold Storage,' previously published in *Without Margins*, by Sukrita Paul Kumar (New Delhi: Bibliophile South Asia, with Promilla & Co. Publishers, 2005).

Asghar Wajahat, for permission to translate two scenes from his play *Jis Lahore Nai Dekhya O Jamyai Nai*, included here as *Those Who Haven't Seen Lahore Haven't Lived*.

Acknowledgements

This book would not have come into being without the interest and perseverance of my co-editors Rakhshanda Jalil and Tarun Saint. I owe them deep thanks for their interest in my work and for taking me on board. Genealogies are always messy, and the origins of this book slightly more so: I was tired with other work commitments and I must confess I did not look forward to the making of an anthology, given that they have cheerless careers, and their motives are always suspect. Nevertheless, the enthusiasm of my fellow editors drew me into this project and I must say my initial resistance turned to interest when I encountered Rakhshanda's passionate arguments and Tarun's measured yet off-beat rejoinders. I recall with fondness the hours we spent arguing, cajoling, decrying and conversing on the ethics of what we were doing, its political goal, its literary merits, and I must assert that the pieces from Bangla, that I was responsible for, owed much of their sustenance to these conversations and arguments.

My deepest thanks go to four extraordinary writers who gave me their incredible stories without a murmur about remuneration or public acknowledgement. The works of Selina Hossain, Joya Mitra, Sunanda Bhattacharya and Jhumur Pandey have somehow remained outside the metropolitan English reading public sphere, and I am happy that they can now be accessible to a set of readers other than their own. They deserve wider critical attention for their deeply contemporary understanding of the subcontinent's history.

Once again, grateful thanks to Manas Ray who has supported my forays into writing with his unstinting generosity in sharing his own work. He gave permission for his piece in an instant, with a kindness that is his very own.

To the poet Sankha Ghosh, I can only say with humility, 'Dhonnyobad.' The poet's painstaking and profound engagement with my translation of his poem made me realise anew why the act of translation is neither for the fainthearted nor the dispassionate. My thanks go to Semanti Ghosh for facilitating these conversations with the poet.

My gratitude to Anil Acharya and Sandipan Sen of *Anustup* for allowing me to translate a poem by Birendra Chattopadhyay, whose work is of great assonance in today's India.

I am grateful to Narayani Gupta for allowing me permission to include an article by Saibal Kumar Gupta, whose brilliant analysis of Dandakaranya's refugee rehabilitation programme has been somewhat consigned to oblivion.

My thanks go to Anwesha Sengupta for her article on the charismatic Dalit leader, Jogen Mandal. Her essay is a valuable addition to this volume.

Many thanks to Farha Noor and Nabina Das for co-translating two stories with me.

Thanks to Shubha Chakraborty and Nandita Basu of the Department of Modern Indian Languages, Delhi University, for their timely help.

Thanks are due to Moutushi Mukherjee of Orient BlackSwan for believing in this book and for her gentle promptings when we lagged behind our schedule. We would especially like to thank the editor, Moyna Mazumdar, for her meticulous work on the volume, which has improved immeasurably as a result.

Acknowledgements are not complete unless I thank Ritwik Saha, my reluctant Muse, whose singular wit and furious encounters with my world keep it alive.

I dedicate this volume to the unknown and often faceless human beings who struggle daily in many corners of this varied land to keep alive the ethics of compassion and conversation and who reject binaries and borders in the face of the hatred and bigotry that have been bequeathed to us through the Partition and well beyond it.

Debjani Sengupta

Debjani's note speaks for us all, except insofar as matters of detail are concerned. We add our deepest thanks to all our contributors and many unsung collaborators for their warm and generous support over the year as we sought to bring this project to a successful conclusion with a specified time-frame in mind. Many thanks to Dr. Vijay Kumar for setting up a panel discussion at the Hyderabad Literary Festival, 2017, on 'Looking Back, But Not in Anger: India's Partition@70,' which enabled an airing of some of the ideas presented here.

A special note of appreciation for the anonymous reviewer at Orient BlackSwan, whose insightful comments helped make this a better book. The faults and omissions remain our responsibility, of course.

New Delhi 2017   Rakhshanda Jalil
                                                 Tarun K. Saint

Introduction

I n the three introductory essays that follow, each of the editors offers comments on the selection of material that came their way, seeking to contextualise the new work—prose, fiction, poetry—and translations presented in this volume.

Partition and Abraded Memory

Looking back, but not in anger? Is it really possible after seventy years to engage in a dispassionate stocktaking of the events of 1947–48? For years, selective historicisation and holes in collective memory on both sides of the border (often as a result of nationalist pressures to forge the memory of the past in predictable ways) have impeded the process of coming to terms with the pain and suffering experienced by many during the Partition and after. Nonetheless, over the last twenty years, especially after the fiftieth anniversary of Independence-Partition, an incremental resistance has taken shape to the censorship and sidelining of the collective violence that took place at the time. Extreme and reciprocal forms of violence ruptured the flow of time, leaving personal and collective memory abraded, as well as etiolated historical narratives. The last twenty years have witnessed the publication of important new historical studies, as well as a series of stories, memoirs and writings in other genres; a second generation perspective was often brought to bear by anthologists.[1] The recovery of lost stories of abducted women by feminist scholars as well as stories from regions earlier neglected such as Bengal and Sindh further extended our understanding of the dark side of 1947.[2] More recently, in early 2016 Salima

Hashmi curated a remarkable exhibition of artwork from both sides of the border in Delhi, 'This Night-Bitten Dawn', taking its title from Faiz's well-known poem 'Subh-e-Azadi' about the disillusionment faced by many in the wake of 1947. This exhibition of installations, paintings (including important work by artist Somnath Hore) and sculptures sought to reinterpret and mediate the differential meanings of the event across the border and over time, circumventing received history as well as reimagining and refashioning the historical narrative, perhaps achieving a cathartic effect in the process (as the curator hoped).[3]

Furthermore, it is remarkable to note that in the past few years, two major initiatives to memorialise the Partition of India have been running concurrently. One is the Berkeley based Partition archives project (initiated by Guneeta Singh Bhalla), which has 'citizen historians' recording interviews with partition survivors from across the world, and making these available on the internet through their website.[4] The other is the effort to construct a Partition-themed museum, helmed by Kishwar Desai, which opened with an exhibition in Amritsar on 24 October 2016.[5] This project also includes the collection of memorabilia, photographs and interviews. So we have the ironic prospect of Partition survivors, whose stories have been largely consigned to oblivion or silenced for seventy years, now actually having a choice about where their memories may be archived. Is this an instance of an excess of memory, a kind of hyperamnesia manifesting itself after years of selective amnesia with respect to the event? It may seem that the questions about the mode of archiving and the ethical dimensions of institutionalised remembrance are less important than filling in the gaps in the official/nationalist narrative and the preservation of stories brought together by such 'citizen historians.' However, the perils (and for that matter, political ramifications) of unearthing traumatic memories much after the event apart, it is evident that there is now a greater space for and receptivity toward such recollections of the moment of 1947 and the major changes wrought by Partition. This logically extends to the domains of fiction, film, art history and also the memoir, in which an imaginative engagement with the ghosts of Partition has begun afresh as new anthologies of stories/poems/graphic narratives/memoirs/plays/films on the event bear out.[6]

For there is no doubt that seventy years after the event, 1947's afterlife, the 'long partition' described by Vazira Zamindar, (indicating that the event was not terminal but rather continues to unfold) bedevils the subcontinent.[7] The Partition of India has had cascading and traumatic effects that still manifest themselves in everyday life for survivors and their families, for the divided Muslim families on both sides of the border (especially once the permit system and passports were introduced), besides the more obvious instances of recrudescence of forms of polarisation and mutual animosity in the public domain (self-evidently between India and Pakistan, but also at times vis-a-vis Bangladesh). As is well known, the decision to partition India was taken by the British Labour government headed by Clement Attlee and acceded to by the Congress and the Muslim League after much bitter recrimination. This was the culmination of the campaign for a separate Muslim state by Jinnah's party, the Muslim League, especially after the Lahore resolution of 1940, also in the face of growing exclusivist and majoritarian tendencies and the rise of Hindu nationalist groups (and despite countervailing efforts to establish a basis for unity by 'nationalist Muslims' and non-communal formations). Whether or not this proposal was a bargaining counter (as Ayesha Jalal argued),[8] or was actively propped up by a utopian vision of an Islamic state—a new Medina—articulated by a section of the Deobandi *ulama* (in Dhulipala's recent study),[9] eventually the Congress leadership accepted this proposal (including, after much heart-searching, Gandhi) and the Boundary Commission was appointed, headed by the British lawyer Cyril Radcliffe, with representatives from different communities.[10] The actual award, after much internecine wrangling, was declared on 16 August 1947, *after* the Independence of the two newly born nation states, Pakistan and India on 14th and 15th August, respectively. The uncertainty accompanying the decision, especially in the border areas, and the accelerated pace at which the implementation took place led to widespread panic and heightened the extant hostility that had resulted from years of communal propaganda and 'othering.' Near genocidal violence and mutual devastation never seen before swept north and eastern India, with women and children being targeted in unprecedented acts of barbarity.[11] At least one million lost their lives, ten to fifteen million were displaced from their homes, and between 75,000 and one lakh women were abducted.

There were of course instances of resistance to the tendency to demonise the 'other'; some Hindus, Sikhs and Muslims did risk their lives to help friends and even strangers, while a few strove to act as witnesses to the descent into depravity at this time. Oases of relative calm did exist. An important case in point is that of Malerkotla, a princely state in East Punjab ruled by Nawab Ali Khan, where many Muslims found succour and sanctuary, even as the rest of Punjab went up in flames (as Talbot and Singh demonstrate).[12] However, as the documentary film *Rabba Hun Kee Kariye* [Thus Departed Our Neighbours] by Ajay Bhardwaj shows, border areas of this state (surrounded by the princely state of Ludhiana on all sides) became a killing zone where mobs waited to attack those from the minority group seeking to find such refuge.[13] Ironically, in east Punjab it was the Dalit followers of Sufi pirs who kept up syncretic practices of worship and performance (integral to the notion of Punjabiyat) at melas like that of Baba Ratan, as Ajay Bhardwaj brings to the fore in the documentary (also part of his Punjab trilogy), *Milange Baba Ratan De Mele Te* [We Shall Meet at the Festival of Baba Ratan].[14] Since the veritable ethnic cleansing of 1947, there have been sporadic attempts in Indian Punjab to rebuild mosques destroyed during the violence of that time, in a gesture of *prayaschit* or atonement. However, justifications of Partition-era violence abound. The artistic/literary response to this ethical catastrophe was muted to begin with. In the years after the appearance of Satish Gujral's representations of the suffering of Partition refugees, the publication of Sa'adat Hasan Manto's dark, ironic short stories and the making of Ritwik Ghatak's remarkable films, a steady series of novels, short stories, memoirs, artistic engagements, cinematic treatments (fictional and documentary) and some, though admittedly fewer, plays and poems have contributed to a deepening understanding of the causes as well as after-effects of the Partition, in societal, cultural and psychological terms.[15]

The idea for this new anthology first came to the fore at the launch of a book on the Partition of Bengal by Debjani Sengupta. Somehow the sense was that the Partition discourse remained one-sided and skewed till this day. The need to bring together writing emanating from the two major theatres of the Partition—the West and the East was perceptible. So I suggested to my co-editors the possibility of a multi-genre and cross-subcontinental volume that would also encompass neglected genres like poetry, drama and the memoir from all three countries worst affected by the events of 1947—India, Pakistan, and Bangladesh. We invited responses, including critical essays and studies from scholars of Partition literature and films and its history; the focus was on trying to assemble material that might indicate a shift in perspective and offer new insights into the realities of Partition and its afterlife. The third and perhaps fourth generation point of view has come to the fore even as we begin to recognise the variegated and at times unpredictable extent of intergenerational transmission of memory.

Indeed, the Partition has even served as the backdrop to a recent (2013) play, *Drawing the Line* by British playwright Howard Brenton, which focuses on the experience of the Head of the Boundary Commission, the lawyer Cyril Radcliffe.[16] The play also features major political players in the domain of 'High Politics' (including Attlee, Lord Mountbatten, Edwina Mountbatten, Gandhi, Nehru, Jinnah and Liaquat Ali Khan) as well as, fleetingly, subaltern peasants from Punjab. While a detailed critical overview is not possible here, one may note the rather uncritical replaying of the scandalous story about India's last Viceroy, Mountbatten, speeding up the process of partition to get Edwina out of Nehru's clutches, as well as Brenton's attempt to revisit and, to an extent, counter the satirical portrait of Radcliffe painted in W. H. Auden's famous poem, 'Partition.'[17] Here, in contrast, Radcliffe appears as a well-intentioned figure caught up in historical forces he is unable to fathom. Indeed, at one point he even summons Krishna to his assistance as he seeks, like Arjuna in the *Gita*, to follow his conscience and do his duty. Brenton, who belongs to the 'angry' generation of British playwrights following the lead of John Osborne, is caustic and unsparing in his treatment of the major historical figures involved in the transfer of power, all of whom have chinks in their armour (especially Mountbatten). They emerge as versions of T. S. Eliot's 'hollow men,' faced with near-impossible existential and historic choices, and often resorting to opportunistic compromises.

In this volume, the essays have been grouped thematically as far as possible. I offer a few brief introductory remarks about the contributions that came my way. At the outset, we seek to reinvestigate the contours of the Partition debate, veering away from the predictable clichés of official historical accounts. Anil Nauriya opens with a reconsideration of the Cabinet Mission Plan, the supposedly last-ditch political plan to avert the prospect of division of the land, making critical reference to later sectarian readings of this moment in history. Sameer Thomas articulates a contemporary viewpoint in his personal account of coming to terms with 1947, crystallised in particular by a visit by students of Lahore University of Management Sciences to Delhi University, which highlighted key differences in the understanding/recollection of the significance of the event amongst young people from opposite sides of the border. Vishwajyoti Ghosh's graphic narrative *Lahore Reporting* provides an ironic personal take on the right wing chorus asking dissenting voices to go to Pakistan, following up on his earlier anthology of graphic narratives on the Partition.[18] Aanchal Malhotra's essay derives from her interest in devising a material history of the Partition and includes extensive reference to the story of a survivor, as gleaned in an interview, as well as photographs that enable childhood memories of Karachi to resurface. In their critical essay on selected instances from Ghosh's graphic anthology, Kajal Tehri and Asmat Jahan show how state-sponsored memory-history can be challenged in the diminutive genre of the graphic narrative. Margit Koves brings in an unusual perspective in her comparison of third-generation Hungarian narratives on the Holocaust and recent graphic narratives on the Partition, as instances of post-memory (in Marianne Hirsch's terms).[19]

In the essays that follow, we further expand our focus beyond the question of literary representation of Partition and its attendant historical trauma to the domains of film and music among others. Here non-textual and non-literary sources are foregrounded. Large-scale reciprocal violence during the period August 1947 to January 1948 left its imprint on syncretic forms of culture (the fabled Ganga-Jamuni tehzeeb) in unexpected and multifarious ways. Ravikant's essay on lesser-known films like *Chacha Zindabad* (1959) and *Mousiqar* (1962) shows how humour and laughter could become subversive strategies in the face of historical transformations of this scale and magnitude. Next, Vidya Rao brings in an insider's perspective as she examines the ways in which the seemingly universal language of music was affected by the displacements of the Partition, with specific focus on the Pakistani qawwali singer Fariduddin Ayaz and the Indian maestro of the same genre, Jafar Husain Badayuni.

In the section featuring literary responses and translations (eclectically chosen, with an emphasis on work previously unpublished in translation as well as with a contemporary resonance), we included some lesser-known stories, poems, plays and memoirs, whether from Urdu, Hindi, Punjabi, Bangla or English, without attempting a representative selection. Meera Sikri's Hindi short story 'Saccho Sach' [Nothing but the Truth] brings in an unorthodox feminist take in its portrayal of a Hindu widow who finds a new path in the midst of the upheaval of Partition. In 'Allah Wale' [People of God], a Punjabi short story by Gurmukh Singh Musafir, the question of survival (and retrieval) of some of the abducted women in the face of social stigma is reflected upon afresh. Sukrita Paul Kumar sensitively evokes temporal distortions experienced by Punjabi migrants in her poem 'Cold Storage' while Tarun K. Saint examines the symbolic ramifications of Radcliffe's exercise in mapmaking in 'Cyril's Map.' Dramatic representations of the historical trauma of Partition have been sadly, neglected in previous anthologies. Alok Bhalla and Nishat Zaidi's translation of the first two scenes of Asghar Wajahat's extremely popular and critically acclaimed Hindi play *Jis Lahore Nai Dekhya O Jamyai Nai* [Those Who Haven't Seen Lahore Haven't Lived] gives an ethically grounded glimpse of dilemmas faced by both migrants and, poignantly, by those who refused to migrate in the wake of Partition. The play memorably features, as a character, the poet Nasir Kazmi, whose conversation with Intizar Husain, included here, allows for intertextual resonance between this Hindi play and the work of the Urdu poet—another way of bridging Partition, perhaps. We thus seek to remedy lacunae in previous anthologies on Partition that have been genre or region specific, as remarks in the following sections by my fellow editors further elucidate. In the process, the hope is that a sense of plurality and ethical responsibility is restored to the remembrance of the Partition (even in its post-memorial forms).

Tarun K. Saint

Batwara vs. *Azadi*: The Urdu Experience

Critics such as Muhammad Umar Memon have argued that the generation of Urdu writers most affected by the Partition actually failed to view it in a historical and cultural context and that the bulk of the writing of this period gives the impression that the writers were *not* trying to describe reality, but avoiding it by focusing their attention on an 'intrinsically less significant element,' namely violence.[20] There is some merit in the argument that the Partition generation of writers, such as Sa'adat Hasan Manto, Krishan Chandar, Tajdar Samri, Ramanand Sagar, did indeed show a bloodcurdling predilection for focusing on the communal violence that spiraled out of the Partition. It is still not clear, seven decades later, whether they did so out of a conviction that the Partition was 'bad' or 'wrong' or from any real understanding of the long-term effects of the Partition. The latter seems unlikely given the knee-jerk quality that marked much of the writings of this period: the writers seemed to be *reacting* to events rather than analysing or introspecting. Perhaps the only meaningful reality for them was the present—not the past that was irrevocably changed, nor the uncertain future awaiting them—even though it contained violence, brutality, degradation and misery. In the present, there was hardly any Muslim family that was untouched by Partition and almost all the writers writing in Urdu—be they Hindu or Sikh writers from the Punjab or Muslim writers from Upper India as well as Hyderabad, Bhopal and parts of the Deccan—were affected by the trauma to some degree or the other. It was no wonder, then, that the violence seized their imagination and the memory of that violence cast a long shadow even when they made it safely across the border, or chose to stay back and dig their heels in against all odds.

The memory of this violence has never really faded. It finds expression every time there is a communal riot in India or whenever pluralism, multiculturalism and secularism come under the onslaught of majoritarian forces. The memory of that violence finds expression in Zakia Mashhadi's story 'The Echo.' A riot in the city brings back painful memories. But this time those who had steadfastly refused to leave their homes in the past pull up their roots and move; they don't have a new country to go to this time, so they move to a neighbourhood, a ghetto, no more than a slum, where others of their community huddle together.

Zakia Mashhadi and Syed Muhammad Ashraf are two major names among contemporary Urdu writers. Not having experienced Partition directly, they have no memories of their own. Nevertheless, they live in a world which is more polarised and more compartmentalised than it was in 1947, a world where the consequences of Partition continue to unspool in newer and ever more tragic ways. Just as communal riots and communal violence is the subject of Mashhadi's story, the ill-will and mistrust that emerged as a bloody after-birth from that painful parturition is the subject of Ashraf's jewel-like story.

Syed Muhammad Ashraf has mastered the ability to speak volumes through just a few broken sentences, allusions and stray thoughts. 'The Other Shore' examines the consequences of Partition, the 'othering' that is all the more painful because it is accepted unquestioningly by the young. Ashraf's story also tells us how those on the other side of the border view us and how that image is so different from the way we see ourselves.

Amena Nazli's 'Allah-ho Akbar' tells a story that is often lost in the jubilant cries of *azadi*. It tells us what happened to the *muhajirs* who crossed over to the Land of the Pure: how the *shervani*-clad Urdu-speaking strangers were mocked, and how the corruption and moral turpitude they thought they had left behind was very much around them in the new country. Finding a Punjabi story by a Pakistani writer would have been difficult were it not for helpful friends. Julien Columeau, a French aid worker who also writes in Urdu and Punjabi, brought this sharply etched extract from the novel by Anwar Ali to our notice; what is more, he also translated it from Punjabi into Urdu, thus allowing Farha Noor to access it and translate it into English for us. *Gwacchiyan Gallan* (translated here as 'Of Lost Stories') reinforces the idea that for those on the bottom of the socio-economic-political pyramid, the partition of the country made little difference. Those who were lepers before 1947 remained lepers after 1947 when they exchanged their Muslim names for Hindu ones and *became* Hindus after chanting 'Ram Chandarji di jay!'

For far too long the genre of reportage has escaped the scrutiny of literary historians or been dismissed as literary jetsam and flotsam with little or no lasting value. Fikr Taunsvi's 'The Sixth River: A Journal from the Time of the Partition of India' is important because it makes an eloquent appeal for the common men and women who suffered most grievously, especially in the fertile 'Land of Five Rivers' where a sixth river ran, the river of blood, during the *annus horribilis* that was 1947. If Taunsvi speaks with the passionate intensity and immediacy of one who lived through those 'sickening and soul-wearying' times and narrates them first-hand, Maya Mirchandani relives those very same days and weeks through the memories of her grandmother, memories that have been shared and retold till they have become as much a part of the granddaughter's sense of identity as the grandmother's. The stone mortar-and-pestle from the grandmother's home in Karachi finds a pride of place in the granddaughter's kitchen and becomes a repository for the 'flavours of home.' The other legacy, more tangible, is a part of her grandmother's wedding sari—the one with bunches of grapes in gold thread—that Maya wears on special occasions as a badge of courage, frayed though it is. The accompanying photograph of her grandmother as a young bride wearing the same sari when it was resplendent and new makes Maya's essay at once heart-warming and evocative.

Memories find their place in a conversation we are privileged to carry: a conversation between two of the finest modern Urdu writers, one a poet, the other a prose writer, one from the Punjab, the other from Uttar Pradesh, but both united in the common experience of being *muhajirs* in their new home. And it is of these early days that they reminisce as one lies critically ill and the other gently peels away layers of memory to probe the newness they had once felt, a newness that gradually got soiled. They had nothing, for they had carried nothing with them except memories of what they had left behind. Despite their penury, they had something then that they lost somewhere along the way: 'But there was something in this condition of not having anything, and it was a great will to live, as if we were the inheritors of this new country.'

Two poems and a photo essay also examine the consequences of Partition. Sahir Ludhianvi, poet and lyricist and active member of the Progressive Writers' movement, was among the first to speak up about the disillusionment that came very quickly in the wake of Independence. In a poem titled 'Twenty-sixth January,' he asks: 'What happened to all those beautiful dreams we had dreamt?' A generation younger and several decades later, Javed Akhtar, also a poet and lyricist and a close friend of Sahir Ludhianvi, paints a terrible picture: the smoke rising from a burnt house, the wasted shops, the deserted streets and the deep silence ask the same question. Salima Hashmi, the daughter of Faiz Ahmad Faiz and an art historian of repute, shares her 'Notes' from an exhibition she had curated in Delhi and two photographs, one by a Pakistani artist and the other by an Indian. Both are women and both explore the idea of a home, a home with four walls that can be a safe haven and also under siege, resilient but also fragile. Then there is the letter from Faiz to his English wife, Alys, written from Lahore in the months leading up to the Partition. His words are lined with empathy and clarity when after commenting, almost dispassionately, on the heat and the 'flare-up' that resulted in thirteen deaths, a 'fresh outbreak in Amritsar' which has caused the condition there to be 'utterly indescribable,' he writes:

> The Muslims have got their Pakistan, the Hindus and Sikhs their desired Punjab and Bengal, but I have yet to meet a person Muslim, Hindu or Sikh who feels enthusiastic about the future. I can't think of any country whose people felt so miserable on the eve of freedom and liberation. Both morally and politically the British could not have hoped for a greater triumph. It is all so depressing.

Slipped in-between the trivia of domesticity and snippets of news about friends and relatives, Faiz has bequeathed us—the literary historians looking for some meaning as we rake the ashes of the past and are helped in our endeavours by the custodians of these precious legacies, in this case the daughter of Alys and Faiz who chose to share this letter with us—a glimmer of insight: the joylessness of those early days which few have chosen to comment on. Shortly afterwards, Faiz would give us his requiem for this bloodied dawn of freedom when he would pen his 'Subah-e Azadi' and lament the 'night-bitten dawn.'

While *taqseem* or *batwara* [synonyms for partition] find as much place as *azadi* [freedom] in a great deal of Urdu prose, the Urdu poet seems to have largely fallen silent when it comes to addressing the events of 1947 with any degree of directness. Partition marked the coming of age of the Urdu short story writer; it all but numbed the Urdu poet. As Rakhshanda Jalil probes in her essay 'The Absent Presence: The Partition in Modern Urdu Poetry,' is the Urdu poet more squeamish than the Urdu short story writer? Or is it the very nature of poetry that clothes itself in the indirect, the oblique, the allusive? Is the difference in output merely due to the inherent difference between poetry and prose? While there can be no easy answers, Jalil's essay documents the disarray, disquiet and dismay that leavens much of Urdu poetry on the Partition.

Rakhshanda Jalil

The Partition of Bengal

> *Is it possible for a moment in present time to become so tumultuous, critical and uncertain, so as to break the linearity of time, deliver the past to the present and thrust the dwellers of the present back into the past?...This is perhaps about imagining simultaneity—us and the dead we admire in an essentially different time, the time that is yet to come.*
>
> —Azadeh Akhlaghi, booth text to her exhibition of photographs, 'By An Eyewitness,' New Delhi, October 2016.

The 1947 Partition of Bengal is significantly different in its aftermath in comparison with the sudden cataclysmic division in Punjab. The Bangla literature that is based on the experiences of Partition is therefore varied and multifarious in its responses to 1947, not simply as an event, but as a metaphor or a trauma or a site of articulation for people living through or resisting communal polarisation, migration, rehabilitation and resettlement in diverse geographical sites. Unlike the sudden and catastrophic violence that took place in Punjab, enunciated through the metaphors of madness, rape and murder, the Bengal region has seen a slower, although no less violent, effect of the vivisection. The literature of this Partition deserves sustained critical attention because it destabilises certain assumptions about 1947 just as it demarcates the way geographical areas, not always contiguous, become the theatres of recuperation, mythmaking and sustainability that give rise to different kinds of literary representations. In the region, literary imagination plays a vital role in a process of recovery for the inhabitants when writers, both Hindu and Muslim, undertake to remap the contours of the mutilated land in a bid to create a site of belonging, habitation and memory while changing the dynamics of fiction, particularly the form and content of the short story and the novel that have responded to 1947 in many heterogeneous ways.

The initial trauma of the Partition is now distant, but its afterlife and 'fantasy aspect' have taken over the subcontinent through a legacy of violence and bigotry. There are numerous studies that have looked at the history of conflict in India, but not enough has been written about the ways whole communities of people remembered and tried to resist in non-violent, elliptical ways the cataclysmic divisions and growth of sectarian hatred over the last few decades after the country was divided. So, seventy years on, the time has come again to look back at that legacy of violence through which the nations of India and Pakistan were born, not to repeat the orgiastic ferocity of their origins but to learn from it.

Even a cursory glance at Bengal's Partition literature lays bare how the vivisection has shaped and moulded the land and people, spanning caste, class, gender and religion as well as geographical sites through the processes of resettlement, migration, border crossings and rehabilitation. Literary narratives that deal with these wide-ranging issues try to reconstruct the lives of individuals and communities, marginal or elite, whose memories of trauma and displacement had dissociated them from their own life stories. Bangla Partition fiction captures the diffusion, through a great degree of self-consciousness, the *longue durée* of continuous migrations and counter-migrations that give refugee-hood a different complexity in Bengal. Reading these imaginative renderings of the diverse facets of Partition becomes therefore an act of creating a literary historiography that is alert to the silences of history, and to become aware of the ways in which individual and collective memories can be brought into play with each other by studying the micro-history of localities and particular communities. This literary account may not have all the facticity of history, but the questions of voice, temporality and lack of closure may say something about the ways in which the Partition is remembered by diverse kinds of people. In these narratives, the less visible and delayed effects of displacement and violence can be seen in the family and community spaces that these texts foreground. They give an added dimension to an event, often unspeakable, and lay bare the notion of how 'literature' transforms the actual into the apocryphal and the mythical.

The stories and non-fiction from Bangla have been chosen with some deliberation. Some of the writers are well-known, others are not. Their fictions represent a new crop of writings that have come out of 1947 in that they have either never been translated previously (and hence are quite unfamiliar to Partition scholars who do not read the language), or their understanding and engagement with 1947 do not follow the beaten track. Saibal Kumar Gupta is a case in point. Gupta was the chairman of the Dandakaranya Development Authority, one of the largest rehabilitation projects undertaken in independent India. His reminiscences, *Kichhu Smriti Kichhu Katha* is a text of great historical significance, particularly because of the essays on Dandakaranya that were first published in *The Economic Weekly* in the late 1960s. The author's *Preface* and sections of the first of his essays on Dandakaranya have been anthologised here in 'Dandakaranya: Some Memories in Words.'

Likewise, stories from Northeast India have hardly gained entry in Partition anthologies; yet 1947 had created significant geopolitical changes in the region whose effects are felt even today. Partition has redrawn the region's map, created new borderlands and borders and pauperised and displaced numerous communities, contributing to sectarian and communal tensions in the area. These complex contours are only now coming to light. The partitioning of Bengal in 1947 necessitated the migration of large groups of people of different ethnicity, religion, caste and class who crossed the borders at different times and at different places. The causes of such migration varied and were not always linked to communal riots or Partition-related violence. Sometimes there was very little migration as in the case of the four *thanas* of the erstwhile Sylhet district that remained in India, so the Hindus living there did not have to migrate. Some of the inhabitants of Sylhet had jobs in the Cachar district in Assam and in the Brahmaputra Valley from colonial times and decided to opt for jobs there after Partition. In the case of Tripura, Hindu refugees had come into the state after the Noakhali riots and were resettled in various areas under the patronage of the Hindu king who was a lover of Bengali art and culture; this was despite the local protests against immigrants which took an organised form right from 1947 when Seng-krak, the first anti-refugee and anti-Bengali political union was established.[21] Tripura shared 839 kilometres of border with East Pakistan and cross-border migrations were common, especially after natural calamities or rising food prices in East Bengal; but the Partition saw a substantial change in the state's demography with the Bangla-speaking refugees settling in the state permanently. In Assam, the landless Muslim peasants had emigrated from East Bengal as far back as 1901 when the British-run tea gardens had attracted labourers from Bihar, Uttar Pradesh and East Bengal; but the Partition brought many changes, and the significance of the question of 'settlers,' 'infiltrators' and 'original inhabitants,' a contentious issue in today's Assamese politics, is a legacy of 1947.

In the Northeast, the migration of people who came to India in 1947 took place in different directions: while one stream crossed into the Brahmaputra and Barak Valleys due to their proximity to East Bengal (rail transport had improved considerably between Eastern Bengal and Assam in the first decade of the nineteenth century), another went to Tripura, Mizoram and Manipur. Many stories from Assam and Tripura (where Bangla is spoken by a large number of people) have addressed issues like porous borders and displacement. Sunanda Bhattacharya (Tripura) and Jhumur Pandey (Assam) are two writers who illustrate through their stories how 1947 lives on in literary representations from this region.

A major aspect of Bengal's Partition was the movement of lower-caste refugees some years after 1947. The Namasudra peasants, mostly agriculturalists and small artisans, had remained in East Pakistan for some time, many believing that the vivisection was temporary and that the upper-caste landowners on whom they depended for work and subsistence would eventually return. Jogendra Nath Mandal, a popular Dalit leader from Barisal and close ally of the Muslim League, had stayed back in East Pakistan. Mandal's decision to stay back had a profound impact on the Namasudra population in East Pakistan. Anwesha Sengupta's essay traces the political trajectory of this charismatic leader, and this is a part of Bengal's post-Partition history that is not often talked about. Widespread food shortage in East Pakistan through 1949 and communal conflagrations in 1950 in Khulna and Bagerhat, however, created a sense of panic among the lower-caste Hindus. The *Amrita Bazar Patrika* (on 23 March 1950) announced:

> people from villages in districts like Dacca, Chittagong, Rajshahi, Mymensingh, Bogra and Rangpur say that large scale movement of Hindus have started. Cattle, stacked paddy and corn, plough and the land offer no more lure to them to keep to their village homes...village smiths, kavirajs, day-labourers, carpenters, namasudras, santhals—in fact every Hindu in Eastern Pakistan is trying to move out.

Many of the agriculturalists and artisans who came into West Bengal after 1950 and even later were systematically pushed out of the state into rehabilitation sites like Dandakaranya, the Andamans and elsewhere.

An unfinished business of the partition in the East has been the border enclaves between India and Bangladesh. In Bengal's Partition fictions, geography becomes deeply implicated in history and politics: the bio-geo-political implications of being a refugee or a minority in a land one no longer belongs to is fraught with issues of livelihood, homelessness and citizenship. The struggle to be heard from the margins then confers on the contingencies of Partition another set of images that articulate other realities— not exile or refugee-hood but being the 'Other' within the space of the nation. As anthropology suggests, margins are not peripheral spaces but are forms and practices through which the state is both experienced and undone and 'margins (are) sites that do not so much lie outside the state but rather, like rivers, run through its body.'[22] In India, portions of Bangladesh can be found in the states of West Bengal, Assam, Meghalaya and Tripura due to the vagaries of the Radcliffe line. The residents of these enclaves do not enjoy the same basic amenities that the mainland citizens of their country possess, for practical problems of access. They find it difficult to travel outside their enclaves as they have no opportunity to obtain

valid travel documents. To all intents and purposes, the residents
of these enclaves are illegible/invisible to their governments
because they possess no documents that mark a nation's citizens,
like passports or identity cards, so often the enclave dwellers resort
to deception even for ordinary tasks like enrolling for schools or
health centres.

The newly-created borders between India and Pakistan covered
some 4,000 kilometres to the east between India and East Pakistan
and Burma, and even after the decisions of the numerous boundary
commissions were implemented, the long periods of uncertainty
and change over actual demarcations of territory remain a
contentious issue between the nations of India, Bangladesh and
Myanmar. The Indo-Bangladesh border was thus a result of
political cartography that is still in a state of flux and is an 'unstable
landscape.' The overlap between migration, politics and national
security makes this border one of the most contingent and hostile
in the subcontinent; yet they have attracted little attention unless
there are shootings between border patrols of the two countries. For
historians, anthropologists and sociologists, this unstable border
remains a challenge 'for narrating border-crossings as interweaving
spaces of loss and abjection on the one hand and material and social
possibilities on the other.'[23] The statistics of border guards shooting
and killing civilians may be disputed by the two nations, yet it is
undoubtedly true that people who continue to cross these borders,
trying to connect with divided families or travelling for work,
without valid documentation face state repression and violence.
In addition to this serious anomaly of the national (and notional)
border, there are also the problems of livelihood and displacement
that beset the enclaves. Both India and Bangladesh have, from time
to time, tried to address these issues politically, rationalising, for
instance, the fact that 1000 kilometres of the West Bengal border
runs through the meandering rivers of the lower Indo-Gangetic
Plain (an active delta region), and their shifting courses and
the sudden rise of *char* land or silt banks and islands which are
often claimed by respective parties as their territory. By the Land
Boundary Agreement of 1974 between the two countries, India

and the newly independent Bangladesh decided to complete the demarcation of the land border between the two countries and the questions of the enclaves also came to be addressed. They listed fifteen sectors of the border that remained to be demarcated and although the Bangladesh Parliament ratified this agreement, the Indian side did not. This long overdue exchange has come into fruition only some time ago when India and Bangladesh exchanged 162 enclaves between them in August 2015. Debjani Sengupta's essay on the enclaves addresses an important issue of the Partition in the East through the optic of a novel set in an enclave named Dohogram. The essay traverses some unfamiliar territory through a novel by Selina Hossain and tries to see how enclave dwellers negotiate, substantiate and represent themselves in the space of a nation.

Joya Mitra's story 'A Face to Hate' is an ironic look at the distortions that 1947 wrought on our collective psyche while Manas Ray's 'Orality of Silence' is an intimate history of the Partition in the domestic and familial space. The poems from Bangla include some never before translations of two of West Bengal's major poets, Sankha Ghosh and Birendra Chattopadhyay, while Kaiser Haq's English poem is a timely reminder of what 1947 has failed to divide. In all the literary pieces, the effort has been to give space to powerful but under-represented writers and poets whose individual and distinct voices allow us to enter the interstices of 1947 that are both liberating and sombre. The anthology thus wishes to address some issues surrounding 1947 that are fecund in the subcontinent's political and social spheres, just as it proposes to usher in a more nuanced understanding of the vivisection's afterlife. Its own afterlife will, of course, be wholly dependent on its gentle readers.

Debjani Sengupta

Notes and References

1. Amongst anthologies, see Ramesh Mathur and M. Kulasrestha eds. *Writings on India's Partition* (Calcutta: Simant, 1976); Alok Bhalla ed. *Stories about the Partition of India* (Vols. 1–3, New Delhi: Indus,

1994; Vol. 4, New Delhi: Manohar, 2012); Saros Cowasjee and K. S. Duggal eds. *Orphans of the Storm* (New Delhi: UBS, 1995); Mushirul Hasan ed. *India Partitioned: The Other Face of Freedom* (2 Vols., New Delhi: 1995); and Muhammad Umar Memon ed. *An Epic Unwritten: The Penguin Book of Partition Stories from Urdu* (New Delhi: Penguin, 1998).

2. See Urvashi Butalia, *The Other Side of Silence* (New Delhi: Penguin, 1998); Ritu Menon and Kamla Bhasin, *Borders and Boundaries* (New Delhi: Kali for Women, 1998); Veena Das, *Critical Events* (New Delhi: Oxford University Press, 1995); Rita Kothari, *The Burden of Refuge: The Sindhi Hindus of Gujarat* (New Delhi: Orient Longman, 2007); Joya Chatterji, *The Spoils of Partition: Bengal and India 1947–67* (Cambridge: Cambridge University Press, 2007). A series of major lectures after the 60th anniversary of the Partition culminated in Urvashi Butalia's edited volume, *Partition: The Long Shadow* (New Delhi: Zubaan, 2015), which included pioneering work on Ladakh and Assam, as well as contributions by psychiatrists Alok Sarin and Sanjeev Jain on the question of trauma based on work with survivors. Rita Kothari innovatively explored the problem of new constraints faced in the post-1947 situation by the nomadic Banni Muslim community (now unable to freely cross the border) in *Memories and Movements: Borders and Communities in Banni, Kutch, Gujarat* (New Delhi: Orient BlackSwan, 2013). More recently, the impact of 1947 on areas like Jammu, the North-east and South India (amongst others) has been discussed in Amritjit Singh, Nalini Iyer and Rahul Gairola eds. *Revisiting India's Partition: New Essays on Memory, Culture and Politics* (Lanham: Lexington Books, 2016).

3. See Salima Hashmi's essay in this volume.

4. See http://www.1947partitionarchive.org/. Accessed 23 September 2016.

5. See http://www.thehindu.com/news/national/amritsars-town-hall-is-site-of-new-partition-museum/article8686932.ece. Accessed 23 September 2016. See also http://www.thehindu.com/news/national/other-states/%E2%80%98How-can-you-partition-the-air%E2%80%99/article17198306.ec. Accessed 6 February 2017.

6. For instance, Bhisham Sahni's *Today's Pasts: A Memoir* includes extensive references to the composition of his major Partition novel *Tamas* (1974, trans., author, New Delhi: Penguin, 2001) after a visit to riot-torn Bhiwandi (which summoned up memories of his own Partition experience in Rawalpindi). He also describes the process

of filming the novel (by director Govind Nihalini). See Bhisham Sahni, *Today's Pasts: A Memoir*, trans. Snehal Shingavi (Gurgaon: Penguin, 2015), a translation of *Aaj ke Ateet* (2004). Also *Tamas*, dir. Govind Nihalini, 1988. Intizar Husain's stories, essays and drama, including his Partition-related masterpiece *An Unwritten Epic*, have been collected afresh in Intizar Husain, *Story is a Vagabond*, eds. Frank Stewart, Alok Bhalla, Asif Aslam Farrukhi, and Nishat Zaidi (Karachi: Oxford University Press, 2015, rpt. 2016), esp. 1–24.

7. See Vazira Fazila-Yacoobali Zamindar, *The Long Partition and the Making of Modern South Asia: Refugees, Boundaries, Histories* (New York: Columbia, 2007), 1–18.

8. See Ayesha Jalal, *The Sole Spokesman* (Cambridge: Cambridge University Press, 1985).

9. See Venkat Dhulipala, *Creating A New Medina: State Power, Islam, and the Quest for Pakistan in Late Colonial North India* (Cambridge: Cambridge University Press, 2015, rpt. 2016).

10. See Dhulipala for an account of Gandhi's correspondence with Jinnah as regards the prospect of partition. Dhulipala, *Creating a New Medina*, 183–88.

11. Also see Faisal Devji, *The Impossible Indian: Gandhi and the Temptation of Violence* (Cambridge, MA: Harvard University Press, 2012), 169–71.

12. See Ian Talbot and Gurharpal Singh, *The Partition of India* (New Delhi: Cambridge University Press, 2009), 79–80.

13. See http://www.ghadar.in/gjh_html/?q=content/sufism-and-east-punjab-dalitassertion-part-i-%E2%80%94-ishtiaq-ahmed. Accessed 23 September 2016. Also Ajay Bhardwaj, dir. *Rabba Hun Ki Kariye* (*Thus Departed Our Neighbours*, 2007).

14. Ibid. Ajay Bhardwaj, dir. *Milange Baba Ratan De Mele Te* (*Let's Meet at Baba Ratan's Fair*, 2012).

15. See Satish Gujral, *Satish Gujral: Selected Works 1947–2000* (New Delhi: Lalit Kala Akademi, 2000); Sa'adat Hasan Manto, *Black Margins: Stories*, ed. M. U. Memon (New Delhi: Katha, 2001); Ritwik Ghatak, dir. *Meghe Dhaka Tara* (1960); *Komal Gandhar* (1961); *Subarnarekha* (1962); *Titash Ekti Nadir Naam* (1973); *Jukti, Takko aar Gappo* (1974). Also see Bhaskar Sarkar, *Mourning the Nation: Indian Cinema in the Wake of Partition* (New Delhi: Orient BlackSwan, 2010) for a critical account of Ghatak's work, esp. 200–239.

16. See Howard Brenton, *Drawing the Line* (London: Nick Hern Books, 2013).

17. W. H. Auden, 'Partition'. See http://www.poemhunter.com/poem/partition-2/. Brenton seemingly draws upon revelations by Radcliffe's secretary Christopher Beaumont (in 1992), especially as regards the controversy about the award of Ferozpur to India. See http://www.telegraph.co.uk/news/obituaries/1394313/His-Honour-Christopher-Beaumont.html. Accessed 10 October 2016.

18. Vishwajyoti Ghosh, curator, *This Side That Side: Restorying Partition* (New Delhi: Yoda Press, 2013).

19. Marianne Hirsch, *Family Frames: Photography, Narrative and Postmemory* (Cambridge, MA: Harvard University Press, 1997).

20. M. U. Memon, 'Partition Literature: A Study of Intizar Husain.' In *Modern Asian Studies* Vol. 14, No. 3 (1980), 381.

21. Gayatri Bhattacharya. *Refugee Rehabilitation and Its Impact on Tripura's Economy* (New Delhi: Omsons, 1988), 12.

22. Veena Das and Deborah Poole eds. *Anthropology in the Margins of the State*, (Santa Fe: School of American Research Press, 2004), 13.

23. Malini Sur, 'Divided Bodies: Crossing the India-Bangladesh Border,' *Economic and Political Weekly* Vol. 49, No. 13 (March 2014), 31.

ESSAYS AND STUDIES

Anil Nauriya
Sameer Abraham Thomas
Anwesha Sengupta
Aanchal Malhotra
Kajal Tehri and Asmat Jahan
Margit Köves
Ravikant
Vidya Rao
Debjani Sengupta
Rakhshanda Jalil
Salima Hashmi

1   Cabinet Mission Reconsidered

ANIL NAURIYA

The vigorous renewal of the Hindutva propaganda holding the Congress responsible for Partition began even as a similar critique of the Congress, albeit from a diametrically opposite perspective, was being developed in some academic writings, especially at Cambridge University. This would, from the early 1980s, come to have an appreciable circulation and also feed into the Hindutva attack. It is therefore necessary to deal with this particular academic critique, as it appears, in spite of its many errors, to be not infrequently repeated.[1] As in the case of the Hindutva position, discussion here too proceeds without recognition of the existence of any British colonial strategic objectives regarding Partition. This is strange considering the attention the British were giving to retaining their control in areas in undivided India's north-west and the north-east.[2]

The hypothesis has been put across from time to time that in the 1940s, Nehru stood in the way of a federal structure which Jinnah supposedly desired.[3] The notion, which has in recent years received some traction, seems to be that Jinnah stood for a more inclusive, broader Union, which was not acceptable to Congress leaders. Generally, the 'loose federal Union' argument is made in the context of the British Cabinet Mission Plan of May 1946. The Cabinet Mission Plan, in paragraphs 6 and 7, rejected the 'larger' and 'smaller' versions of Pakistan that had been placed for consideration, and overtly envisaged an undivided India. The Plan was to be subject to re-consideration at the instance of any province after ten years and every ten years thereafter. It envisaged three Groups A, B, and C; Group B would consist of the Muslim-majority provinces in the north-west and Group C of the eastern provinces of Bengal and Assam. The Groups would come together at the Centre in respect of specified subjects.

The two underpinnings of the 'loose federal structure' argument are, first, that this is an adequate description of the character of the Cabinet Mission Plan of 1946 and, second, that Jinnah had 'accepted' this Plan. The view, first expressed by the then Viceroy Wavell and later popularised by Cambridge scholars as well as some Bombay-based lawyers, was that the Cabinet Mission Plan was 'accepted' by Jinnah and the Muslim League and that this implied that the Pakistan demand had been given up. This view has been widely circulated, sometimes with the qualification that the demand was *effectively* given up.[4] This was not in fact correct. The resolution passed on 6 June 1946 by the Council of the Muslim League, by which the Plan was supposedly 'accepted', made it clear that Pakistan remained its 'unalterable objective.'[5] Curiously, this part of the resolution was not emphasised either by Ayesha Jalal in her work on Jinnah published by Cambridge University Press, or by H. M. Seervai in his work on Partition.[6] Jalal and Seervai also did not deal with the League's (1941) Madras session, where it had been made clear by an amendment to the League's Constitution that its demand for the partition of India was not a 'bargaining counter.'[7] Both these writers were the principal propagators, after Wavell, of the idea that the League had 'accepted' the Cabinet Mission Plan, which had, prima facie, rejected the Pakistan idea. Gandhi's wry comment on the 6 June 1946 resolution of the League Council was: 'It speaks volumes for me.'[8]

The second and third paragraphs of the League's resolution of 6 June 1946 reiterated that Pakistan remained 'the unalterable objective' of the League and that the Cabinet Mission Plan was for it only a step towards Pakistan, which it saw as '*inherent in the Mission's Plan.*'[9] It is not as if the League had 'accepted' the Cabinet Mission Plan, and the Congress and Nehru simply came and torpedoed it. The League's options with respect to the Cabinet

Mission Plan were restricted as the Labour Government in Britain at this stage was not willing overtly to go further by way of a direct Pakistan commitment. The Mission's Plan *ostensibly* rejected the Pakistan concept; even so, as the League noticed, an alternative route to Pakistan was implicit in the Plan. In the third paragraph of the League Council's 6 June 1946 resolution, it was observed that 'it will keep in view the opportunity and right of secession of Provinces or groups from the Union, which have been provided in the Mission's Plan by implication.'[10] There was on the League's part no intention to work the Plan except as a route to attain Pakistan.

While later withdrawing its 'acceptance' of the Cabinet Mission Plan, the Muslim League had cited, inter alia, a statement of Nehru's on 10 July 1946 at a press conference, in which he had declared that the Constituent Assembly would be sovereign.[11] Yet, given the fact that the League had, just a month earlier, on 6 June 1946, reiterated the Pakistan objective, it is hardly fair to blame Nehru's statement for a withdrawal of a League 'acceptance' that did not really exist in the first place.

Besides, the Congress had already made it clear, through Maulana Azad's letter of 20 May 1946 to Lord Pethick-Lawrence who led the Cabinet Mission, that it would look upon the Constituent Assembly as a sovereign body for the purpose of drafting the Constitution 'unhindered by any external authority.' This letter was drafted by Nehru. What Nehru said on 10 July 1946 was, therefore, not entirely new.

A federal structure requires that the provinces have some control over themselves and their fate. In their submission to the Cabinet Mission four days before the Plan was announced, the League had somewhat brazenly referred to Assam as a 'Muslim province.'[12] The Cabinet Mission obliged the League by placing Assam in Group C along with Muslim-majority Bengal. There was hardly any upholding of the federal principle here. In placing Assam in Group C the British would have known that they were including in the Plan a 'deal-breaker.' The statement issued by the Cabinet Mission on 16 May 1946 required under Paragraph 19 (iv) that the provincial representatives to the Constituent Assembly would divide up into three Sections (corresponding respectively to Groups A, B and C). Paragraph 19 (v) of the statement further required that these 'Sections shall proceed to settle Provincial Constitutions for the provinces included in each Section and shall also decide whether any Group Constitution shall be set up for those Provinces.' Maulana Azad pointed out in the letter (drafted by Nehru) to the Cabinet Mission on 20 May 1946 that Bengal would thus play a dominating role over Assam as the Plan required the Provincial Constitution to be 'settled' not by the Province but by the Section, that is Constituent Assembly members belonging to Group C, comprising Bengal and Assam. Rules framed by Group C could thus nullify the theoretical option given to a Province to opt out of a Group at a later stage. Azad pointed out that similarly in Group B, Punjab would dominate over Sind and the North-West Frontier Province (NWFP). Incidentally, those familiar with the workings of politics in Pakistan today would readily endorse the validity of this apprehension. In the form in which it was presented, the Cabinet Mission Plan cannot be treated as coterminous with or equivalent to setting up a 'federal structure.' In actual fact it had the effect of covertly throttling provincial federalism at the Group level.

There were other features militating against inclusiveness. Some of these were immediately obvious. Others unfolded in the course of the Cabinet Mission's deliberations. Sikhs were left out on a limb in Group B. Jinnah also resisted a role for non-League Muslims in the Executive Council envisaged under the Cabinet Mission Plan. Thus he sought to determine not only the League's representation on the Council but also the composition of the Congress representation. In this context, Zakir Husain was to Jinnah a 'Quisling.'[13] To describe such positions as federalist or inclusive in any way is hardly tenable.

Speech-making apart, Jinnah had difficulty not only with the federal principle but also with a pluralist approach on Pakistan. In the course of his talks with Jinnah in 1944, Gandhi had suggested a referendum in the Muslim-majority areas to ascertain by adult suffrage of 'all of the inhabitants of the Pakistan area' whether they wished to be part of a separate state. The offer is recorded in

Gandhi's letter of 22 September 1944 to Jinnah. He also suggested in the letter that a 'third party or parties' be called in 'to guide or even arbitrate between us.' Jinnah responded on 25 September 1944 by demanding that the voting in such a referendum be confined to the Muslims in the area.[14] Thus he was not inclined to permit the Sikhs, Hindus, Christians and others in the so-called Pakistan to have a say in the future of the region that was their home. Such positions sit ill with civil libertarian claims.

Throughout the relevant period, the British resisted any suggestions for resolution of the inter-communal question which did not involve a key role for themselves. They saw themselves as arbiters in an inter-communal dispute. Gandhi and Maulana Azad had called this particular bluff more than once in statements usually neglected by historians. On 8 August 1942, a few hours before his arrest the next day, Gandhi dictated a letter to a citizen of Bombay, backing Azad's offer to the League that if it cooperated fully in the demand for Indian independence, the Congress would have no objection 'to the British Government transferring all the powers it to-day exercises to the Muslim League on behalf of the whole of India, including the so-called Indian India.'[15] On 8 May 1946 also Gandhi had suggested that an 'impartial non-British tribunal' go into the points of dispute.[16] But it was difficult to get the British to agree. In fact, the provision in the Cabinet Mission Plan regarding a review after every ten years also contained within it the likelihood of continued British supervisory presence.

Parenthetically, we may note that within independent Pakistan too, Jinnah was not enamoured of federalism or its implications. Although Bengalis constituted a majority in Pakistan after its formation, Jinnah, in a speech at Dhaka on 21 March 1948, declared that Urdu and 'no other language' would be Pakistan's state language.[17] It was this early disinclination to grant a due place to the Bengali language in Pakistan that contributed to the movement for secession of its eastern wing.

The oft-heard lament for the Cabinet Mission Plan and the attempt by diverse forces to pin its 'failure' upon the Congress and Nehru is especially surprising considering some other particularly obscure features of the Plan, which have historically not received adequate attention. These features relate to the complicated tie-up envisaged in the Plan between four future events and processes: (i) the lengthy Constitution-making process required under the Plan, (ii) the transfer of power and sovereignty in the form of independence to India, (iii) the condition relating to the formulation of a treaty between the United Kingdom and the Constituent Assembly and (iv) the stationing of British troops in India and the terms on which these troops would be withdrawn. An examination of this intricate inter-relationship indicates that the Cabinet Mission Plan was not a document simply offering a 'loose federal Union.' We may, for the present, consider features seriatim.

First, *the length of the Constitution-making process envisaged under the Plan*; for it was only after this process was complete that sovereignty was to be transferred under the Plan. In a statement issued the same day as the Plan was announced, Stafford Cripps declared: 'So the three Sections will formulate the Provincial and Group Constitutions and *when that is done* they work together with the States representatives to make the Union Constitution. This is the final phase.'[18] Thus work on the Union Constitution would start only *after* the Provincial and Group Constitutions were ready. That meant that each Group could take its own time settling its own Constitution and the constitutions of the Provinces comprising the Group. Then work would start on the Union Constitution in association with the (princely) States. Paradoxically, the Cabinet Mission Plan simultaneously declared [in Paragraph 14] that British paramountcy over the Princely States would *not* be transferred to the new Indian government on attainment of Indian independence.[19] Thus even while expressing the hope that the Princely States would co-operate, the Cabinet Mission Plan offered the States the enticing prospect of their own independence *if they did not co-operate* in the making of a Union Constitution.

Second, *it is not generally appreciated or understood that the matter of transfer of sovereignty was deferred under the Cabinet*

Mission Plan. The Secretary of State for India, Pethick-Lawrence, as leader of the Cabinet Mission, wrote in his letter dated 22 May 1946 to Maulana Azad that *'independence cannot precede the bringing into operation of a new Constitution.'*[20] He added: 'When the Constituent Assembly has *completed its labours,* His Majesty's Government will recommend to Parliament such action as may be necessary for the cession of sovereignty to the Indian people...'[21] [italics added]. Even at that stage, this transfer of sovereignty was to be subject to certain provisos. Oddly enough, these vital issues have often escaped attention.

A third aspect *concerns the Treaty envisaged under the Plan.* Paragraph 22 of the Cabinet Mission Plan made it 'necessary to negotiate a treaty between the Union Constituent Assembly and the United Kingdom to provide for certain matters arising out of the transfer of power.'[22] The Cabinet Mission did not envisage any transfer of sovereignty in the form of independence without the Union Constitution having been drafted and in the absence of such a Treaty having been negotiated. The inevitably long-drawn Constitution-making process intrinsic to the Plan also implied the possibility of continued British supervisory presence. What shape would this take? Moreover, what was there to prevent this supervisory presence from telescoping into the review after the ten years envisaged in the Plan? [It may be noted parenthetically that it was only on 20 February 1947, by when it had become fairly clear that the Cabinet Mission Plan was not working, that the British Prime Minister announced a 'definite intention' to hand over power to Indian hands 'not later than June 1948.']

Finally, *there is the inter-related matter of the stationing of British troops.* In the Nehru-drafted letter of 20 May 1946, Maulana Azad had pointed out to the Cabinet Mission that its notion of British troops remaining in India 'till after the establishment of the Government in accordance with the instrument produced by the Constituent Assembly' would be 'a negation of India's independence.'[23] Nehru made this point several times. For example, on 20 August 1946, he observed: 'I am sure that when British armed might is removed from India, it will be easier for all of us to face the realities in India and arrive at mutually advantageous agreements.'[24]

The Cabinet Mission, while confirming in its statement on 25 May 1946 that there was 'no intention of retaining British troops in India against the wish of an independent India under the new Constitution,' maintained that 'during the interim period' it was 'necessary' that 'British troops should remain.'[25] By 'interim period' was meant the entire elongated period leading up to the framing of the Union Constitution under the Plan, which would be a sequel to the framing of the Provincial and Group Constitutions, and finally the formulation of a Treaty between the Constituent Assembly and the United Kingdom. Not surprisingly, in his letter dated 20 May 1946 to Pethick-Lawrence, Gandhi had also observed that with British troops in India, 'independence would in fact be a farce' and that 'it can in no way be contended that in the face of the troops, there would be natural behaviour in the Constituent Assembly.'[26] On the provision concerning the Treaty envisaged under the Cabinet Mission Plan, Gandhi had also noted in this context: '...the treaty must be a voluntary act on the part of Independent India. If it pre-supposes compulsion, there is no Independence.'[27] Such matters which were vital in the thinking of Gandhi, Nehru and Azad, who were all familiar with the Egyptian experience where a nominal independence recognised in 1922 had been subverted through stationing of troops and by power purportedly exercised pending, and ultimately under, a treaty, are generally overlooked by academic and other writers in their projection of the Cabinet Mission Plan.[28]

Thus in the obviously long-drawn Constitution-making process envisaged under the Plan, with no transfer of power or sovereignty in the form of Indian independence, and with one political party still committed to its objective of Pakistan, the continued British presence, including the presence of British troops, had the distinct prospect of playing off Groups, Provinces, and Princely States against one another.

The Cabinet Mission Plan was quite different from the current perception of it in sections of the academic community and intelligentsia. That this perception has acquired an appreciable hold is, in part, to be accounted for by the resources still available to colonialist historiography. Far from being the blueprint of a loose federal Union, the Cabinet Mission Plan contained within it no early, clear and definite prospect of Indian independence as such. Instead it set out a Constitutional route for dissolution, a possible prelude to a larger Pakistan and even to the prospect, under colonial auspices and under the watch of British troops, of the separate independence of various Princely States.

Looked at from any angle, therefore, it appears that attempts to shift the primary responsibility for failure of the Cabinet Mission Plan and consequently for Partition upon Nehru individually or upon the Congress collectively, whether these attempts be made on behalf of Hindutva or on behalf of the League or by colonialist historiography, are less than convincing and historically dubious. This is so particularly because each one of the forces involved or associated with such targeting usually excludes its own role from the analysis. It is necessary that this record be set straight as the sectarian accounts tend to become elements in the contemporary political and electoral arena.

Notes and References

1. For an earlier critique of such perspectives, see Anil Nauriya, 'Some Portrayals of Jinnah: A Critique', in *Minority Identities and the Nation-State*, eds. D. L. Sheth and Gurpreet Mahajan (New Delhi: Oxford University Press, 1999), 73–112.
2. We may cite one of various indications of a British expectation of a foothold in the so-called 'Pakistan' areas. On 25 April 1946, a few days before the Cabinet Mission Plan was announced, one of the contingency arrangements put forward by Sir William Croft, the Deputy Under Secretary of State, India Office, was 'that we should withdraw from Hindustan and leave it to its own devices while staying in Pakistan by agreement which he estimated would be forthcoming...' (*The Transfer of Power, 1942–7*, Vol. 7, London: Her Majesty's Stationery Office, Document 138). Upon this Viceroy Archibald Wavell said that he 'had considered this possibility in consultation with the Commander-in-Chief, and thought that we

might have to contemplate something of the sort' (idem.). At his meeting with the Cabinet Delegation on 31 May 1946, the Viceroy said that 'he did not feel that there were final grounds for rejecting the possibility that we might remain in North-Eastern and North-western India for an indefinite period' (*The Transfer of Power*, Vol. 7, Document 415). This line of thinking was understandable also because, so far as British control of India was concerned, Wavell, his administration and provincial governors were naturally more in sync with the policies maintained by the previous British government headed by Winston Churchill than with the post-War Labour government. Earlier, when on a visit to England soon after the change in government, Wavell had on 31 August 1945 called on Churchill, the latter's parting advice had been to 'Keep a bit of India' (Archibald Wavell, *The Viceroy's Journal*, Delhi: Oxford University Press, 1973, 168).

3. In an article published on 18 August 2009, Jaswant Singh was reported as follows. According to him, Jinnah envisaged that some areas of the new country would have Muslim majority areas and some Hindu majority areas and believed a federal system that kept the country as one was desirable. Nehru, by contrast, demanded a system that was centralised. 'Nehru believed in a highly centralised policy. That's what he wanted India to be,' Singh went on. 'Jinnah wanted a federal polity. That, even Gandhi accepted. Nehru didn't. Consistently he stood in the way of a federal India until 1947 when it became a partitioned India.' http://www.independent.co.uk/news/world/asia/search-for-the-real-villain-of-partition-divides-india-again-1773486.html [Retrieved 6 Sept 2016]

   See also: 'Nehru was as much to blame as Jinnah for Partition' (January 2016). Rediff interview with Nisid Hajari (author of *Midnight's Furies: The Deadly Legacy of India's Partition*, Viking/Penguin, Gurgaon, 2015). http://m.rediff.com/news/interview/nehru-was-as-much-to-blame-as-jinnah-for-partition/20150813.htm [Retrieved 6 Sept 2016]. In the interview to Rediff, Hajari asserts: 'Up until the spring of 1946, a political compromise that would have preserved a united India, was still possible. The Congress—Nehru in particular—would have had to grant the Muslim areas that (eventually) became Pakistan more autonomy than he was willing to grant, and have had to accept a weaker Central government than he wanted.'

4. See, for example, Aijaz Ahmad, "'Tryst with Destiny"—Free but Divided,' *The Hindu*, Independence Day Supplement, 15 August 1997, 22–23.
5. For text, see Maurice Gwyer and A. Appadorai, *Speeches and Documents on the Indian Constitution, 1921–47*, Vol. 2 (Bombay: Oxford University Press, 1957), 601.
6. Ayesha Jalal, *The Sole Spokesman: Jinnah, The Muslim League and the Demand for Pakistan*, (Cambridge: Cambridge University Press, 1985); and H. M. Seervai, *Constitutional Law of India*, Vol. 1, 4th edition (Bombay: N. M. Tripathi Pvt. Ltd., 1991).
7. Syed Sharifuddin Pirzada ed., *Foundations of Pakistan: All India Muslim League Documents: 1906–1947*, Vol. 2 (Karachi: National Publishing House, 1970), 371–372. Liaquat Ali Khan said in the course of the debate that the amendment 'would be an effective reply to those who had alleged' that the demand for Pakistan was 'merely a counter for bargaining' (Pirzada, op. cit., 376).
8. Letter dated 12 June 1946 to Frederick Pethick-Lawrence, in *Collected Works of Mahatma Gandhi* (*CWMG*), Vol. 84 (New Delhi: Government of India, Publications Division, 1981), 323.
9. Gwyer and Appadorai, *Speeches and Documents on the Indian Constitution, 1921–47*, Vol. 2, 601.
10. Idem.
11. Gwyer and Appadorai, op. cit., 619.
12. *Terms of Offer made by the Muslim League as a basis of agreement*, 12 May 1946; see Gwyer and Appadorai, op. cit. 573. These were communicated by Jinnah to the Cabinet Mission on the same day (*The Transfer of Power, 1942–7*, Vol. 7, Document 259 with enclosure). Earlier, on 7 February 1946, Viceroy Wavell, in a cable to Pethick-Lawrence had accepted that Assam (apart from Sylhet district) was not a province to which there could be 'a reasonable claim' on behalf of the projected Pakistan (ibid., Vol. 6, Document 406). When the Cabinet Mission Plan was yet in the making, the Mission offered to Jinnah on 16 April 1946 the possibility of a Union Centre limited to essential subjects and envisaging also 'in one federation the whole of the Provinces of Sind, Baluchistan, North-West Frontier Province, the Punjab and Bengal *plus* perhaps the Sylhet district of Assam' (ibid., Vol. 7, Document 116). By the time the Cabinet Mission Plan was announced the following month, Assam *as a whole* was to be added to a third Group comprising Bengal and itself. The Mission was fully aware of the unfairness of this, particularly as the Group

would essentially determine the Provincial Constitutions as well. A note by W. Croft and F. F. Turnbull, Secretary to the Mission, circulated on 25 April 1946, and by these two men and G. E. B. Abell, Private Secretary to the Viceroy, on 2 May 1946, presaged the change in the manner the Mission would deal with Assam as a whole (ibid., Documents 140 (enclosure) and 179). While these documents were not *overtly* endorsed by the Cabinet Mission, they decisively affected the evolution of the Mission's proposals. This was reflected in the revision of the proposals made on 4 May 1946, (whereby it was proposed to have three Groups instead of two) in which Bengal and Assam as a whole were nonchalantly placed in the third group, which would later be known as Group C (ibid., Document 189). The document sent to the British Prime Minister by the Cabinet Mission and Viceroy Wavell on 5 May 1946 thus had Bengal and the whole of Assam in the same group, that is, Group C (ibid., Document 193). While Croft, Turnbull and Abell thus succeeded in inverting the original intent of the Cabinet Mission's proposals, the ultimate responsibility for this must be borne by Viceroy Wavell and the Cabinet Mission itself.

A further inflexibility was introduced in terms of restricting the possibility of any Province opting out of the particular Group in which it had been placed. At the outset, on 27 April 1946, it had been proposed that provinces could voluntarily form groups in order to deal with certain subjects in common (*The Transfer of Power, 1942–7*, Vol. 7, Document 156, paragraph 15). This was later modified: Groups would be pre-specified and a Province could opt out only *after* the new constitution was settled (ibid., Document 193, paragraph 15). After initially suggesting that 'Provinces should be free to form groups....,' a formulation that still remained in Paragraph 15 of the Cabinet Mission Plan, the same document went on to nullify this by further specifying in Paragraph 19 (viii) that 'opting out' by a Province from the Group could only be after 'the new Constitutional arrangements come into operation' *and* 'after the first general election under the new Constitution.' The change in Paragraph 19 occurred primarily as a sequel to a cable on 9 May 1946 from F. Burrows, the Governor of Bengal, whose views had also been sought by Wavell (ibid., Document 231). Burrows wanted also to ensure that the voting system *within the Group*, for formulation of the *Constitutional* arrangements, be such that decisions would be by *simple majority*. The *anti-federality* and inherent unjustness of this was conspicuous also in relation to the NWFP and similarly placed provinces. In any explanation of Partition and analysis of sectarian politics, the role of officials like Croft, Turnbull, Abell and Burrows who pointedly introduced and encouraged sectarian demands needs close evaluation. The arrangements devised and promoted by them appear to have been programmed to ensure the failure of the Cabinet Mission even before the publication of its Plan. The Cabinet Mission, with its own ambiguities, waverings and flip-flops, perhaps failed to see that Wavell and his administration in India, and in most of its Provinces, were attuned to the *preceding* British government, not to the one that had sent out the Cabinet Mission to India. How the smorgasbord that emerged out of this surrealistic encounter within India between two successive British regimes could be projected for decades in scholarship and in 'popular' writing as 'loose federal arrangements' and Nehru accused of opposing these without justification, remains quite inexplicable. What both the successive British establishments that came to operate simultaneously in India in the summer of 1946 shared, however, was a desire to project to the world that it was not the British who were holding up Indian independence but the Indians themselves who were unable to come to an agreement and, more importantly, that the British themselves were not averse to an undivided India. In this projection the Cabinet Mission Plan would serve a purpose: the world would know primarily of the *fact* of the Plan, not of the devils so scrupulously introduced into its details.

13. Wavell, *The Viceroy's Journal*, 296.
14. Syed Sharifuddin Pirzada, *Quaid-e-Azam Jinnah's Correspondence* (Karachi: East and West Publishing Company, 1977), 124.
15. *Collected Works of Mahatma Gandhi* (CWMG), Vol. 76, 382.
16. Ibid., Vol. 84, 123.
17. Quaid-i-Azam Mohammad Ali Jinnah, *Speeches and Statements as Governor General of Pakistan 1947–48* (Islamabad: Ministry of Information and Broadcasting, Government of Pakistan, 1989), 183.
18. Gwyer and Appadorai, op. cit., 585; italics added.
19. On 10 April 1946, Gandhi had told Stafford Cripps: 'You are transferring power to Indian hands. The authority which takes your place in British India should exercise that paramountcy after you hand over power.' Cripps had maintained that was 'not the law,' upon which Gandhi had enquired: 'Was not it law in 1858 and in 1935?' ('Talk with Sir Stafford Cripps,' CWMG, Vol. 94, Supplementary Volume 4, 261).

20. Gwyer and Appadorai, op. cit., 591.
21. Idem.
22. Gwyer and Appadorai, op. cit., 583.
23. *Selected Works of Jawaharlal Nehru*, Vol. 15 (New Delhi: Orient Longman, 1982), 177.
24. Ibid., 303.
25. Gwyer and Appadorai, op. cit., 595.
26. CWMG, Vol. 84, 173–174.
27. CWMG, Vol. 94, Supplementary Volume 4, 276.
28. For Gandhi and Nehru's familiarity with the Egyptian experience, see (i) Jawaharlal Nehru, *Glimpses of World History*, (Bombay: Asia Publishing House, 1962, reprint 1975), 761–775 (for Nehru's writings on Egypt, 'Egypt's Fight for Freedom' and 'What Independence Under the British Means' dated respectively 20 and 22 May 1933, along with his note dated October 1938; and (ii) Anil Nauriya, 'Soundings in Kindred Struggles: The Egyptian Voice in Gandhi,' *Identity, Culture and Politics* Vol. 12(2): 43–66, December 2011.

In Other Words

SAMEER ABRAHAM THOMAS

The first time I learned about Partition was in college. That is not to say that it was the first time I had heard about Partition. Of course I'd heard about it, but there's a difference between knowing of something and knowing something about it. No doubt there had been mention of it in our history textbooks in school, but I never read the full chapter on it until I was in college. The CBSE reserves that information for those who choose to study the humanities in much the same way as more detailed sex education is reserved for the (ideally) pre-med science with biology students. Unlike most people my age that I know, I had never watched *Border* (I still haven't), so I could neither ironically quote that movie, nor could I unironically share clips from it on social media to 'educate' people about the nuances of Indo-Pak relations. I was too shy to ask my parents' friends, any of my relatives, or strangers, and being raised in a family of history students counterintuitively put me off from going anywhere near the many books on the subject that were threatening to crowd us out of our home. I am, of course, saying all this in order to feel better about my complete lack of curiosity in such matters during my childhood, something that baffles me today as I try to trace the roots of my ignorance.

I had never been to Pakistan, never even met a Pakistani. My mother had. She went to Lahore as part of a panel for a conference. She had told me about the mobile wonders that are Pakistani trucks, the food and the people. At the conference, she was seated next to a Pakistani scholar who only spoke Urdu. This posed a problem as my mother had never learned to speak that language. The two of them decided that the Indian scholar would speak in Hindi while the Pakistani scholar would speak in Urdu and somehow they would try to communicate. As it turns out, my mother told me, they didn't face any trouble at all. They might as well have been speaking the same language. Even the Persian words were familiar to my mother, who had either heard them used in Bollywood films or was accustomed to using them as a part of what all but the most intractable and devout ultra-nationalists would call 'Hindi' in their everyday life outside of the realm of academic linguistics.

So in what way did I engage with Partition and with the two countries it produced? I had the India-Pakistan cricket matches where my brother sitting in Delhi rooted with the Marathis, Gujaratis, Punjabis et al, the Indians in the stadium, for the Indians on the pitch. He cursed when 'we' lost and crowed when 'we' won in this battle for bragging rights between Manichean opposites locked in an eternal struggle, our devs against their asuras, our ahuras against their daevs. I believe the newspapers refer to this as 'cricket diplomacy.' I had the press for whom Pakistan was sometimes the place where terrorists come from and criminals flee to, and at other times India's long-lost twin who had fallen in with the wrong crowd. The former necessitated military and bureaucratic intervention while the latter required the kind of tearful familial reconciliation Ambuja Cement sold us as a dream made impossible by indestructible industrial walls of steadfast cement. Of course, India was both Amitabh Bachchan and Shashi Kapoor in this relationship; we had wealth as well as tradition. Then there was Attenborough's *Gandhi* with Alyque Padamsee's Jinnah as the Mephistopheles of Partition and Gandhi as the sacrificial Christ who stopped the riots almost single-handedly. That movie had an afterlife in my mind in conversations apportioning the blame for Partition to one or the other of these big names, with Nehru added to the line-up for good measure. The most intellectual conversations I had about Partition as a child among children always involved trying to identify the Keyser Soze of 1947.

Things changed when I became a student at Hindu College. Thanks to my teacher, Dr Tarun Saint, what would otherwise have been one among many short stories forming a single unit of our Indian Literature paper became a crash course in Partition Literature. Everything I knew about Partition became, that most favourite of words in a Literature student's arsenal, problematic. In particular, the debates about culpability changed. Not only were the British added to the line-up, the violence, that had otherwise been only an acting motivation for Ben Kingsley or a statistic to be memorised by a schoolboy more interested in the numbers on his report card, was made painfully visible. The rapes and the murders seemed less like regrettable, avoidable misunderstandings and more like the covenant of blood through which two countries learned their own names. My country had had a psychotic break at the moment of its birth and somehow this was not something we talked about every day. Instead, we tried to forget that neighbours could become killers and then morph back into normal people without being charged, tried or sentenced. We built up walls between the two countries which seeped into our own lives, until we began to look askance at our own countrymen and countrywomen for speaking in a tongue that not too long ago might have been mistaken for our own. And still the violence and the endless blame games without any clear culprits continued.

It was only relatively recently, we were told, that people like Urvashi Butalia started collecting stories from those who survived the violence before they died taking those stories with them. In the classroom and outside it, we did our bit too by asking each other about the experiences of our families during and as a result of Partition. I discovered that the grandfather of one of my friends left Lahore with almost nothing and settled in Delhi where he designed his own house and started an automobile parts business. Another friend's grandparents had ended up in West Bengal by mistake, thinking they were heading towards Bangladesh. But I had no such stories. My family was from Kerala, so we didn't have any relatives across the border. If there had ever been any friends or neighbours or family members who had suffered in 1947, their names had been forgotten. How was it that my friends and I could claim a common identity when our experience of such a crucial moment in our nation's history differed so greatly? Could I call myself an Indian if I hadn't shared in the wounds of my country's past?

This is not to say that my family was completely untouched by Partition. I had always heard that my maternal grandfather, a well-known writer in Malayalam, had written a Partition novel in that language. I learnt from Dr Saint that this was possibly one of its kind and that I should do my best to get it translated. I myself do not know the language, so I asked my father about it. He seemed oddly unwilling to talk about the book. Eventually, I discovered why. According to my father, what my grandfather had written was, to put it generously, heavily inspired by Khushwant Singh's *Train to Pakistan*. This was a bit embarrassing and anyway the book would be difficult to find in the librarian labyrinth at home, so I didn't pursue the matter.

So much for my side of things. I had the opportunity to learn about the other side of the matter in my final year when a group of students from Lahore University of Management Sciences (LUMS) visited Hindu College in order to present papers they had written on Partition Literature. While the papers themselves were interesting and well-researched, what sticks in my mind is the discussion we had afterwards, where both the Indian and Pakistani students shared the images they had been raised with of the other country. When one of the visitors said they had been surprised by the fact that Delhi women were not, as they had been led to believe, all forced to dress modestly and traditionally by conservative-minded patriarchs, the Indians in the room exchanged glances. We couldn't deny that some diet-racist part of our minds had consciously chosen not to be surprised by the fact that most of the Pakistani students were women wearing make-up and dressed in Western attire. 'Not a veil in sight!' the Pakistani students said of us, and the Indian students thought of them. We began to realise that we weren't so different after all.

This impression seemed to be strengthened by the fact that in Pakistan too, Partition was not something that was discussed very often. Like us, the students we met had only engaged with Partition as a result of the course they did. However, what one of them said threw a whole new light on the relationship between our two countries. While telling her parents that she was learning about Partition, they seemed confused about what she meant. She repeated herself a couple of times and then finally mentioned1947, at which point she was firmly corrected:

'Not Partition. Azadi.'

In India, we are taught that Partition and Independence happened simultaneously, but when we refer to them, it is as two distinct events. The two are not synonymous, which perhaps they should be, but one word certainly doesn't delegitimise the other. But here was the implication that perhaps 'azadi' was not merely from the British, but from India too. Which made sense if Pakistan was imagined, as it was, to be a refuge for Muslims who would otherwise suffer discrimination, violence and inequality in the newly independent nation that would have been had there not been a miscarriage (or perhaps it was an abortion). This was a far cry from 'Aman ki Asha' or the Google Reunion ad. In other words, India and Pakistan appear not as friends who have had a misunderstanding or have become estranged, but as oppressor and oppressed, imperial power and refugee state. The question of whether any of these relationships are real or true misses the point. The point is that 'imagined communities' are more than a critique of national difference that first year liberal arts students use self-importantly without having read Benedict Anderson; imagined communities also produce distinct imaginaries, and, with them, distinct imagining communities. How can dialogue take place in such a situation? How can people communicate when they not only speak different languages but use the same language in very different ways, to refer to different realities, to imagine differently? How can two countries co-exist if one of them uses the word 'freedom' to refer to what another calls 'violence'?

Fast forward to 2016. Once again, we have people demanding azadi—for Kashmir; from caste, corruption and poverty—and people firing back that we don't need another Partition. Ironically, it is some among the latter who are dividing the country in other ways as well, and not along religious lines alone. We live in times when Urdu writers have to sign an undertaking that their writing will not contain anti-national material. We live in times when it's condemnable to say Pakistan is not hell. We live in times when those who criticise the government are encouraged to go to Pakistan as if it were India's own Siberia. Yet we also live in times where to say you want to leave the country because you fear for your safety is a sin; but if you want to leave the country because you fear for your wealth, no one will stop you. You are even rewarded with the coveted NRI tag if you leave the country to work, as long as you keep sending money 'home' as penance for crossing the black waters. We live in times where it is becoming increasingly clear that a nation is not divided by religion alone, but by the ways in which different people imagine the nation. All this is not to say that we are headed towards another Partition. We may instead be headed to another Khalistan Movement, with no redrawn boundaries, but plenty of bloodshed all the same. And in India, unlike Macondo, the trail of blood grows longer but it needn't stop at anyone's door.

Are we doomed to repeat history because we didn't study it in time? Has the incoherence of the past translated into the incoherence of the future? Frustration takes hold of me. If I cannot make sense of the past, and I cannot make sense of the present, what do I write? It is then that I remember that my education started with 'Toba Tek Singh' written by Saadat Hasan Manto. Tormented by the incoherence around him, split between two countries, he wrote all of that incoherence into a story, but not incoherently, not as a formal defect, but as a record of incoherent times. The story is about the incoherence of Partition, the incoherence of history, the incoherence of politics, the incoherence of geography, the incoherence of violence, the incoherence of sanity and insanity, and the incoherence of language itself. Manto wasn't alone in recording the horrors of Partition in literature, and such literature lives on to this day. It was Partition literature that made me think about 1947 differently, that brought the LUMS students to my college, and that inspired my grandfather to try to write about Partition in a language that had been untouched by it. Perhaps the literature that will emerge from our present will also be a literature of incoherence that will lead our children and their children to retrospectively find meaning in the meaninglessness that surrounds us.

Regardless, we need to make an effort not just to record incoherence but to forge coherence, to harmonise the dissonant voices yelling at each other today in order to make them sing together, each in its own register. To do this, we must start listening to each other's stories, because stories are histories told in other words, directed Otherwards, in words other than our own. We need to try to imagine each other's realities, despite how repugnant they may seem to us. This will not happen so long as we cling to our binaries of bhakt versus antinational or sanghi versus sickular. It requires us to tell our stories even if they are not heard, and to listen to stories even if they are not ours. We must learn the humility and the courage to edit our stories and perhaps even rewrite them if our faith in them is challenged by the stories of others. Until we do, we will keep having the same fruitless arguments, again and again, never changing, even if they are framed in other words.

3   **Partition and Dalit Politics in Bengal**
The Figure of Jogendra Nath Mandal

ANWESHA SENGUPTA

Introduction

This paper studies the complex nature of Dalit politics in Bengal during the times of Partition. It focuses on Jogendra Nath Mandal, a popular Dalit leader from Barisal (now in Bangladesh) who was also an ally of the Muslim League.[1] Through a study of Mandal's political career, the essay reflects on the nature and scope of caste politics in Bengal in the late 1940s and '50s and consequently complicates our understanding of 'partitioned times.'[2]

Mandal was the leader of the Scheduled Castes Federation (SCF), a party that had been in alliance with the Muslim League in undivided Bengal. When Bengal was partitioned between India and Pakistan, SCF remained with the League. Mandal joined the Pakistan cabinet as its first Law and Labour Minister. His stint was brief as he resigned and migrated to Calcutta in October 1950. Thereafter, he attempted to organise the low-caste refugees in West Bengal in demand for better relief and rehabilitation from the government. However, neither as a minority minister in Pakistan nor as a refugee leader in West Bengal was Mandal successful. One may say that Partition destroyed his hitherto brilliant political career. Caste as the basis of political mobilisation became somewhat marginal at this juncture, but it remained relevant otherwise, particularly as a governmental category in both East and

West Bengal. This essay focuses on these points to understand the changing nature of caste politics and Jogendra Nath's role in it.

Jogendra Nath in Pakistan

Jogendra Nath Mandal chaired the inaugural session of the Constituent Assembly of Pakistan. He was handpicked by Jinnah for this occasion.[3] This was a well calculated step. Jinnah had repeatedly claimed that once Pakistan was achieved, everyone would be treated equally in his country, irrespective of caste, creed and religion. Choosing Mandal as the chair for the inaugural session was definitely an attempt to show that Jinnah and his government were eager to practice what they were saying.

As mentioned earlier, Mandal was the first Law and Labour Minister of the Pakistan Cabinet. He was important to Pakistani politics for a number of reasons. First, his appointment was meant to show that even if Pakistan was an Islamic state, it was a liberal, democratic and modern nation. The League had always criticised the Congress as a party of caste Hindus. Mandal's politics corroborated this position. Among the Hindus who had remained in West and East Pakistan, the majority belonged to scheduled castes. Having Mandal in the cabinet was also a gesture towards winning their confidence and support.

That the League had high stakes in Mandal was perhaps best reflected in the 'Mandal Day' celebrations held across Pakistan on 19 June 1949. 'Mandal Day' was announced to mark Jogendra Nath's forty-third birthday, which was on 29 January. A 'Mandal Day Celebration Committee' was formed to organise the event. Celebrations began with morning prayers in various scheduled caste localities of Karachi where people prayed for his long life. In the evening, Mandal was given a grand reception at the famous Khaliqdina Hall of Karachi. Cabinet ministers, ministers of Sindh, important bureaucrats, ambassadors of various countries and a few prominent caste Hindus who were still in Karachi, were invited. This was followed by a tea party at a hotel, attended by Mandal and several central ministers and all the state ministers of Sindh. At a huge hall, tea was served to a few women and children of the local Dalit communities also. At night, scheduled caste localities were decorated with colourful *diyas*, bulbs and festive illuminations.[4] 'Mandal Day' was also observed in Dhaka where the function was attended by prominent League leaders like Nurul Amin and Choudhury Khaliquzzaman. Nurul Amin mentioned that the high position occupied by Mandal was 'proof of the kindly intentions the Quaid-e-Azam had towards the Scheduled Castes Community.'[5]

The alliance between the Pakistan government and Mandal, however, did not last long. From the beginning, there had been minor tiffs between Mandal and the League on various issues, particularly regarding the inclusion of a scheduled caste minister in the East Bengal cabinet.[6] Once Mandal had even warned the East Pakistan government that 'he might have to "revise his policy" and come to some understanding with the caste Hindus in the Congress Party, much as he distrusted them,' if a minister was not appointed from his party within a month or so.[7] But these bargains and threats had not signaled any major trouble prior to the February Riots of 1950.[8] Communal disturbances began towards the end of 1949 when in Kalshira village of Khulna district (East Pakistan), a house belonging to a Namasudra family was raided and the residents were tortured by the police for giving shelter to some Communist Party members.[9] Trouble soon spread over almost the entire province of East Pakistan and also to eastern India.[10]

Mandal was deeply disturbed by this incident. Letters reached him with vivid descriptions of assaults on scheduled caste communities. Mandal wrote to Liaquat Ali Khan that 'widespread oppression and persecution is carried on the Scheduled Caste people irrespective of their fault or guilt.'[11] He warned that these atrocities 'will only lead to mass exodus of the Scheduled Caste people and creation of a feeling that they are not entitled to get protection of law in Pakistan.'[12] The communal situation, however, deteriorated even further in February 1950. Mandal's politics, based on solidarity between Muslims and Hindu scheduled castes, began to look irrelevant now. He no longer insisted that his followers stay on in East Pakistan. According to a report published in the

Anandabazar Patrika, Mandal apparently wept like a child while describing the communal situation in Bakarganj to the media.[13] Mandal's activities during the riots and his criticism of the authorities did not go well with the Pakistan government. He was now an embarrassment for them. Not surprisingly, therefore, Mandal's recommendations were completely ignored when in accordance with the provisions of the Nehru-Liaquat Pact,[14] an MLA from the minority community was appointed as the Minority Minister of East Pakistan. The new minister, Dwarakanath Barori, though a member of SCF, was not a Mandal loyalist. Mandal had earlier commented that Barori 'represented nobody but himself as a Minister' and that 'educationally and intellectually he was absolutely unfit to become a minister.'[15] On 15 October 1950, Mandal formally resigned from the cabinet, accusing the Pakistan government of communalism and anti-scheduled caste policies.[16] His personal issues with Barori, who was now a close ally of the League High Command, also pushed him towards resignation. Barori himself gave a five-page long statement where he described Mandal's resignation letter as one of the 'greedy refugees' tale of miseries and misfortunes invented for the purpose of liberal relief.'[17]

A Separate Scheduled Caste Identity: Caste Politics of the Muslim League

For a moment let us look beyond Jogendra Nath Mandal to try and understand the Muslim League's attitude towards Pakistan's Dalit population. The League was eager to constitutionally maintain a separate scheduled caste identity as opposed to a common Hindu identity. This was evident from various debates in the Constituent Assembly and Legislative Assemblies of Pakistan. I will discuss two such debates briefly: a) the debate around declaring the practice of 'untouchability' a punishable offence; and b) the debate around a separate electorate for scheduled castes in Pakistan.

While the Congress members of the Pakistan Constituent Assembly had demanded that 'untouchability' be declared a punishable offence in Pakistan, the Muslim League was unwilling to support such a measure.[18] The League's representative from East Bengal, Maulana Akram Khan, argued in the Assembly that though 'untouchability' was a sin, banning it would mean interfering in matters of Hindu customs and society. Nurul Amin argued that Hindus themselves by their behaviour made this distinction between scheduled castes and caste Hindus, and that those speaking in favour of abolishing 'untouchability' would probably not speak in the same way before an exclusively Hindu audience. Muslims could never think of 'untouchability,' Amin said, adding that these members should try to eradicate the practice by setting examples through their own behaviour in daily life without the help of legislation. The League leaders, though theoretically opposed to 'untouchability,' were not ready to provide constitutional safeguards against it. Finally, it was decided that if the Hindu members of the House were unanimous on this, 'untouchability' would be declared illegal. Thus the practice of 'untouchability' became a punishable offence.

Similarly, the Pakistan Congress and the Muslim League had a long-drawn conflict over the nature of the electorate. The League supported a separate electorate for the scheduled castes while the Congress, like always, pushed for a joint electorate. In the Constituent Assembly of Pakistan on 12 March 1949, Srischandra Chattopadhyay (Congress member from Comilla, East Pakistan) said that the Congress would fight against the idea of separate electorates because the 'people of Pakistan, Muslims and non-Muslims, consist of one nation and they are all Pakistanis.'[19] The issue was fiercely debated in the Constituent Assembly in April 1952 when the existing electoral law was amended to provide a separate electorate for scheduled castes. Congress saw this as an attempt towards the 'vivisection' of the Hindu community. The strong opposition from the Congress and majority of Hindu members in the Constituent Assembly on the issue finally produced a compromise in the form of Article 145, which declared that an Act on the electorate issue would be formulated after ascertaining the views of the provincial assemblies.[20] Finally, when Huseyn Shaheed Suhrawardy became the Prime Minister of Pakistan, a compromise bill was proposed that provided for a joint electorate in East Pakistan and a separate electorate in West Pakistan. This bill was introduced in the Assembly on 10 October 1956 and was passed.[21]

Mandal's resignation might have shaped such a 'divide and rule' policy of the League Government. The 1950 communal riots, perhaps the primary reason for Mandal's resignation, did not make a distinction along caste lines, resulting in the first massive migration of Dalits from East Pakistan since Partition. The riot also delegitimised the longstanding alliance between the League and a section of the scheduled caste leadership. In such a context, re-emphasising the fault lines within the Hindu community was important for the League government. Moreover, one needs to keep in mind the ongoing language controversy in East Pakistan while studying the minority politics of this time. Many among the Urdu-speaking ruling elite of Pakistan perceived Bengali or Bangla as a Hindu language and the Hindu *bhadralok* as the major troublemakers in this Urdu-Bangla conflict. In this context, keeping Dalit Hindus (who were still more numerous) separated from the upper castes, constitutionally and otherwise, was one possible way of keeping the opposition in check.

Jogendra Nath Mandal in West Bengal

Let us now go back to Jogendra Nath to understand the scope of Dalit politics in post-Partition West Bengal. Mandal's resignation and migration to India did not win him the confidence of the Congress Party. 'Mr. Mandal's past record is so unsavoury from India's point of view that it is hardly possible for us to accept him or his statement as completely *bona fide*,' commented Prime Minister Jawaharlal Nehru.[22] Nehru also pointed out that 'throughout the gravest crises, including the holocaust in August and September 1947, Mr. Mandal continued to serve Pakistan.'[23]

In West Bengal, Mandal dabbled with refugee politics and, in particular, attempted to organise the Namasudra refugees staying in various camps. But his attempt to 'reinvent his political leadership as a refugee leader'[24] was only marginally successful. As Sekhar Bandyopadhyay and Anasua Basu Ray Chaudhury write, 'Mandal's leadership of the refugee movement [did not] help him launch a new political career in West Bengal. He failed to win a single elected office and died on 5 October 1968 while conducting an election campaign.'[25] Mandal's failure shows that caste had lost its political significance for most of the refugees in West Bengal. Secret reports of the Intelligence Bureau on the political activities of refugees staying at the Sealdah station also show how Mandal was losing support among them. One such report records the events of 6 February 1958 when a protest rally of refugees was scheduled in Calcutta:

> .... At about 11.30 hrs Shri Dhirendra Bhowmik (Praja Socialist Party) accompanied by ...Shri Jogendra Nath Mandal, (Ex-Pak Minister) again visited Sealdah ...to arrange for the proposed procession of the refugees of the place. It was secretly learnt that during talks with the refugees Shri Jogendra Nath Mandal expressed that the partition of Bengal was caused due to the fault of the caste Hindus whereas the sufferance due to such partition goes to scheduled caste people. At this the majority of the refugees of the place were annoyed and also protested against such remarks of Shri Mandal and asked him not to entrench such sort of feelings among the refugees of the place, thereby denouncing their unity, and they also decided not to participate in the rally of the refugees as requested by Mr. Mandal. However Mr. Mandal and Mr. Bhowmik continued to exert their efforts to persuade the refugees to attend the rally...
>
> Ultimately having failed to persuade the refugees of Sealdah R.S....both Shri Dhirendra Bhowmik and Shri Jogendra Nath Mandal left Sealdah R.S. at about 14.15 hrs after talking for a minute or two with Shri Bhajan Haldar, Madhu Sudan Biswas...
>
> Since about 15.15 hrs said Shri Bhajan Haldar and Shri Madhu Sudan Biswas were not found at Sealdah R.S. Subsequently it was learnt that about 5/6 refugees of the place including Shri Bhajan Haldar and Shri Madhu Sudan Biswas, a man of Shri Mandal's community, being specially

requested by Shri Jogendra Nath Mandal at the time of his departure from Sealdah, had left the station individually to join the rally at Raja Subodh M. Square. ...At about 18.50 hrs Shrimati Sudha Roy (BPI) and Shri Chitto Nath (UCRC) had visited Sealdah Railway Station and asked the refugees to join the proposed meeting at Raja Subodh M. Square on 9.2.58 at 16.00 hrs in large numbers. It was learnt that they condemned the above stated remarks of Shri Jogendra Nath Mandal against the caste Hindus and supported the refugees of Sealdah R.S. They advised them to be united and not to lend their ears to such remarks of Shri Jogendra Nath Mandal.[26]

The above extract indicates that caste was losing its relevance, at least for the time being, in the refugee politics of West Bengal. However, 'caste' as a category was still important in case of various government rehabilitation policies, especially in the scheme of 'dispersal.' Under this scheme, Bengali Hindu refugees were sent to sparsely populated areas within and outside West Bengal from congested zones like Calcutta. The purpose was to reduce the demographic pressure on certain areas and to provide cheap labour in underdeveloped, thinly populated regions like the Andaman Islands and Dandakaranya. Those dispersed were mostly Dalit refugees from East Pakistan. Though the government did not have a stated policy of keeping the upper castes in Calcutta and driving the Dalits away, in practice this was effectively the case. The fact that even in face of this 'divide-and-disperse' policy, the refugees tried to present a united opposition shows that Mandal's mode of politics was perhaps a thing of the past. As caste became marginal in popular politics, new alliances were forged in terms of class under the Left opposition in West Bengal. But this did not mean an obliteration of caste-based practices. Far from it, the schisms in society and the refugee population in particular were often reframed in terms of 'colony residents' and 'camp dwellers.' Manoranjan Byapari, a Dalit refugee, wrote in his autobiography:

Among the refugees from East Bengal, there were two classes. The educated, well-to-do, upper caste *bhadraloks* among them had good connections with the influential people of this country. They despised the low caste subaltern camp residents. They utilized their connections and occupied plots in and around Calcutta. I have read that there are 149 such colonies. No poor, low caste, illiterate person got a place here in these colonies...The camp refugees had no leader...no one remembered them. Suddenly the government woke up from its slumber and decided to rehabilitate us. Where? In Dandakaranya.[27]

Conclusion

In this short essay, I have tried to understand the scope of caste politics in East and West Bengal (and also in Pakistan in general) in the aftermath of the Partition. On one hand, by focusing on Jogendra Nath Mandal's political career, I have tried to understand the scope of Dalit mobilisation in partitioned Bengal; on the other, by briefly discussing various policies I have attempted to show the Pakistan government's eagerness to keep the Dalits and upper castes segregated. Mandal (or any other leader for that matter) was not successful in making caste crucial to Bengal politics after 1947. Bandyopadhyay and Basu Ray Chaudhury have argued that the Partition disintegrated the Namasudra community and weakened their capacity to mobilise politically.[28] Indeed, Partition had a deep impact on the Namasudras. Some of them stayed on in East Pakistan; the rest migrated to West Bengal and were resettled in various parts of the province and also in areas like Andaman, Bihar, Orissa and Dandakaranya. Moreover, new binaries were emerging in postcolonial times. Competing trends of mass mobilisation could be identified where Hindu-Muslim, Bengali-non-Bengali (in East Pakistan), and mobilisation along class lines became important. However, caste remained important for governments on either side, whether for the 'developmental' needs of Nehruvian India or to keep the primarily non-Muslim opposition in East Pakistan divided in times of trouble over state language. Consequently, caste as identity remained crucial for Dalits in shaping their experiences of decolonisation, even when it failed to become a major factor in the politics of Bengal.

Notes and References

1. Dwaipayan Sen has extensively worked on Jogendra Nath Mandal. Please see Dwaipayan Sen, 'No Matter How Jogendra Nath had to be Defeated: The Scheduled Castes Federation and the Making of Partition in Bengal 1945–47,' *Indian Economic and Social History Review* 49, No. 3 (2012): 321–364. See also Dwaipayan Sen, *The Emergence and Decline of Dalit Politics in Bengal: Jogendranath Mandal, the Scheduled Castes Federation and Partition, 1932–1968,* (Unpublished PhD Dissertation, University of Chicago, 2012). However, Sen's work is in the nature of a biography. My research adds to Sen's work as my primary aim is to understand the locations of religious minorities in East Pakistan, keeping caste as an important entry point. Jogendra Nath is important to my research, but not its main subject, though in this short piece the primary focus is on Mandal. See Anwesha Sengupta, *Breaking Up Bengal: Land, People and Things, 1947–1952* (Unpublished PhD Dissertation, Centre for Historical Studies, Jawaharlal Nehru University, 2016).
2. The phrase 'partitioned times' has been coined by Ranabir Samaddar, who has argued that the experience of decolonisation in South Asia has been shaped by the Partition of British India to the extent that it is more appropriate to refer to 'post-colonial times' as 'partitioned times.' See Ranabir Samaddar, 'The Last Hurrah that Continues,' in *Divided Countries, Separated Cities: The Modern Legacy of Partition,* eds. Ghislaine Glasson Deschaumes and Rada Ivekovic (New Delhi: Oxford University Press, 2003), 21.
3. See Jagadish Chandra Mandal ed., *Mahapran Jogendra Nath,* Vol. 4 (Kolkata: Chaturthho Dunia, 2004), 23.
4. *Mahapran Jogendra Nath,* Vol. 4, 94–95 (translation mine).
5. 'Weekly Report from British Deputy High Commissioner in Dacca to British High Commissioner in Karachi No. 25 for the period ending June 25, 1949,' IOR/ L/Pj/5/325, British Library.
6. East Pakistan and East Bengal have been used interchangeably throughout the essay as both were in official usage till 1956. After 1971, East Pakistan became a sovereign nation state known as Bangladesh.

7. 'Weekly Report No. 24 for the period ending June 20, 1948,' IOR/L/ Pj/5/322, British Library.

8. For details on February Riots in East Pakistan, see the entries in Tajuddin Ahmed, *Tajuddin Ahmed's Diary*, Vol. 2 (Dhaka: Pratibhash, 2000), 76. Also see A. G. Stock's Memoir, translated into Bengali by Mubbasera Khanam in *Daccar Smriti*, ed. Muntassir Mamoon (Dhaka: Maula Brothers, 2001). The riots spread in West Bengal and Assam with equal intensity. For details, see Sekhar Bandyopadhyay's, 'The Minorities in Post-Partition West Bengal: The Riots of 1950,' in *Minorities and the State: Changing Social and Political Landscape of Bengal*, eds. Abhijit Dasgupta, Masahiko Togawa, and Abul Barkat (New Delhi: Sage Publications, 2011), 3–17; and Anasua Basu Ray Chaudhury, 'Remembering the Communal Violence of 1950 in Hooghly,' *Journal of Borderland Studies* 27, No.1 (2012): 45–59.

9. See Dilip Haldar, *Atrocities on Dalits since the Partition of Bengal: A Human Right Question* (New Delhi: Mittal Publications, 2008), 19–20.

10. This was one of the major events that led to the February Riots of 1950, but not the only one. There were economic causes too that strained Indo-Pakistan relations, particularly between East and West Bengal.

11. Letter dated 19 January 1950. Jagadish Chandra Mandal (son of Jogendra Nath Mandal)'s personal record collection.

12. Ibid.

13. *Anandabazar Patrika*, 12 April 1950.

14. The Nehru-Liaquat Pact was signed on 8 April 1950 to deal with the communal situation in East Pakistan, West Bengal and Assam. Among other provisions, it took measures to stop harassment of religious minorities who were migrating across the border, recognised the refugees' rights to return, set up an enquiry commission to probe recent disturbances, included a minority minister in the West Bengal, Assam and East Bengal ministry to restore confidence amongst religious minorities.

15. Excerpt from *The Civil and Military Gazette*, 9 July 1950, in *Mahapran Jogendra Nath*, Vol. 4, 155–156.

16. See Jogendra Nath Mandal's resignation letter. http://bengalvoice. blogspot.in/2008/05/appendix-1-jogendra-nath-mandals.html. Accessed 26 April 2015.

17. Reported in *Hindustan Standard*, 19 October 1950, taken from *Mahapran Jogendra Nath*, Vol. 5, 38–39.

18. See *Dawn*, 9 October 1952. After the creation of Pakistan, Congress was the main opposition in both the Constituent Assembly and East Bengal Legislative Assembly. The Indian National Congress would soon declare that its counterpart in Pakistan was a separate independent party. A new party would also be formed by some Congress leaders of East Pakistan. And gradually, the Muslim Awami League would emerge as the main opposition of the Muslim League.

19. M. G. Kabir, *Minority Politics in Bangladesh* (New Delhi: Vikas Publishing House, 1980), 31.

20. Ibid., 57.

21. Ibid., 60.

22. Nehru's letter to Chief Ministers, 16 October 1950, in *Selected Works*, Second Series, Vol. 15, Part 1, 554.

23. Nehru's letter to Chief Ministers, 16 October 1950.

24. Sekhar Bandyopadhyay and Anasua Basu Ray Chaudhury, 'In Search of Space: The Scheduled Castes Movement in West Bengal after Partition,' *Policies and Practices*, No. 59 (Kolkata: Mahanirban Calcutta Research Group, February 2014), 10.

25. Ibid.,12.

26. Copy of Secret Report No. Nil dated 6.2.58 from R.I.O. Sealdah, File on Sudha Roy (Bolshevik Party of India), F. No -67/39; Part III, 1939, Intelligence Bureau Records, West Bengal State Archives (WBSA), Kolkata.

27. Manoranjan Byapari,'Ananta Ratrir Chandal,' in *Deshbhag: Binash O Binirman*, ed. Madhumoy Pal (Kolkata: Gangchil, 2011), 212–213.

28. Bandyopadhyay and Basu Ray Chaudhury,'In Search of Space.'

4   A Sepia-Toned Past
A Photo Album Travels from Maghiana to Delhi

AANCHAL MALHOTRA

'I think,' her words hung light and hopeful, 'I should still be able to find my way from our home to the school, if nothing has changed in Maghiana.'

The woman looked up at me and smiled, and then her eyes went back to the old album full of sepia-toned photographs. Her soft, brown hands held between thumb and forefinger a delicate, wrinkled sheet of butter paper. Drawing the dull golden translucency aside, she revealed an image of a seascape, and with her fingers, traced its edges. 'Yeh dekho, look at this, Karachi!'

She gestured for me to come closer, and I peered down at the print. The photograph was held in place by two exquisite gold corners carefully stuck onto the page. Sliding it out, she wiped the surface and carefully studied the image. A small ship docked at a distance stared back. Turning it over, she read the inscription printed in a quick blue scrawl. *MANORA BEACH, 1946.* The photo beside it showed a family sitting in a boat, the wide expanse of the sea visible behind them.

'Manora Beach is now *sarhad paar*, across the border in Pakistan,' she said, pointing at her blurry child-like self in the photo. '*Kya hawa thi wahan ki!* I was very young here, but I can still feel the salty air of the sea. Actually, things from that time seem so clear, it feels almost impossible to believe that one will never see them again,' she smiled sadly.

'Were you born in Karachi?' I asked.

'No, but my family was from there. The year was 1939, and it was the onset of World War II. People had dug up bunkers all over the city to hide in case of an explosion or attack. My mother was pregnant with me and due any day, and so to ensure her safety and also as per custom, my parents travelled to her *maika*, her father's house in Maghiana for the delivery. My father was a devout man and had taken a vow of silence during the pregnancy to pray for the good health of a child that would grace his house after six long years. Their journey lasted two–three days, but her labour pains began mid-way in a town called Sukkur.'

As she spoke, I made note of her lexicon—Hindi for the most part, but peppered with English words. She had pronounced Sakhar as Sukkur, and within her voice was embedded an inherently Punjabi accent.

'When my parents finally reached, my mother was writhing in pain. In those days, there was no electricity, so amidst the dim light of many *diyas*, I was born on the midnight of 2 October 1939.'

As the story concluded, she turned the pages of the album to a leaf with two photographs—one of a small child, presumably her, sitting in the lap of a very old woman whose head was covered with a dupatta, and the other, of a principled looking moustached man in a regal white turban. Squinting at the small square frames, looking at the faces of her ancestry frozen within their sepia-toned lives, I wondered if it was possible to encapsulate the sentiments towards a place of the past within a photograph. Could the filmy grain contain a father's love, a carefree childhood, the memories of a celebration, the smell of a soil, the association of home? This lone photo album, the only evidence of a family's time spent in a land that had now become Pakistan, could it serve as a portal into the past? Years of storing it behind the closed doors of an almirah had caused its pages to be caked in a thin film of olden dust. But what time had also done was to infuse each page with an immeasurable surge of nostalgia, a likeness of which also swam in the eyes of the woman sitting before me.

We sat in the living room of a Karol Bagh house, bought by the family in 1973. Within its old-fashioned marble-chipped floors, impossibly high ceilings, rusted locks and decaying doors was suffused the same wear and nostalgic charm that could be found within the photo album. Following my gaze, the woman, too, looked around the room and then with a sigh, said, 'The haveli of my childhood was far grander than any house I've ever lived in. *Woh zamana*, that time, there is just no parallel to it. Though we lived in Maghiana, we would come back to Karachi for the holidays. My father owned cotton and textile mills, and we lived quite a comfortable life. Within our residential compound, my father had made a makeshift swimming pool, like a *hammam* with tall brick walls on all sides. *Sab dupkiyan lagate thhe*, we'd all take dips in it! In the unbearable summer heat, he would buy crates of mangoes and douse them in the cold water of the hammam and tell us to jump in and enjoy them!'

Laughing, she pointed to a photograph of a row of boys, skinny legs and knobbly knees, standing in front of the hammam, each modestly clad in his swimming trunks. 'You see, here are my brother and cousins! Oh, and near the pool was a long, beautiful, lush green corridor made with strong wire, upon which hung *angoor*, grape vines that were often visited by tree snakes! Beyond that was a vegetable garden and on the side were stables and sheds for horses and other animals. We used to have a Musalman *coachvaan*, Mummadeen, who drove us around in the horse-carriage.'

Her voice became impossibly childish as she visited the memories of her past. The Kashmiri floral *kadhai* on her shawl danced as she drew images of the old house in the air before us; her large red *bindi* leapt from side to side as she animatedly recounted tales; her long hair tied into a braid swung forward when with her fingers she traced the expanse of a leafy corridor. Remembrance, it appeared, was a living, breathing thing, bodily and visceral, which only grew exponentially with the passing of time. An excess of memory now appeared before her eyes—a childhood that had all but been forgotten, a carefreeness long consigned to oblivion—as if the gateways of recollection had finally been unlocked.

'*Batware ke samay*, during the Partition, we were forced to leave all of this behind.' A note of heartbreak suddenly pierced her jovial spirit, 'Sab kuchh, everything was lost. Land, respect, a comfortable life. We were young, I was barely eight years old but I remember, in a small room of the house, my father had set up a wireless radio and wahan se, he would hear what city was being engulfed in communal riots. From Maghiana we had to leave quickly, but our family in Karachi came out much, much later and safely by ship, because there were no riots there until November 1947 when the Musalman refugees, the Muhajirs finally started pouring in from India.

'My father had tremendous foresight, for in these early months of the riots he got all our money and gold transferred to a bank in Kanpur. Then, though we lived in a Hindu neighbourhood, he fortified the front of the house with a large iron gate and constructed walls higher than the ones currently standing.' She pointed again at the portrait of the moustached man in the white turban, her father, and in the background, showed me the front of the house, where even the windows were fastened safely with iron bars. 'But it was all in vain, for one day, our own household help looted our house, stole our grain and fled! You see, beta, there was madness in the air those days, pagalpan, violence and anger. The same Musalmans who looted us had served us for years and so it was difficult to believe that they were bad people. Bas, mahaul kharab thha, the atmosphere was bad; it made people do regrettable things. In the beginning of August, our father suddenly declared that we were leaving the house and moving to a makeshift camp where we would be safe.'

'What did you think was happening?' I asked, attempting to understand the psyche of a child amidst the changing the political climate of the time.

'Well, we were four sisters and one brother, all so young. What did we know? Suddenly, we weren't allowed to go anywhere. Schools were shut and there was talk of migration to another city, far away. We were afraid but were told that it was just temporary and that we'd come back to our home, to Maghiana. Our parents told us we were going to India, but I couldn't understand that, samajh hi nahin aya...Weren't we already in India? They said something was happening in the governments at the centre, the angrez were leaving, and that all this violence would die down after a few months. For the time being, to keep us safe, we would migrate. When your parents tell you that, you believe it.'

The immediate and extended family was relocated to a makeshift camp in an area called Mandi within the Hindu neighbourhoods of Maghiana city. Abandoned shops lined the bottom of the streets and homes dotted the tops. From the balconies, the women and children would look out at the transforming terrain they had once called home. Meanwhile, Hindu women had begun to be abducted and kept hostage by men, taking advantage of the tumultuous environment.

'My father would travel from morning to night, risking his life, finding these young women and bringing them to our camp. Some were so young, just children my age, and it hurt our hearts even then to imagine what would have happened to them otherwise. My father vowed he would not leave the city until he recovered every abducted Hindu girl. There was a small Hindu child, maybe five or six years old, whom the Muslim neighbours had found hiding in a large *tandoor* after her family had been slaughtered. They wanted to keep her, but my father wouldn't let them. *Itni khoobsurat thhi*, such a beautiful child, he brought her to our house and eventually my uncle's family adopted her, having no children of their own.'

But amidst this violence, amidst terrible riots, there were still glimpses of hope and humanity. 'Do you remember Mummadeen, our coachvaan?' her face broke into a smile. 'Well, even after we moved to Mandi, he continued to come and see us. Everyday, he'd bring fresh milk for us children from the cows we had abandoned at the haveli. He would call out to my mother, and she would say, "*Kaafir, zeher mila ke laya hai*," suggesting that he'd mixed poison in the milk. But after years of serving the family, he knew well that embedded within that outward insult was a longing to be proved wrong, a latent trust. And smiling, he would pour some milk out in a small *katori*, drink it himself and only then would mother be satisfied and accept it. *Aise hi chala*, this is how the days went by and before we knew it, we had to pack up and leave again, this time for Lahore, from where we would finally be transported to India.'

'What were you able to take from the haveli when you first left it?'

'*Kuchh nahin.* My mother had packed one box in haste, some clothes, a few kitchen utensils—a *lassi* glass, a *garva* for storing water, two *sagliyan*, bowls in which she cooked dal, which now my sister has with her in the UK, and...this.' Her hands patted the album in her lap. 'I don't know why she thought of bringing it, but in that moment, no sense prevailed. You took whatever your hands could find, you didn't think of need or want, and then years later these things became mementos...almost like souvenirs from another life.'

4.1: A photo album.

Courtesy: Usha Chaudhary.

What would I take if I had been in her mother's place, I found myself wondering. If I had had time, if I had known that my family would likely never come back to Maghiana. Would I have picked up all the constituents that make up a matrimonial life?

Bringing me back to the sunlit living room in Delhi's Karol Bagh, the woman completed the tale of their migration. 'From

Lahore, we were taken finally to Jalandhar. We heard that the border had already been drawn by then, but there was no physical line yet. Where Pakistan ended and where India began, we didn't know. We never felt it. We were just put on a train and told to remain silent. All the windows were shut; the air inside was heavy and recycled, and it led us to our new life. From Jalandhar, we went to Kanpur to stay with our cousins for a while and then, we came to Deh-li.'

So delicately she pronounced the name of the capital city, making it sound musical and fanciful, so far removed from the circumstances that had brought them here.

'I don't remember much of those first few years in Dehli, just that life was difficult. From Kanpur, we picked up the money our father had deposited in the bank and arriving in the capital, we first lived near this house itself in a small community with other refugees. School began, daily activities began and Maghiana became a distant memory...' She sighed deeply, her words dissolving in the air.

'Do you think about it ever? Do you wish you could go back?'

'Beta, ab kya sochna, now we do not think about it ever. So many years have passed. We don't consider ourselves from there anymore. In independent India, we rebuilt our lives. We were forced to. So now, if by chance, memories of Pakistan do visit me, I open these pages...' gracefully, purposefully, her flat palms caressed the pages of the ancient photo album, an heirloom, '...and find myself back in time. The swimming pool, the house, the buzzing of the bees around the grape vines, Mummadeen... that is all I remember. The disarray of Partition has all but faded away and what remains are these memories. Square frames of an idyllic, carefree childhood. Bas.'

With finality, she closed the photo album, a knowing smile spreading on her lips, memories brewing in her mind.

Acknowledgements

I am grateful to Mrs. Usha Chaudhary for allowing me to reproduce, in parts, the oral history interview conducted at her Delhi home on 22 January 2014 for my MFA dissertation [defended in 2015] at Concordia University, Montreal, entitled, 'Remnants of a Separation—A History of the Partition of India through Material Memory.' I am further grateful to her daughter, Anshu Bedi for providing additional information.

5   History, Memory, Genre

A Critical Reading of *I Too Have Seen Lahore* and
Milne Do from the anthology *This Side That Side*

KAJAL TEHRI AND ASMAT JAHAN

The 1947 Partition of the subcontinent with its warped legacy of uneasy equations between the nation states, ossified cultural attitudes and ambivalent structures of feeling towards the 'other' is seven decades behind us. Or is it? Scholarly anxieties about the ramifications of the Partition and its reenactments once again stand vindicated in the theatre of military action manifested in the surgical strike on terror camps in parts of Pakistan Occupied Kashmir (POK) widely reported recently in print and electronic media. The differential narrativisation of the surgical strike in India and Pakistan makes visible the interface of masculinity, national honour and discourse even as the surgical strike itself became a battleground for competing and contradictory discourses within the spaces of the body politic which cast aspersions on the strike as a politically motivated fictive discourse. The narrative(s) and counter narrative(s) endorsed by the nation states thus illuminates the oppositional political project of historiography which can be traced back (in this particular case) to the Partition. The evacuation of villages close to the border in the eventuality of a likely war resulting in the dislocation of hapless people partially refracts the Partition with its multiple violence(s) and the costs of warfare (whether organised or diffuse, whether state-sponsored or not) for common people on both sides of the border. The two polities thus continue to 'compulsively reenact the original divide.'[1]

This paper tries to locate spaces and sites which contest the othering of the 'other,' a dangerous socio-political discourse which releases its destructive energies in a spiral of hatred and animosity between the two nuclear states. The calcification of the image of the vengeful, violent and distrustful 'other,' an offshoot of the processes of nation-building across the two nation states, stands subverted in civil society initiatives which address the needs of common people across the border(s) for peaceful coexistence as also in the spaces of personal memory of a generation now in its twilight, memories which run counter to state-sponsored memory and history.

The monolith of state-sponsored history has been interrogated by a number of scholars. The fiftieth anniversary of the Independence and the Partition generated a spate of research works which took cognisance of the valence of alternative historical archives to understand the Partition and its protracted ramifications in its fullness. Studies by scholars like Alok Bhalla, Duggal and Cowasjee, Mushirul Hasan, M. U. Memon, Urvashi Butalia, Menon and Bhasin, Veena Das and Tarun K. Saint among others initiated a deeper enquiry enabling a nuanced understanding of the human losses of the Partition while also interrogating 'History.' Literary witnessing came to acquire an additional salience as a mode of alternative truth telling.[2]

Into the seventieth anniversary of the Independence and the Partition, the present paper seeks to analyse select narratives in the graphic format, interrogating how the lived realities of people's lives across makeshift borders are inflected with the (im)perfect collective past of both the nation states, while also tracing the affective ambivalences at the core of the relationship of the self with the 'other.' The paper traces the trajectory of negotiations of the founding trauma at the individual and collective level in the framework of memory (both individual and state-sponsored), state policies and civil society initiatives gesturing towards the pressing need to disseminate a politics of tolerance through initiatives which enable healing of the wounded psyche of the individual and the nation, while also recognising the humanity of the 'other.'

The entry of the graphic novel into the canon of literary witnessing(s) of the Partition is a recent phenomenon. The choice of the graphic genre for the enormity of the Partition raises certain questions about the congruity or otherwise of the form and content. However, several precedents from the West erase doubts about suitability of form and content in the register of the graphic.[3] Back home too, a number of graphic novels such as *Corridor* and *Delhi Calm* among others were published in the first decade of the twenty-first century.[4] The innovativeness of the anthology *This Side That Side* lies in articulating a polyphony of voices from different subject positions from across the border(s), thus attempting to open up spaces and sites for dialogue in the register of the literary. Located at an intersection of literature and art, these narratives that interrogate longing, belonging and unbelonging are Janus-faced, looking back at histories they are products of, and imagining futures in spite of these histories.

The silence around the Partition is ruptured in an inter-generational, inter-ethnic exchange to reclaim peaceful coexistence of the communities (and nations) lost not only to violent historical excesses but also to ossified attitudes and stereotypes. The text, I argue, contributes towards the opening up of spaces for a genuine dialogic interaction with the 'other' in a politics of peaceful coexistence in spite of the cataclysm of 1947. The text gestures towards the creation of redemptive spaces while subtly destabilising the hegemony of memories of the cataclysm as being 'the' signpost in the lives of people of the subcontinent.

This paper analyses two narratives from the aforementioned anthology—*I Too Have Seen Lahore*, and *Milne Do*. *I Too Have Seen Lahore*, by Salman Rashid and Mohit Suneja, is the story of Darshan Singh, who is delighted when the narrator-protagonist and his friend, Shabnam, come all the way from Lahore to Jalandhar to locate Shabnam's father's home (which might have been abandoned in the wake of the Partition) now on this side of the border. This motif of reclaiming lost ancestral spaces to memory stems from a founding curiosity about that part of the self which is now lost as the 'other.' In extension of Vazira Zamindar's trope of 'Partition Effects' or 'the ways in which Partition is rhetorically invoked and socially remembered,' the narrative gestures towards the continued affective pull of the othered people and spaces felt by those who were forced to leave parts of their lives elsewhere.[5]

While the house has been brought down, it is through Darshan Singh that the two of them become aware of the valence of these fading memories for an entire generation of displaced Punjabis even as they acquire an understanding of the therapeutic potential of these memories which escape the problematic seamlessness of the state-sponsored complex of history, memory and affect. Darshan Singh recounts to the young people his idyllic days in the village Klasswala where he was born and where he lived before the carnage broke. Darshan Singh's tenuous connection with his native village is available to him now only through a couple of fragmented images—the peepul tree, and inter-ethnic friendship with Hindu, Muslim and Sikh friends. In an inter-generational transmission, Darshan Singh shares with them his memories of 1947 which are firmly anchored in his mind despite the time lag. While on the surface, Darshan Singh's narrative seems to relay the metaphorical images of bewildered refugees on train tops and on foot in long columns with meagre possessions, his reminiscences create space for the humanity and kindness of the Muslim mob which let unarmed Sikhs cross over to the other side of the Ravi, unharmed. This imagining, while without precedent in the register of literary cultural productions, is significant in its refraction of cultural attitudes towards the 'other.' The narrative subconscious creates a moment of empathetic identification with the unarmed members of the 'other' community, a reckoning of the humanity of the 'other.' Also, the valence of the telling lies in the preservation of a redemptive memory in spite of the historically inflected, culturally conditioned memories of the Sikh community.

Butalia illuminates the fact that the Sikh community keeps the memories of its martyrs alive in ritual remembrances held at gurudwaras every year.[6] For a community which founds its ontological core in the affectively overcharged concepts of martyrdom and suffering at the hands of erstwhile Muslim rulers, this literary witnessing is an affirmation of the pluralistic contours of memory which escape the monolithic meta-narratives of the community and the nation, thus becoming a space and site for salvaging a sense of humanity. Therefore, Darshan Singh's membership into the community does not erase multiple ways of being and belonging, and the residual affect is a split sense of longing and belonging which does not map neatly onto the cartographic sensibility created by forces of history.

It needs to be answered whether the scars of history have healed at the individual and collective level. Through the subject position of Darshan Singh we discern a movement towards a reconciliatory future. Reckoning the presence of God in every individual irrespective of her/his religious affiliations, Darshan Singh's ethical model holds on trial members of both the communities who committed crimes against humanity instead of taking recourse to retributive discourses which feed into the never ending spiral of hatred. Darshan Singh thus bears out Susan Sontag's concern that while too much premium is being paid on remembering, not enough is put on thinking, which constitutes an ethical act.[7] Thus, while the narrative representation does not elide the remembrance of the wrongs of Partition, it is the processes of ethical thinking which liberate the now elderly Darshan Singh from the vicious spiral of discourses of hate and othering.

The significance of Lahore to the narrative or to Darshan Singh's life cannot be missed. The much anthologised cosmopolitanism of the fabled city is echoed in several registers—films and theatre productions, for instance.[8] Like so many displaced Punjabis, for Singh too the cosmopolitan city becomes a hyper signifier, an important signpost of his memories of the place which also anchors his sense of self. It is important to note that Darshan Singh has been to Lahore only once and that too as a child of six or seven. However, Lahore becomes a conduit through which he can connect himself to the village, city and country of his birth and reclaim a lost sense of belonging and a way of life. His only memory of Lahore is of 'an aquarium in which a frog kept trying to swim to the top but kept going under.'[9] It is through this overcharged image that the memories of the fabled city are kept afloat. The narrator's failure to photograph Singh's two-storeyed house in Klasswala gestures towards the urgency now implicit in the project of documenting and archiving the memories of first-generation Partition survivors, most of who are now in the twilight of their lives, an urgency articulated through the two frustrated projects—Shabnam's search for her ancestral house, and the narrator's promise to Darshan Singh, to photograph his house in Klasswala, which he could not keep.

In extension of the thematic of longing and belonging, Beena Sarwar's narrative *Milne Do* gestures towards fatigue with the carefully nurtured afterlife of the Partition which materialises in the discourses of 'othering,' and differential treatment and ghettoisation of the members of the 'other' community. Directed towards the nameless, faceless agents of the state, the title in the imperative mood is a tacit acknowledgment of the political agenda of the state and its agents which runs counter to the lived realities of the lives of common people.[10] The narrative is actually an extension of Sarwar's commitment to the peace-keeping project, Pakistan-India Peoples' Forum for Peace and Democracy (PIPFPD), a forum which was set up to promote peace and democracy in India and Pakistan in 1994, when acrimony between the nation states had increased and the threat of nuclearisation loomed large over South Asia.[11] Initially a small group comprising human rights activists from both countries, the ambitious civil society initiative—which swelled to include the membership of ministers, activists, scholars, business people and retired government officials—aims to put together 'an "alternate relational narrative of India and Pakistan" instead of the antagonistic and statist one.'[12] The project's larger concept aimed at a joint production of resource books, pamphlets, literature, people to people contact and cultural productions to curb hostilities which were unleashed in the 1940s and continue to hold sway.

Beena Sarwar's narrative also traces the differential trajectory of evolution in the relationships of both countries. While the access of journalists to the 'other' country have improved greatly with the erosion of barriers facilitated by social media, the panoptical surveillance maintained by both nation states betrays an anxiety over borders and intermingling which is an ironic subversion of sporadic aims at bridging the divide. While the narrative asserts that the two nation states are inching towards normalcy, the recent souring of relationships in verbal exchanges of the leaders of the two countries testify to the dispensability of common people's feelings which are sought to be disciplined and aligned according to state policy and ideology while also reenacting fissures between state policies and common people's lives. The haunting image of multitudes on both sides of the border who eagerly await reunification with their loved ones on the other side even as the soldiers as representatives of the state engage in ritual performance at the border again plays out the apathy of the state(s) to the agonisingly slow process of reunification. Interestingly, the concern over stringent visas between the two countries has also been articulated by members of the PIPFDP. In the tenth anniversary celebrations of the forum, the longstanding demand for easy and citizen-friendly visas was reiterated even as the governments of both countries were urged to review and revise school curricula to expunge it of hate material while also upholding the introduction of peace education as a part of the school curricula.

Both the narratives, then, are a counterpoint to the exclusionary practices and violent legacies of the Partition with a redemptive potential. Several scholars have addressed the erasure of Partition violence, especially gendered violence, in state-sponsored history. It is our contention that representation of the Partition and its lived realities in this new genre is an opening up of spaces for dialogue and reconciliation in the spaces of the popular. This anthology thus opens up another space for Partition Studies with potential appeal to a wider reading public. In the lopsided discourses around Partition, while the repressed memories of violence continue to enjoy an afterlife in the post-independence spaces of the nation, it is the 'other' of this violence, the syncretic modes of being and living, which have not enjoyed the same robustness, overwhelmed as our historical memories are with the violent excesses of the Partition. This renewed negotiation thus bears testimony to fissures in our national histories and personal memories even as it tries to interrogate exclusionary practices and calcified attitudes towards the 'other,' and dismembering cultural myopia, a pathological state which impedes widespread dissemination of memories of shared cultural values and syncretic living.

What is common to *I Too Have Seen Lahore* and *Milne Do* is fatigue with the legacy of violence and hostility, and its reenactments which are far removed from the business of everyday living in both the countries, the narratives suggest. The offspring of the children of violence are looking to break stereotypes and discover the 'other' through untinted glasses. However, while the narratives create spaces for dialogic interaction between the two communities, the narrative reimagining stops at the borders. The solid materiality of the borders of the nation states etched in the bloodshed of millions in 1947 thus circumscribes narrative imaginings which stop short at hoping for reconciliation, for peace or for ease of visas while not interrogating the continuing valence of these borders. What is interesting about the memories of people like Darshan Singh is their duality which escapes the monochromatism inherent in national memories of post-Partition generations. The duality of memory—the fading memories of a past of peaceful inter-ethnic coexistence and the later memories singed with the scars of the Partition—gives to the protagonist a split sensibility which resists appropriation in the dominant culture of inter-ethnic hostility.

The state-sponsored memory-history of the Partition relays historical wrongs in the form of massive dislocation and loss of life and property, but this hegemonic discourse eclipses other memories which are actively repressed in the meta-narrative of the body politic. It is our contention that narratives such as Darshan Singh's and Beena Sarwar's serve as valuable cognitive tools as they shift focus from annihilating violence to redemptive kindness. The unsung heroes of the multiple narratives of Partition are the nameless, faceless people represented by the mob in the story who resisted the urge for retributive justice in the face of rampant retaliatory violence as also members of civil society who tried to look beyond the manufactured discourses of absolute othering, beseeching the governments of both countries to open up channels of communication and people's interaction. It is these unsung heroes who redeem our lost humanity even in times of extreme polarisation and ethical breakdown.

Notes and References

1. See the introduction to Suvir Kaul, *The Partitions of Memory: The Afterlife of the Division of India* (New Delhi: Permanent Black, 2001).

2. For a detailed discussion, see the introduction to Tarun K. Saint, *Witnessing Partition: Memory, History, Fiction* (New Delhi: Routledge, 2010).

3. I specifically allude to *Maus*, which became the first graphic novel to receive serious academic attention as an award-winning documentation of the experiences of the author's parents during the Holocaust. See Art Spiegelman, *Maus: A Survivor's Tale* (New York: Pantheon Books, 1986).

4. *Corridor* is the first Indian graphic novel, first published in 2000. See Sarnath Banerjee, *Corridor* (New Delhi: Penguin, 2004). See also Vishwajyoti Ghosh, *Delhi Calm* (New Delhi: Harper Collins, 2010).

5. See Vazira Fazila-Yacoobali Zamindar, *The Long Partition and the Making of Modern South Asia: Refugees, Boundaries, Histories* (New York: Columbia University Press, 2007), 238.

6. Urvashi Butalia alludes to the centrality of martyrdom for the Sikh community. See Urvashi Butalia, 'Community, State and Gender: On Women's Agency during Partition,' *Economic and Political Weekly* 28, No. 17 (1993): WS12–WS24. http://jstor.org/stable/4399641.

7. See Susan Sontag, *Regarding the Pain of Others* (New York: Picador, 2003), 86.

8. The cosmopolitanism of Lahore and its enchantments are evocatively alluded to in the title of Asghar Wajahat's Hindi play, *Jis Lahore Nai Dekhya O Jamyai Nai* [One Who Hasn't Seen Lahore Hasn't Even Been Born], an excerpt from which is included in this volume in Alok Bhalla and Nishat Zaidi's translation.

9. See Salman Rashid and Mohit Suneja, *I Too Have Seen Lahore*, in *This Side That Side: Restorying Partition*, curated by Vishwajyoti Ghosh (New Delhi: Yoda Press, 2013), 218.

10. See Beena Sarwar, *Milne Do*, in *This Side That Side*. *Milne Do* is also the title of a 2006 documentary by Sarwar which foregrounds the perception of the common Pakistani about the people of Kashmir, and the erosion of these stereotypes as a consequence of dialogue with the 'other.' It is also the title of one of the campaigns of the peace initiative, *Aman ki Asha*, flagged off by the Jang Group, Pakistan and *The Times of India* which, among other things, foregrounded the need to ease out visa restrictions between the two countries.

11. *Bridging Partition* foregrounds stories of activists who believe that it is through dialogue and peace initiatives that the two countries can ever reach a resolution of longstanding disputes. One such example is Kuldip Nayar's *People to People Contact*, his own story of post-Partition activism whose success, though limited, lay in opening up channels of interaction with the 'other.' See Kuldip Nayar, *Scoop! Inside Stories from the Partition to the Present* (New Delhi: Harper Collins, 2006); and Smitu Kothari and Zia Mian, eds., *Bridging Partition: People's Initiatives for Peace between India and Pakistan* (New Delhi: Orient BlackSwan, 2010), 87–95.

12. See Papiya Ghosh, *Partition and the South Asian Diaspora: Extending the Subcontinent* (London: Routledge, 2014), 214–216.

Photo-framed Installations
Second and Third Generation Narratives
about the Partition and the Holocaust

MARGIT KÖVES

T he Holocaust and the Partition, even after seventy years, have not become settled issues of the past. Even though the generation which was immediate witness to them has mostly passed away, these events affect us in some way or the other and force us time and again to rethink our basic notions of victimhood, trauma and memory. Their aesthetic reflection and artistic elaboration also went through various changes with a new generation which has different modes of witnessing and receiving, and this also broadens our aesthetic horizons.

New forms of art and their expression require the anticipation, the presentiment of new unimaginable aspects of the reality of modernity and postmodernity. It is no longer possible to integrate these events in our earlier conceptions of history and to give a transparent meaning to historical events, and establish a tranquilising meaning on them.[1] The arts and aesthetics of Partition and Holocaust need to be open to the paradoxical aspects of the reality of the penal colony and the concentration camp. George Steiner suggests in his essay 'K' about Franz Kafka that '*In the Penal Colony* foreshadows not only the technology of the death-factories, but that special paradox of the modern totalitarian regime—the subtle, obscene collaboration between victim and torturer.'[2] The arts of Partition and Holocaust demand an aesthetics that gives space to the generation of a narrative through loops, gaps, and the palimpsest of shifting contexts. This way in the course of reading the reader can interpret his/her understanding of these events.

In a dialogue between Suresh Sharma and Javeed Alam,[3] the issue emerged as to what extent the comparison between the Partition and the Holocaust was possible. Alam underlined the role of the state that in the case of the Holocaust built up a long and powerful campaign to suppress, to remove and to liquidate the minority and used all its resources.

The history of the decades preceding the Holocaust and the history of World War II when Hungary was an ally of Germany shows that Hungarian society and state were complicit with the extermination of 600 thousand Hungarian people of Jewish origin. But collective amnesia about the events leading up to the Holocaust in Hungary prompts common people and many historians to blame only the Germans. Similar issues emerge in India connected to selective remembering and selective forgetting where each group forgets its complicity with the persecution of the other groups and remembers its own victimhood.[4]

Suresh Sharma stressed the use of the newest technology employed in the Holocaust, but he also spoke about the elements of forgetting and remembrance. This paper highlights this aspect in the context of second- and third-generation remembrance, 'postmemory,'[5] which assumes that children, grandchildren and contemporaries of survivors come into the memories of the survivors through stories and material objects. The work of the artists of *This Side That Side: Restorying Partition*, an album curated by Vishwajyoti Ghosh[6] and *We Are On Our Own*[7] by Miriam Katin, the first dealing with narratives of Partition and the second, a memoir of the Holocaust by a Hungarian child survivor. The child survivor with very few or no memories is called '1.5 generation' by Leo Spitzer.[8]

Saadat Hasan Manto and the Hungarian István Örkény, first-generation survivors of the Partition and Holocaust, in their short fiction anthologies *Siyah Hashiye* and *One Minute Stories* respectively, used narrative strategies which countered accepted forms of the canon.[9] These few line stories form a marginal genre, which Manto called 'avsananch' and Örkény, 'egyperces' [one-minute story], something between a short story, joke and dramatic scene.

In the story 'The Sweet Moment' (Saat-e Shirin) by Manto, the title and the event of Gandhi's death serves as a challenge; in 'Out of Consideration' the daughter is not killed in front of her father but stripped and kept with the other women out of kindness. As Ashis Nandy has pointed out, 'Manto was one of the few who "faced... the psychopathic and sadistic aspects of the carnage."'[10] Similarly Örkény's one-minute stories like 'In Memoriam Dr. K.H.G.' expose the paradox between the existential situation of Dr. K.H.G., the Hungarian Jewish prisoner, and his German guard. It consists of a dialogue that presents Dr. K.H.G.'s urge to explain and teach German literature and culture to the guard, who shoots and kills him at the end of the dialogue. These works by Manto and Örkény, like the Polish writer Tadeusz Borowski's stories on Auschwitz, This Way for the Gas, Ladies and Gentlemen, are grounded in an ironic sensibility and the rejection of sentimentality and moral judgement. They enable the reader to deal with the benumbing effects of the experiences of Partition and World War II and avoid identifying with the roles of either the victims or the perpetrators.

In the nineteen nineties and the twenty-first century, visual media and artifacts of the earlier generation[11], photography and visual traces were invoked, superimposed and emplotted by the second and third generation who were born after the Holocaust and whose ideas about the Holocaust were shaped by the narratives of the earlier generations. Photographs are considered to be testimonies and are specially powerful material links to the past, as Marianne Hirsch has pointed out. István Örkény, like Franz Kafka before him, had a special talent for anticipating new forms of narrative and formulating contradictions in the form of paradoxes. The photograph as record and narrative tool figures in his one-minute story, 'Two Onion-domes in a Snowy Landscape,' a photograph of the Russian winter. The photograph presents the onion cupolas of a Russian church, the face of a four-year old girl, and Hungarian and German soldiers in the snow. Intimate details of the motives of the participants and use of the first-person plural by the narrator suggests a close acquintance and participation in their everyday life recalled on the basis of a photograph, which calls forth the hanging of a Russian partisan, a woman. The tone of the story reminds the reader of Kafka's *In the Penal Colony.* László Márton's novel *Shadowy Main Street*[12] narrates events in a provincial city through characters in an album of photographs. These characters were all taken to concentration camps, and the indication of their absence re-draws the outliness of the city. Photography as visual trace and evidence figure in the Oscar-winning film, *Son of Saul,* by László Jeles Nemes where in a scene Saul takes photographs of a group of women before their execution.

This can be considered a transitional point between first-, second- and third-generation narratives of the Holocaust, which focus on visual elements. The work of the second and third generation brings into play visual imagery and photographic images of the Holocaust and connects to other legacies of colonialism like Partition.

Maus: The Story of a Survivor by Art Spiegelman builds the narrative on the radical form of the graphic novel that was, until recently, considered a marginal genre. Installation art and the growth of graphic novels and digital arts in the last few decades has catapulted the form into the focus of attention.

Memories and experiences of the Partition and Holocaust in fiction and graphic novels give space to the voice of the individual as s/he remembers his/her victimhood and/or complicity with the perpetrators.[13] Geoffrey Hartman points out that using a graphic approach for his story on the Holocaust, Spiegelman asked the question: what are the possible ways of knowing the Holocaust exhaustively, completely. *This Side That Side* invites the work of artists from across India, Pakistan and Bangladesh, and this widens the history of the Partition in the subcontinent. This history counters the official recorded history of these three countries. *90 Upper Mall or 1 Bawa Park* asserts that the narrator, Ahmad Rafay, found out during conversations with Martand Khosla that 'India was other than the opinions I'd picked up from schoolbooks, television and the press.' The official view of the Partition and

Holocaust is often distorted, ascribing responsibility to outsiders. The responsibility of the state, and often its complicity with the persecution, emerges in these stories.

> Using the same footage, history keeps changing its story at every border....The nights look younger now than those evenings of listening to the same old grandiose stories told by grandparents. Those fictions are now photo-framed installations of memory....To listen to the subsequent generations and the grandchildren and how they have negotiated maps that never got drawn, *This Side That Side* is a tiny drop in the river of stories that must be told before the markers run dry.[14]

The aspect of oral fiction is clear from the remark that the book grew out of conversations. Likewise, Miriam Katin's memoir also reflects that her book grew out of her mother's and her own memories, mediated by her after a gap of sixty years. In the coloured panels of *We Are On Our Own*, she is also shown talking to her mother on the phone about the winter of 1944–45 in Hungary. Katin's narrative is, first and foremost, built on her mother's account, but Lisa, the narrator, also tends to speak for her.

Women went through specific experiences during the Holocaust and Partition, and this aspect links several of the stories in Katin's graphic novel; for instance, Esther is picked to be the German officer's lover, and later she offers herself in place of her daughter to the Russian soldier. In *This Side That Side*, women are the carriers and narrators of persecution, abuse and dispossession of home in *Water Stories* by Arundhati Ghosh and Apuppen, or deprival of work in *Know Directions Home?* by Nina Sabnani, or being debarred from education and the opportunity of planning their future in *Little Women* by Syeda Farhana and Nitesh Mohanty.

Katin's book starts with mother and daughter reading the *Genesis* in Hebrew and the title *We Are On Our Own* reflects the loss of belief that is the result of loss, death, betrayal and persecution and the father's secular influence as it is exposed in the 'Afterword.'[15] Most of the stories in *This Side That Side* as well as in

We Are On Our Own are narrated on two and, quite often, three planes of time—on the third plane, the memories of the intervening years play out. While the first plane of time is black and white, the alternative planes are in colour. The oscillation between these different planes of time is a characteristic feature of 'postmemory'.

There are a number of allegories in *This Side That Side*; for example, the first narrative is *An Old Fable*,[16] an adaptation of the *Caucasian Chalk Circle*, the allegory of the baby, an undivided India, claimed by a woman 'in green' representing the Muslim side and by another woman 'in saffron' representing Hindus and 'the wise King who was famous, in his own words, for Reason and Law.' The desperate mothers offer to give up their half of the baby when the king decides to cut the child into two. As it could not be decided whether the baby should be cut horizontally or vertically, it was decided to cut him into three. Priya Kuriyan's figures give the allegories an iconic, tale-like character. The large figures of the king, the oversized baby and the crowd scenes require much space. Page layout is an important aspect of *An Old Fable*; the panel borders are porous and the king's shadow spills over into other panels, making an internal connection between panels of different sizes. Hands—whether those of the newborn baby or the crowd's—stretch across the panels. One large panel can occupy the equivalent of a smaller one-third or a larger two-third of the page.[17] The one-third and two-third sized panels can also occupy an entire spread of two facing pages of the book.[18] When the king announces that the baby shall be cut horizontally as well as vertically on the left side of the page, he is shown to be deep in thought while the courtiers celebrate him, and below on the right the two women are depicted weeping and wringing their hands. On page 29, on the right, the baby is cut into four, horizontally and vertically. The juxtaposition of contrasts on the pages underlines the division of power and the expectation of privileges by the upper and middle class. Graphic narratives are first of all visual, but Tabish Khair's text, the formulation of the tongue-in-cheek 'royal' pronouncements in the speech balloons, the mix of languages and his witty summary of the tale are integral to the narrative. 'We always knew that two women could not have a baby together. We always said so. It stands to Reason.'[19] British rule is represented by the king who stands for Reason and Law.[20]

90 Upper Mall or 1 Bawa Park is a graphic narrative by Ahmad Rafay Alam and Martand Khosla[21] which maintains an autobiographical perspective. Rafay and Khosla were both born long after the Partition, and the filters and methods of mediation through various sources are foregrounded in their respective family histories. The narrator, Ahmad Rafay, makes explicit reference to the educational expectations of the family he was born into, where it was assumed that one would 'complete one's studies at a Western university,' specially 'reading law in the United Kingdom.'

During the narrator's stay in London in Mecklenburgh Square in a building popularly known as 'Willie G,' he meets Martand Khosla. Rafay is a first-person narrator, whose photograph is pasted in front of a large, packed bookshelf. Photographs inserted or pasted on drawings are part of the style, the missing detail is complemented with a drawing. Rafay tells us about his life on Willie G and his friendhip with Martand, who is also first introduced in a drawing from an angle high above his head seen from the back, and our view of him covers his back and his desk with a mug and drawings all over. First the picture of a truck, and then a group of trucks[22] indicate Partition and the shift to the new countries. In the next panel, Lahore and the Lahore Government College, where the grandparents of both Khosla and Rafay studied, are depicted.[23]

In *90 Upper Mall or 1 Bawa Park*, notions of official history as contained 'in school textbooks, television and the press' about the Partition surface as completely irrelevant and Rafay and Khosla discover the shared past of the pre-Partition Indian upper middle class. 1 Bawa Park was built by Bawa Nath Singh, Martand Khosla's great-grandfather and Chief Engineer of the Canals; the park is surrounded by sprawling gardens.[24] The Khoslas had to leave Lahore suddenly because they never anticipated the violence that broke out in the middle of 1947. The Alam family migrated, as did many muhajirs, to Pakistan, and were compensated for the property they lost by the house the Khoslas left behind. The house that was inherited by Shakuntala Khosla, grandmother of Martand

Khosla, was taken over by the Rafay family. Ahmad Rafay writes about the 'absurd and arbitrary nature' of Partition as life histories and experiences are shared by the grandchildren of the two families in London, where they chance to meet and stay together.

Water Stories by Arundhati Ghosh and Apuppen[25] focuses on the nature of memory and how it is mediated to the second and third generation that had no direct experience of the Partition. Memory is fluid like water, and the water motif is repeated through the narrative and gives a rhythm to the story of grief and regret about the missing mother, the wife and the river Padma. Thierry Groensteen refers[26] to the 'pantomime strip', the silent graphic novel, where reiteration of the motif gives the story its rhythm. *Water Stories*, which contains many silent panels, is an example of the silent strip. In the first-person narrative, the girl, who is the narrator, listens to her father's stories of the Padma and she is seen between the panels,[27] which indicates her gradual absorption into her father's narrative. Her father's face, lined with wrinkles and folds, looks like the surface of the huge river. The Padma was an essential part of the father's childhood; the river 'swallowed' his mother on the eve of the Partition and also 'cursed' his wife, the narrator's mother. The river Padma as 'Rakshasi' affects the narrator with a longing that could be similar to the longing of a 'childless woman for a child.'[28] In the closing panels of the narrative, the narrator herself merges with the river. Water and river as an allegory of memory, grief and the regret of later generations is part of the Partition stories.

This Side That Side presents graphic narratives of fourteen-fifteen pages and *We Are On Our Own* is a 127-page long graphic memoir. Both graphic narratives can be considered to be albums assembling stories, displaying photographs and letters. They also present alternate histories, partial memories in black and white. The incidents in *We Are On Our Own* are all connected to the narrator's mother, Esther Levy; the memoir is also dedicated to the mother 'who taught me to laugh and forgive.' The interchange of black and white and coloured pages adds rhythm to the narrative apart from other rhythmic elements. The size of frames offers variety; the opening and closing frames are of the size and style of an old black and white photograph with serrated edges.

The 'idea of black' according to Adorno was a response to the 'black hole' of Auschwitz, to the mass executions, and also an answer to the market conditions of artistic creation. *This Side That Side* consists of graphic narratives entirely in black and white and *We Are On Our Own* has only seven of its 127 pages in colour. The panels in colour indicate a different plane of time; they show Katin as a young mother in New York in a telephone conversation with her mother, Esther who reminds Katin of their escape from the village in winter early 1945.[29] The colour panel indicates a historical change when the German flag falls and the Soviet flag with the hammer and sickle goes up.[30] Though Lisa, the narrator, is also supposed to be a witness, in the above-mentioned phone conversation she admits to not remembering the events.[31] On the last pages of the book, along with photographs of some letters and postcards in Hungarian, part of a personal family archive, she reiterates, 'I could somehow imagine the places and the people my mother told me about but a real sense of myself as a small child and the reality of the fear and confusion of those times I could understand only by reading the last few letters and postcards my mother had written to my father.'[32]

The titular phrase 'We are on our own' is declared first by Esther at the time when she burns the family Bible before hiding with fake papers in the countryside. Esther transforms herself into a village woman with an illegitimate child with the help of her friend Éva and her maid Anna, and arranges for evidence to show that she had committed suicide by drowning herself in the Danube. The kindness of the maid, who is the only witness, is contrasted with the wickedness of Mr. Barossi, the concierge. The inmates of the housing block where Esther and Lisa live, and where the father Károly Levy had lived before being called for military service to fight the Russians, express their grief over their death. Esther and Lisa find refuge in a village where a family permits them to stay, and Esther is discovered by a SS officer who uses his position to force her to become his lover. As the Germans withdraw in early

1945 and the Russians occupy the part of western Hungary where Esther and Lisa stay, Esther and the other women of the village are raped by Russian soldiers. Esther finds one of the soldiers dead in her bed, and she has to run to escape arrest. *We Are On Our Own* presents Hungarian village people of great kindness along with some other peasants who want to profit from Esther's and Lisa's troubles. In Borosvár, near the Jewish centre in the market, some peasants comment on the presence of Jews even after the war 'Getting by without working. Like always.'[33] When after a few weeks Esther realises that she is pregnant she decides to move and find help in the city of Borosvár to have an abortion.

The book is a women's memoir, and the daughter recounts her mother's life experiences while also revisiting them, the places she lived in, and in the process of remembering, she identifies with her mother's emotions after a gap of decades. At the same time the book gives an account of the slow erosion of secular positions in Israel and in the United States. The narrator, Lisa wites about her father's secular convinctions, her own atheism, which she had to adjust to a conservative Jewish lifestyle to conform to their surroundings after they emigrated from Hungary.[34] The graphic memoir is written in English; its authenticity for the Hungarian reader is maintained by the Hungarian personal names and place names, the billboards in Hungarian, the typical buildings in Pest with the circular galleries.

This Side That Side and *We Are On Our Own* are works of postmemory by second- and third-generation survivors of the Partition and Holocaust. The works in these two books connect many countries, stories, memories and histories in an aesthetic space that is embedded in installations, graphic narratives and digital arts, which were earlier considered to be marginal in comparison with the 'high arts.' In the last few decades, there has been an aesthetic shift in Holocaust literature and the graphic narratives avail of the opportunities of visual culture and the wide possibilities offered by the web and by private and public archives. The testimonial quality of visual material is important, and the graphic narrative form provides a space with loops and gaps where imagination and fiction can enter and mingle with history and fact.

Notes and References

1. Tamás Kisantal, *Túlélő Történetek, Ábrázolásmód és Történetiség a Holokauszt űvészetében* [Survival Stories, Artistic Method and History in the Art of the Holocaust], (Budapest: Kijárat, 2009), 35–71.

2. George Steiner, 'K,' in *Language and Silence, Essays on Language, Literature and the Inhuman* (New York: Atheneum, 1967), 121.

3. 'Remembering Partition, Dialogue between Javeed Alam and Suresh Sharma,' *Seminar* 461 (January 1998): 98–103.

4. Urvashi Butalia, 'Communications,' *Seminar* 463 (March 1998): 71–74.

5. Marianne Hirsch, *The Generation of Postmemory: Writing and Visual Culture After the Holocaust* (New York: Columbia University Press, 2012), 3–6.

6. Vishwajyoti Ghosh curated, *This Side That Side: Restorying Partition* (New Delhi: Yoda Press, 2013).

7. Miriam Katin, *We Are On Our Own*, (Montreal: Drawn & Quarterly, 2006).

8. Hirsch, *The Generation of Postmemory*, 14.

9. Margit Köves, 'Telling Stories of Partition and War: Saadat Hasan Manto and István Örkény,' *Economic and Political Weekly* 32, Nos. 33 and 34 (August 1997): 16–23.

10. Ashis Nandy, 'The Days of The Hyaena: A Foreword,' in *Mapmaking: Partition Stories from Two Bengals*, ed. Debjani Sengupta (New Delhi: Amaryllis, 2011), xiii.

11. Marianne Hirsch, 'Past Lives, Postmemories in Exile,' *Poetics Today* 17:4 (Winter 1996): 659–686.

12. László Márton, *Árnyas Főutca* [Shadowy Main Street] (Pécs: Jelenkor, 1999).

13. Butalia, 'Communications,' 71–74.

14. Vishwajyoti Ghosh, 'Curator's Note,' in *This Side That Side*, 12.

15. Katin, *We Are On Our Own*, 124. There is no part in this book entitled 'Afterword.' I use this to refer to pages 124–127, which are not numbered in the book. Page numbers stop at 122 after the mother, father and child reach Budapest, their original home. 123 is a blank page, followed by what I call the 'Afterword,' which begins with the author telling us: 'This book is the story of our escape and life in hiding during the year 1944–45.' It continues with the depiction of the memory of the child—now an adult—with text and pictures, upto page 127.

16. Tabish Khair and Priya Kuriyan, *An Old Fable*, in *This Side That Side: Restorying Partition*, curated by Vishwajyoti Ghosh (New Delhi: Yoda Press, 2013), 15–29.
17. Khair and Kuriyan, *An Old Fable*, 25.
18. Ibid., 18–19.
19. Ibid., 29.
20. Ibid., 16.
21. Ahmad Rafay Alam and Martand Khosla, *90 Upper Mall or 1 Bawa Park*, in *This Side That Side: Restorying Partition*, curated by Vishwajyoti Ghosh (New Delhi: Yoda Press, 2013), 177–190.
22. Alam and Khosla, *90 Upper Mall or 1 Bawa Park*, 180, 183.
23. Ibid., 181.
24. Alam and Khosla, *90 Upper Mall or 1 Bawa Park*, 184–185.
25. Arundhati Ghosh and Apuppen, *Water Stories*, in *This Side That Side: Restorying Partition*, curated by Vishwajyoti Ghosh (New Delhi: Yoda Press, 2013), 129–136.
26. Thierry Groensteen, *Comics and Narration* (University Press of Mississippi, 2013), 114–115.
27. Ghosh and Appupen, *Water Stories*, 131.
28. Ibid., 134.
29. Katin, *We Are On Our Own*, 6, 63, 70, 84, 101.
30. Ibid., 47.
31. Ibid., 70.
32. Ibid., 125.
33. Ibid., 106.
34. Ibid., 125.

7 Undoing Partition
Flight of Utopian Fantasies across Borders

RAVIKANT

Badi cheez hai pyar mohabbat, aisi taisi jhagde ki
Ho jaye sarkar mohabbat, aisi taisi jhagde ki[1]
        —A song from *Chacha Zindabad* (1959).

Phagua Brij dekhan ko chal ree[2]
        —A *hori* from *Mousiqar* (1962).

The compromised and controversial release of Karan Johar's *Ai Dil Hai Mushkil* (2016) following the ongoing cycle of attack and counter-attack on the Indo-Pakistan border in Kashmir is not atypical of the manner in which the two states and certain populist, sectarian and even extremist non-state actors have conducted their bilateral affairs in the post-Partition period.[3] It can be historically demonstrated that every time there are wars or serious skirmishes on the border or terrorist strikes inside, cultural bilaterality stands collaterally damaged, and mutual flows are violently disrupted. The warring camps spar by other means too: if cricket matches were the favourite targets of the Shiv Sena in the last century, cross-over film releases or musical shows continue to be vulnerable, as evidenced in the recent cancellation of Ghulam Ali shows in India. Taking advantage of the high investment and advance planning involved in such events, these actors manage to snap trade, diplomatic and even 'normal' exchange of formal and informal variety, and force producers of cross-over events back into nationalist enclosures. A state of 'Emergency' kicks in, leading to the suspension of scheduled conferences, meetings and even the bus journeys launched with much fanfare in more peaceful, optimistic and 'normal' times. In other words, sharing cultural artefacts that remind citizens of a utopian continuity into the present of a shared past is a precarious undertaking fraught with the risk of crossing borders without visas: Manto's story 'Tetwal ka Kutta' from the '50s and contemporary films like *Filmistaan* (Nitin Kakkar, 2012) and *Bajrangi Bhaijan* (Kabir Khan, 2015) highlight this in their own darkly eloquent, if melodramatic, ways, just as they underline the indisputable fact that marginal citizens on either side have not really been averse to this kind of risk-taking.[4] Add to the physical borders a technology-enabled, extra-terrestrial, ethereal or virtual dimension, and what we have is a less-than-absolute imagination of Partition at work.[5]

To Javed Akhtar's natural metaphors of 'birds, rivers and winds gushing over the mountains unhindered' (*'Panchhi, nadiya, pawan ke jhonke/Koi parvat na inhein roke'* from *Border* (J. P. Dutta, 1997), one could add a rich history of the consumption of printed material, gramophone records, radio broadcasts, telecasts, cassettes, compact discs and virtual podcasts travelling across the sovereign geographies of South Asia.[6] An innocent and incessant popular desire for sharing that in a sense amounts to undoing Partition; its persistence has created chinks on the borders and allowed seepage to take place, leading quite often to policy rethinks. A five-year highbrow ban on film music on All India Radio (AIR) and a similar turning away of Radio Pakistan from its Indian roots led to the dramatic emergence of Radio Ceylon (later Sri Lanka Broadcasting Corporation) as a dominant channel of auditory entertainment in South Asia, forcing the Indian Government to re-embrace film music via Vividh Bharti and even the Urdu Service of AIR. Ameen Sayani of *Geetmala* fame became an icon within and beyond the subcontinent, just as Noor Jahan and Lata Mangeshkar talking to each other over phone and throwing tantrums to set up a meeting with each other across the Wagah border made heartening news headlines for their fans still united in their supposedly divided loyalties.[7] Pakistani plays, *qawwals*, *ghazal* singers—even television serials aired on Zee TV until recently—had always been popular in India, but filmmaker Yousuf Saeed documented the 'real' claimants of the *Dilli gharana* of Hindustani music practitioners in Lahore and even a musician who devoted a lifetime to making his own perfect version of the veena.[8] Delhi-based Urdu magazines such as *Shama* and *Jasoosi Duniya* were read for decades in Pakistan, while writers such as Manto, Faiz, Qateel Shifai, Ahmad Faraz, Zahida Hina and Intizar Husain continue to be read (and heard) here in legal, pirated and online editions appearing in Nagri and Urdu scripts. Bapsi Sidhwa famously reported a *Ramayan-Mahabharata*-like teletime curfew in Lahore when Doordarshan Amritsar chose to telecast Kamal Amrohi's *Pakeezah* (1972) one afternoon in the 1970s.[9] So much so that her servants struck work on her refusal to buy a television set for the household!

This essay presents a layered and ambivalent response to the oft-quoted sardonic quip, made in the wake of Partition, whether art and literature would also be divided.[10] It also elaborates on Bhisham Sahni's comment on the possibility of mixing humour with trauma while revisiting the Partition. It is well known that Partition historiography underwent a tectonic shift in the early 90s as it moved from enlisting causes to mapping effects, from high political machinations to subaltern physical and emotional suffering, and from official archive to oral, literary and filmic testimonies.[11] Subsequent to the appearance of at least two monographs and several hitherto unnoticed films on YouTube, even though the filmic archive remains to be exhaustively explored, we can safely say that there was no such dearth of cinematic representation after all, as was believed by the first generation of revisionist Partition historians.

Laughing about Partition: A Poetic Cartography

Let us begin with one such find from the filmic archive, now completely wide open thanks to popular and corporate uploads on YouTube: *Chacha Zindabad* (or Long Live Uncle, by Om Prakash, 1959). It is an allegory about the Partition wrapped in an unusually comic mode. It is allegorical because the main line of conflict involves two Hindu neighbours—friends for several generations, living in houses facing each other—who decide to marry their children. The couple in question is played by Anita Guha (AG) and Kishore Kumar (KK), happy-go-lucky college-going offspring of a judge and a colonel, both retired. The fathers go for morning walks together and play chess in the ample free time at their disposal. The trouble is that while Kishore and Anita are good friends, they are not interested in marrying as they are culturally quite different from each other. So they conspire in creating a wedge, indeed a 'partition,' between the fathers. A greedy, miserly contractor, Om Prakash tries to fish in the troubled waters by pushing his worthless son Anoop Kumar's candidature for Anita's marriage, with an eye on her father's property. After a couple of tense post-partition reels, the seriousness of the rift finally dawns on the lead pair and they agree to marry, as in the meanwhile they have also fallen in love with each other, overcoming their deep cultural and aesthetic divergences. KK prefers a Western lifestyle, uses a lot of English words, celebrates Western music and rhythms, wears coat-suit-necktie, and calls AG an 'ishtehar [ad] of Khadi Bhandar.' She, a lover of classical music and dance, retaliates by calling him 'technicolour,' 'cartoon' and 'Filmfare akhbar.' The film piles up layers of playful banter between other pairs of characters as well: the judge and the colonel; Om Prakash and his wife Manorama; Bhagwan, the driver in the judge's household and his wife Tuntun, the maidservant in the colonel's house. So when the partition is effected between the two friends, these interdependent relationships naturally also get affected as the subalterns are ordered to snap all ties and lines of communication between the rival camps, which also reminds us of Padosi (V. Shantaram, 1941).

That this is a post-Partition film is clear from the very outset. The credits start rolling or rather flying in and condensing as cloud-clumps on the screen surface, like jigsaw pieces of a cartographic representation of various regions that ultimately go on to become an undivided India. When the map reaches completion, we see the set of faint lines demarcating the internal regions dissolving into India and a set of thicker lines denoting the newly erected international borders on its west and east. The director's name (pronounced Om Parkash) comes flying into the frame and gets broken into three parts: 'Om' sticks to India, 'Par' (which may legitimately be read as 'Paar' [across in Hindi] in the Roman script) flies into West Pakistan and 'Kash' [literally, sigh or I wish!] to East Pakistan, not yet Bangladesh (see image 7.1). This is a shrewd, even poignant, articulation of a heartache felt across the subcontinent at the event of Partition: *'Is dil ke tukde hazar hue/Koi yahan gira, koi vahan gira'* [This heart broke into a thousand pieces/Some fell here, and some fell there], where *yahan* and *wahan* could be read as references to 'this' and 'that' side of the border. The film works towards opening up the possibility of displacing attention from Partition as a mammoth tragedy by rendering it as a cartographic whimsy, facilitating laughter by offering a slightly detached perspective, which is achieved through the abstraction of the map and an all-Hindu characterisation.[12] The opening instrumental music has a prankish quality that nudges us towards a playful mindset from the outset.[13]

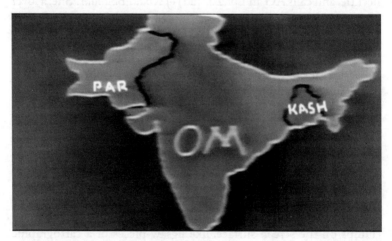

7.1: A still from the credits of *Chacha Zindabad*.
Courtesy: Pramilla Chhabra and Om Prakash.

KK and AG are initially very happy to see their plan work, and in their elation they sing, *'Bach gaye, bach gaye hum donon phanste phanste'* [Both of us escaped unwanted entanglement], a duet in which AG showcases her Yaman Kalyan, and KK his Western music including yodelling and a certain irreverence towards Hindustani classical music.[14] However, when the rift starts taking its toll, including on their own love life, they ask, *'Yeh kaisa partition hai? Pitaji aur Chachaji ek taraf, ab to naukar bhi ek doosre se nahin mil sakte'* [What kind of partition is this? Forget the elders, even the servants can't meet each other now]. The comic rendering of the partition logic extends to the jointly-owned motorcar, which the two rivals take apart piece by piece in a choreographed exercise where they mirror each other's actions, as if in a ritual army drill on the Wagah border, or in Manto's 'Tetwal ka Kutta.' Saddened by separation, KK starts practising classical music and AG starts wearing Western clothes, and singing Western tunes. In a remarkably enacted Parsi theatre-style song, KK brings together diverse musical sources: Indian classical music, Arabian music as well as Urdu, Brajbhasha and Hinglish lyrics. Finally, they manage to undo the partition between the uncles and their two households, with a bit of help from the inevitable melodramatic twist. The bride faints on her wedding night, and Anoop Kumar's wedding party is turned back. In the denouement scene, the motorcar is reassembled on the beats of the *mukhda* cited above as an epigram. The following *antaras* follow:

KK: *Pyar hai do nainon ki bhasha, na Urdu na Hindi*
AG: *Na koi zer zabar ka jhagda, na syahi na bindi*
Both: *Dil se dil ka taar mohabbat, aisi taisi jhagde ki...*
KK: *Parle darje ke ziddi thhe Laila-Majnu ke Abba*
AG: *Isiliye to gol ho gaya donon hi ke ghar ka dabba*
Both fathers: *Kar lo barkhurdar mohabbat*/KK: *Chakai ke chakdhum makai ke satuva*
Both fathers: *Kar lo barkhurdar mohabbat*/AG: *Nee dhapa dha pamapa magaresa....*
KK: Love is a language spoken by eyes, neither Urdu nor Hindi

AG: It's not a battle between diacritics, or of inscriptions in print
Both: Love is a link between wired hearts, to hell with the fight...
KK: Laila and Majnu's fathers were idiots of the highest order
AG: That is why both their homes were ruined
Both fathers: Okay, children, go fall in love.

The film was clearly a satirical utopian fantasy in the context of the emergent rivalry between India and Pakistan in general and a comment on the aggressively divergent cultural policies pursued by the two new governments in particular, somewhat like in Manto's personal essay, 'Kal Savere Jo Meri Aankh Khuli.'[15] On the specific question of Hindi and Urdu, the first antara is a defiant declaration of love over rivalry and celebrates the triumph of a direct visual communication between eyes, declaring love as the medium connecting two hearts, unmediated by the deadly fight carried out in the print domain over *bindi*, *zer* and *zabar*.[16] The last antara lampoons the received tale of Laila-Majnun, a staple medieval tragic romance re-enacted in numerous *dastaans*, plays and films, and blames their fatal end on their fathers' wooden, orthodox obstinacy. A script bought by Madhubala, who was by now indisposed to play the role, it was put together by her cohorts as an auto-critical, even irreverent satire that urged viewers to culturally undo a cartographic blunder called Partition.

A Pakistani Detour via *Mousiqar*

To further elaborate the point about cultural flows, let us travel three years down the line and cross over to Pakistan and consider Qadeer Ghori's *Mousiqar* (1962), a romantic musical anchored in Hindustani classical music.[17] It is a triangular love story between a folk singer Ragini (Sabiha), who is also a fan of the hero Sawan (Santosh Kumar; real name Syed Moosa Raza), and a rich woman socialite and patron of music, Nazneen (off-screen name Meena).[18] Sawan is a classical singer and the film opens with his public performance being broadcast live. By way of introduction, the socialite theatre-owner Nazneen says: 'Main janti hun ki aap sabko Mr. Sawan ki awaz se ishq hai, lekin aap yeh nahin jante ki main to inki puja karti hun' [I know that you are all in love with Mr. Sawan's voice, but what you do not know is that I worship him]. It is a dialogue she has just stolen from Ragini, who calls him devta [deity/god] and says 'Main inki puja karti hun' in a desperate effort to buy a seat for his concert. The classical piece, in the voice of Munir Husain, goes:

> Mitwa tarse mori ankhiyan
> Jab jab aaye yaad tihari (2)
> Tadpe hai pyaasi ankhiyan ... mitwa...
> Tujhko dekhe kai jug beete
> Haar gaye ab jeete jeete
> Sun le pukar....mitwa....
>
> My eyes yearn to see you, my mate
> Each time I think of you
> My eyes thirst for you
> Eons have passed since I saw you
> I have grown weary of life
> Won't you answer my call, my mate...

Ragini has sold her jewellery for the concert ticket, but it is houseful and she has to make do with listening to it on the radio. Next we hear Ragini singing in a fair, 'Gayegi duniya geet mere, sureele ang mein, niraale rang mein, bhare hain armanon mein...' [The world will sing my songs in sweet new melodies, full of dreams and aspirations], and Sawan, suitably impressed, tries to meet her, but she runs away from the stranger. When the stranger's true identity is revealed, she tracks him down and performs right outside his house:

> Tum jug-jug jiyo maharajre, ham teri nagariya mein aaye
> Taras raheen mori ankhiyan tere daras ki pyasi
> Pyas bujhaja, saamne aaja (2)
> Bin dekhe na jaun aajre
> Tujhsa nahin koi jag mein, nagar nagar teri dhoomein
> Mukh dikhla ja, rup ke raja (2)

mere sapnon pe tera raaj re...ham teri nagariya...
tum jug-jug jiyo maharajre![19]

May you live long, maharaj!
I have come to your town
These eyes thirst for just a glimpse of you
Pray, o' come, quench my thirst
Today I won't leave without seeing you
There is no one in this world like you
Your fame is spread far and wide
Pray, show me your face, o' king of beauty
You rule my dreams...
May you live long, maharaj!

Sawan takes her under his wing and transforms her into a great professional classical singer. Her first performance goes something like this:

Doha: *Haar singar lagayke, deun main baat bataay*
Sab sur mere piyavar hain, sampuran jyon raag.

Having adorned myself with all ornaments, let me proclaim
That all the notes are my lovers, coming together in a perfect composition.

The next line mentions *vadi, samvadi* and 'Raga Yaman' and the *sargam* gets recited by seven women, each sitting with sitars on giant-sized drums. Ragini, the lead singer, intones: 'Raseele more rasiya, najariya mila' [O' my colourful connoisseur/admirer/beloved, meet my eye]. *Najariya,* and not *nazariya,* reminds us of the famous Asha Bhosle thumri, 'Najar laagi raja tore bangle par'[20] (*Kala Pani,* Raj Khosla, 1957), or the Rajkumari number 'Najariya ki maari'[21] from *Pakeezah* (Kamal Amrohi, 1972). As if indicating a flow of aesthetic elements across centuries and forms, with suitable changes in linguistic registers and virtuosity, *Mousiqar* makes references to Tansen, Acchan Maharaj, Uday Shankar and Vyjayanthimala in the dialogues of various comic characters. Sawan has a past life, a girlfriend who was killed, and he drinks regularly. Ragini tries to disabuse him, but fails. The machinations by Nazneen create a rift between the two. After a heated exchange with him, Ragini leaves.

Heartbroken, he becomes a confirmed alcoholic. Finally, Sawan gets an invite to a classical music competition with a seasoned singer, Banne Khan; but he does not practice at all, is completely inebriated and unable to perform on stage. The Rag Basant song is a traditional *hori*, [sung during the Holi festival] elaborated here for more than six minutes by the Nazakat-Salamat Ali duo and Naseem Begum: *Phagwa Brij dekhan ko chal ree.*[22] Sawan switches off within a minute, and Banne Khan appears triumphant. Ragini comes to his rescue, saying, 'It is unfair, Sawan has not lost; he is drunk. *Mausiqui ka matlab sirf taan palta nahin hai balki sur ka lagaav bhi hai, jaisa main pesh karti hun.*' Ragini goes on to give a fitting and winning reply to the legendary performer, who runs away from the competition with his tail between the legs. The hori is a musically faithful, if lyrically enhanced, rendition, and it ends with the urban cosmopolitan audience chanting, 'Radha! Radha! Radha!' in the Brij-Vaishnav style. What a mirror image, almost a true copy of *Barsaat Ki Raat*, released a couple of years earlier and whose qawwali-driven theme was inspired by a performance in Bombay of visiting Pakistani qawwals![23] *Mousiqar* also has a special scene in the form of a tortured and melancholic male ghazal lamenting falling into neglect and loss, before Sawan decides to go back to Ragini's village and win her back by singing the same song of supplication which she had sung to break into his discipleship, albeit with suitably modified lyrics: *Tum yug-yug jiyo maharaj re, ham teri nagariya mein aaye.*[24] She comes out, touches his feet, and they embrace. We see a woman lurking behind the bushes and hear a gunshot, in a repetition of the film's opening scene in which Sawan's original girlfriend was murdered. To the relief of the audience, a repentant Nazneen kills herself, and history is saved from the blushes of repeating a tragedy.

By way of conclusion we may suggest that Indian filmmaker Yousuf Saeed and his well-researched documentary on Hindustani classical music in Pakistan, *Khayal Darpan*, could very well have benefited by footnoting the rich musical and linguistic repertoire of Pakistani films like *Mousiqar*. The song lyrics of the film cited above are a natural mix of Avadhi, Brajbhasha, Hindi and Urdu, straddling both urban and rural registers. At least two of these four languages might have failed in securing official recognition in India or Pakistan; but Pakistan was geographically carved out from a cultural-linguistic whole and inhabited in part by muhajirs from regions that hosted these languages. A longer tradition of classical Hindustani music in its myriad popular forms had used all these linguistic registers and was appreciated through live performances, broadcasts and gramophone records, and of course Hindustani cinema, the classic convergent form. *Mousiqar* re-enacts the fantasy and flow of that continuity and its continued resonance.[25]

Taken together, the two films discussed in this essay seem to be making an interesting point about cultural flows and their reception. Cultural forms and linguistic habits are formed in the longue duree, and they cannot suddenly be destroyed by arbitrary strokes of the pen or unilateral official fiats: cultures, by virtue of their embedded momentum and unpredictable memorialisation, reproduction and recycling by humans, are neither so vulnerable nor as readily amenable to clinical partitions and erasures as non-demographic cartographies apparently are. The fact that commerce and profit were central to these cultural productions across India and Pakistan, across Hindi, Urdu, Punjabi, Bengali and other languages is obvious but worth remembering. As the pioneer historian of Pakistani cinema, Mustaq Gazdar concluded, 'It proves beyond any reasonable doubt that the film world, since its inception, has always been motivated by commercial considerations and the marketability of its product. It belies the notion of ethnic and parochial reasons for the production of films in any particular vernacular.'[26]

Notes and References

1. Rough translation:
    Love is great, to hell with the fight
    Let's fall in love, o lady/government/lord, to hell with the fight
2. Let's go to Brij to watch Holi festivities.
3. Gyan Prakash, 'Karan Johar Controversy Mirrors Rising Populist Politics,' *The Indian Express*, 4 November 2016.

4. Ravikant and Tarun Saint, 'The Dog of Tetwal in Context', in *Translating Partition*, eds. Ravikant and Tarun Saint (New Delhi: Katha, 2001).

5. For an elaboration of the argument, see Ravikant, *Media ki Bhasha- leela* (New Delhi: Vani Prakashan, 2016), especially the 'Bhumika'.

6. Consider, for example, a listener, Narendra Jain's voice, in radio announcer Manohar Mahajan's memoirs: 'The relations between India and Pakistan were not quite cordial back then, but the music played from Radio Ceylon had kept the ties between the two countries alive, which could not have been accomplished even by veteran leaders.'
   —*Yaadein Radio Ceylon Ki* (299–300).

7. In a reception organised for Noor Jahan in Bombay (now Mumbai) in 1982, Dilip Kumar memorably remarked, 'We have waited for you exactly as many years as you have taken to be here.' The audience applauded enthusiastically and with tearful eyes. See https://www. youtube.com/watch?v=FLlOepvJVvM. The video has recorded more than half a million views till date. Describing her songs as property shared by Indian audiences as well, Noor Jahan prayed for a better relationship between the two countries so that 'we could meet every once in a while.' Although very good friends, they never sang together; still, a search for Lata Mangeshkar on Noor Jahan on YouTube yields videos with a large number of views. When Manohar Mahajan interviewed Noor Jahan for Radio Ceylon, the unplanned event was enthusiastically reported in the Hindi film magazine *Madhuri*, 11 April 1975.

8. *Khayal Darpan* (A Mirror of Imagination) *Classical Music in Pakistan: A Journey by an Indian Filmmaker* (Yousuf Saeed 2006). For his reflections, see Yousuf Saeed, 'Fled is That Music', *India International Centre Quarterly* 35, No. 3/4 (2008): 238–249. http:// www.jstor.org/stable/23006263.

9. Bapsi Sidhwa, 'The Way It Was: The Television Boycott', reproduced on the Sarai Reader List: http://www.mail.sarai.net/pipermail/ reader-list/2002/001616.html

10. See for example, Bhisham Sahni's memoirs *Apni Baat* (1980) and *Aaj Ke Ateet* (2013), New Delhi: Rajkamal Prakashan. Reflecting on the future of Pakistani films exactly a year after Partition, still in shambles, Manto raised forthright questions in his typical ironic tone: 'Will actresses too have to work in Burkas?' and 'Should there be Hindu characters in films?' He concluded, 'We are a long way from knowing what it is about our cinema that is authentically Pakistani.'

See Saadat Hasan Manto, 'Pakistani Film,' introduced, translated and annotated by Ali Nobil Ahmad, *BioScope* 5, No. 2 (2014): 163–166. With the passage of time, certain other fictional projections became optimistic with regard to the future of cultural bilaterality. See for example, Faheem Azmi's story 'Art ka Pul,' translated into Hindi from the Urdu by Shambhu Yadav, in *Vibhajan: Bharatiya Bhashaon ki Kahaniyan, Khand-II*, ed. Narendra Mohan (New Delhi: Bharatiya Gyanpeeth, 2009), 214–218.

11. Gyanendra Pandey, 'The Prose of Otherness,' in *Subaltern Studies VII*, eds. David Arnold and David Hardiman (New Delhi: Oxford University Press, 1994); Bhaskar Sarkar, *Mourning the Nation: Indian Cinema in the Wake of Partition* (New Delhi: Orient BlackSwan, 2010); Kavita Daiya, *Violent Belongings: Partition, Gender, and National Culture in Postcolonial India* (Philadelphia: Temple University Press, 2008).

12. *Chacha Zindabad* presents a remarkable contrast to what Alok Rai calls the 'pornographic' literary recreation of violence during Partition: 'The Trauma of Independence: Some Aspects of Partition Literature, 1945–47,' *Journal of Arts and Ideas* (January–March 1984), 19–35.

13. The role of cartographic visualisation in cinema for the nationalist cause demands serious scholarly attention, for there is plenty of material here starting with the famous Kavi Pradeep patriotic number in *Kismet* (1943), 'Door hato ai duniya walo, Hindustan hamara hai.' It is a dance number set to a marching tune picturised on the stage with India's map and Bharat Mata's icon on the screen. The song escaped British censorship by virtue of clever references to German and Japanese imperialism during World War II, but the audience got its intended 'Quit India' spirit, evidenced by several 'once more' demands in cinema halls. It made a record continuous run in Roxy theatre, Calcutta, which could only be broken decades later by Ramesh Sippy's *Sholay*. Bharat Mata and India's map as icons were common enough in the popular print culture and cinema takes it forward, so we see the iconography multiplied in the films of the 1950s and '60s as well. To repeat, the innovation on the received carto-iconography—of constitution and reconstitution of the map as if indexing the nation states' constructed nature—was an artistic master stroke of *Chacha Zindabad*.

14. A playful facet of Kishore Kumar's singing style, which was thematically elaborated in Mahmood's *Padosan* (Jyoti Swaroop, 1968).
15. 'When I Woke Up Yesterday,' compiled in *Manto Ki Rajneetik Kahaniyan*, ed. Devendra Issar (New Delhi: Indraprasth Prakashan, 1988). For a fine recent study of Manto, see Ayesha Jalal, *The Pity of Partition: Manto's Life, Times and Work across the India-Pakistan Divide* (New Delhi: Harper Collins, 2013).
16. The Hindi-Urdu-Hindustani debate has produced volumes and continues to engage scholars. For an historian's pithy and ironical recall, see Shahid Amin, 'Will Recognition of Urdu Slow Down Hindi's Progress?', *The Times of India*, 19 October 1989.
17. Available on YouTube: https://www.youtube.com/watch?v=mDEw2UcZ2nc. For full credits, see http://en.wikipedia.org/wiki/List_of_Pakistani_films_of_1962.
18. Mustaq Gazdar informs us that Santosh Kumar and Sabiha were married, and together with the former's younger brother Darpan, and his wife Naiyer Sultana, they dominated the Pakistani film industry for more than a decade. See *Pakistan Cinema: 1947–1997* (Karachi: Oxford University Press).
19. https://www.youtube.com/watch?v=Js6Lp6iqQj4. The song has been a favourite with itinerant Mirasi as well as Sufi singers. For example, here is an instrumental rendering at Khwaja Nagar Shareef, Hassan Abdal, Pakistan: https://www.youtube.com/watch?v=8F1kGXBSCqY. For a raw, down-to-earth rendition, see https://www.youtube.com/watch?v=XXs1wPe7faE. It is a hagiographic verse, a prayer to the master/lover for immediate *darshan*. Its form and structure is a not-so-uncommon mix between a *bhakti pada* and a qawwali.
20. https://www.youtube.com/watch?v=6DxCg8bCvA8
21. https://www.youtube.com/watch?v=Yg23Stzr0N8
22. YouTube has several renditions of this by masters old and new. The version by Ustad Abdul Karim Khan (1872–1937): https://www.youtube.com/watch?v=l2fsrJjdXhI; and a more recent one by Pandit Bhimsen Joshi: https://www.youtube.com/watch?v=eL2BHFaleqM.
23. Interestingly, one cannot miss the obvious shades of *Mousiqar* in Lucky Ali's *Sur* (2000), made in Bollywood several decades later. *Barsaat Ki Raat* and *Mousiqar* are also interesting replicas of each

other in the sense that while Bharat Bhushan essays the role of a Muslim poet, Aman Hyderabadi, in his home production, Santosh Kumar and Sabiha were given Hindu-sounding names—Sawan and Ragini—as classical Hindustani singers in the Pakistani film.

24. Note the transformation of 'jug' into 'yug.' All *antaras* are completely different in the two versions. The film's meta-language is Urdu, but some characters, especially the peasants from Ragini's *qasba*, speak in Bhojpuri-sounding Purabiya.

25. For a recent study of the mixed and syncretic genealogies of commercial Hindi cinema, see Anjali Gera Roy, *Cinema of Enchantment: Perso-Arabic Genealogies of the Hindi Masala Film* (New Delhi: Orient BlackSwan, 2016). For the early origins of 'Islamicate' cinema, especially the genre known as 'Muslim Social,' see Ravi Vasudevan, 'Film Genres, the Muslim Social and Discourses of Identity C. 1935–45,' *BioScope* 6(1), 2015.

26. Mustaq Gazdar, *Pakistan Cinema*: 180–181.

8

Twins, But not Identical

Music in India and Pakistan

VIDYA RAO

n 1947, when the subcontinent was suddenly and brutally torn apart, did music also become divided into 'Indian' music and 'Pakistani' music? Can music be partitioned? Is that at all possible?

I remember, as a very small child, being taken by my mother to listen to a ghazal singer whom everyone called Rauf Saheb. The *mehfil* was in the home of my uncle (my mother's brother), a great music lover and connoisseur. Several people were crammed into a small room—floor seating, no microphones, and so little space that I had to sit in my mother's lap right through—quite unlike today's rather grand events. I listened, spellbound, to Rauf Saheb's wonderful voice, and his gentle persona as it shone through in his singing, understanding little else of either music or *shairi*. I heard and watched Rauf Saheb's deep involvement and effortless singing. I saw my mother's eyes fill with tears as she listened and, now, remembering, am amazed—my mother knows no Urdu! It was the singer's voice and presence, his *gayaki* that had moved her so deeply. And the fact, too, that one of Hyderabad's living treasures had returned home across the newly drawn border—back to his beloved city, his listeners, his own space. Perhaps the fact, too, that he had felt the need to travel in 1947 to a now 'foreign' country because politics deemed it was 'his country' more than the Dakkhani soil where his family had lived for generations. But now, after an absence of some years, he was back, and his music was back, and that mehfil was the first celebration of welcome and gratitude.

Today, remembering and thinking about that moment, I begin to understand just a little of the complexity of emotions that singers and listeners face when confronted with the horror of an artificial line drawn upon the earth, separating homes, families and cultures.

A sense of the romantic, of nostalgia even, might prompt us to declare that culture has no boundaries; it cannot be divided up. And that is absolutely true. Music truly knows no boundaries.

But what is equally true is that musical styles, responses to the performance of music and even what is heard at all do change. They change over time. And they change from area to area, varying ever so slightly depending on so many factors—for instance, the landscape (how singers throw their voice in riverine areas is quite different from the throw of voice in the desert or the mountains, or indeed in enclosed spaces like mehfils and modern concert auditoriums). Styles change with singers' linguistic comfort and linguistic and oral shifts that shape the modulation of sound and tonality. They change in response to changes in lifestyle and taste. And certainly, music changes in response to what audiences and the powers that be want to hear. And most certainly, music responds to and changes given cataclysmic events like the 1947 Partition of the subcontinent.

I will attempt here to think about some of the ways in which music both remained the same and changed consequent upon Partition. I will do this by speaking of my understanding of the styles of two wonderful qawwals—Fariduddin Ayaz of Pakistan and the late Jafar Husain Badayuni of India. I will also refer to the gayaki of other singers as I write. But my focus will be on these two, whose music I love, whom I have had the privilege to hear very often, and the privilege, too, of meeting many times. And I write this based on my own experience of listening and understanding and responding to what I hear. It is not a scholarly essay!

Let me begin with Fariduddin (Farid) Ayaz.

Farid Ayaz is a performer par excellence—and I emphasise the word 'performer.' His singing and persona are dramatic, larger than life. He dominates the space of the performance, and is both aware of his ability to do so, and enjoys it. The first time I heard him I was struck by his wonderful singing, but also by his ability to seize the stage and reign over it like an emperor. But what was also very evident was a certain very conscious classicizing of his opening phrases. Opening his recital with the steady clapping typical of qawwali, moving on to the use of percussion and then to his own opening *alaap*—you could see this was an extremely well-choreographed piece. Moreover he chose to open his performance with a somewhat less frequently used (today) *tala* in qawwali— *jhaptala*. And he began not with a brief *aakaar alaap*, not the flourish of a 'sher,' but with a fairly lengthy *nom-tom alaap*.

This use of nom-tom alaap brought to the performance an interesting quality—a different quality of gravitas and weightiness that one does not generally expect or hear in contemporary qawwali. (While the weightiness—albeit of a different kind; it is surely more playful—of *tarana bols* is used in *manqabat*, as in the wonderful 'Man kunto Maula,' nom-tom alaap is not something one hears or expects to hear as the opening phrases of a qawwali.) Farid Ayaz's nom-tom alaap immediately brings to mind the Agra *gharana* and also *dhrupad*. This is perhaps significant because it suggests to the listener the connection that dhrupad and Agra gharana share, and also that qawwali and *khayal* share. Agra gayaki uses many facets that are reminiscent of dhrupad gayaki, including this nom-tom alaap. But also, Agra gayaki, especially that of Faiyaz Khan, clearly underlines the origins of khayal in the music of the Qawwal Bacche gharana—a gharana deeply connected to qawwali itself as the name testifies, and from which, as many scholars believe, khayal gayaki derives its form.

Farid Ayaz's use of this style of alaap in qawwali, reminiscent of the majestic Agra gayaki, is interesting. He himself claims allegiance to the Dilli gharana (more on this later), which itself has close links with the Qawwal Bacche gharana and indeed with the Sufic *khanqahi* styles. In fact, as the khalifa of Dilli gharana in India, Iqbal Ahmed Khan, is quick to point out, qawwali, *sufiana qalam* and Dilli gharana have a common origin in the dargah—one branch of the family took their music and adapted it to the darbar, while the other branch stayed within the Sufic tradition and space. However, to the best of my knowledge, none of the singers of Dilli gharana in India, and none of the qawwali singers in India currently begin their performance with nom-tom alaap.

So here is an extraordinary thing! Despite his allegiance to the Dilli gharana, Farid Ayaz chooses to open his performance (on that occasion and others too where I have heard him) with a style of alaap more associated with Agra and dhrupad. Why does he do this?

I can only speculate about this, raise a few questions.

Is he trying to stress the 'classicism' of his qawwali by forging an aural link with that majestic gharana of khayal (Agra), and also with dhrupad, a form not just austere (and therefore 'serious') but also tinged with the patina of age—a very ancient form as we are given to understand? Something is being conveyed here. And it is not just Sufiana passion and devotion—though as Ayaz continues to sing, there is that in abundance too. It seemed to me, as I listened that day, that Farid Ayaz was perhaps indeed claiming a connection for himself with 'high classical' music—with not just khayal, but with dhrupad, too (sometimes people are wont to think of dhrupad and Agra gharana as high classical forms, while qawwali, thumri, ghazal etc. are thought of as 'semi-classical,' not serious forms). And using the nom-tom of Agra and dhrupad gayaki seemed a very appropriate gesturing towards that claim of high classicism.

Farid Ayaz is not alone in his unexpected use of nom-tom alaap. Such an alaap is also heard in the singing of Nasiruddin Sami, an absolutely stunning khayal singer of the Dilli gharana based in Pakistan. Ayaz describes his nom-tom alaap as *layi-layi ki alaap*. However Nasiruddin Sami does not use this phrase to describe his own alaap. Also there are differences in the way both these singers negotiate the nom-tom alaap.

For now, let me turn to Ayaz's phrase 'layi-layi' to understand the difference and its significance. Layi-layi... the words cause me to make several connections. There is the most obvious one with *laya*, rhythm. And indeed nom-tom does create a sense of a rhythmic alaap. Farid Ayaz's layi-layi ki alaap is more rhythmic, and even playful, as compared to that of the Agra gharana or dhrupad or even of Nasiruddin Sami. But might there also be another connection to the word layi? Layi also means soldier, warrior. I hear the word frequently in verses from the Sozkhani tradition. In one particular *nauha* based on Raga Malkauns that describes the arrival of Abbas onto the battlefield (to fetch water for the thirsty children of Husain's clan), the layi or soldiers of Shaam (Syria/Damascus) are filled with fear and consternation to see Abbas coming towards them/towards the river Alquman (Euphrates):

> *Hulchul hai fauj-e-Shaam, Abbas aate hain*
> *Murh-murh ke layi dekhte hain, thartharate hain*

Seen from this perspective, I could ask: might Ayaz's use of the phrase 'layi-layi ki' be a way of describing his alaap as strong and energetic? His alaap has a tremendous quality of energy, certainly. But there is also a quality of playfulness, a quality that is not so evident in Sami's more meditative nom-tom. Ayaz's layi-layi surprises us and then it quickens the blood—it is exciting, thrilling, and not only because it is so unexpected. And oddly enough, one's breath comes faster rather than slowing down, as we might expect it to do in response to a traditional nom-tom alaap. Ayaz's layi-layi stirs us up rather than calms us down. This is Ayaz's brilliance! To use a meditative form to actually create quite different emotions!

Despite what I imagine might be his claims to classicism, his nom-tom/layi-layi is therefore not as meditative as dhrupad's might be. So, might his describing his alaap as layi-layi suggest the more tandav-like qualities of dhrupad, the strength and solemn ruggedness of music, of khayal and Agra gayaki rather than its equally *rangeela* qualities? Might Ayaz's layi-layi be reminding us that Hazrat Ali, so present in the qawwali tradition, is both Iman and Sher-e-Khuda, both Maula and great warrior?

Could the phrase layi-layi also be harking back to the wonderful word and the idea it embodies—*lehan*? Lehan has resonances with that other South Asian word, *naad*—the primordial sound, the hum of the universe, the fine perfection of *swar*[1] and *swar ka nikaas*[2]. Through this connection, layi-layi acquires a sense of the mystical, the perfection, un-nameability and in-articulatability of the pure swar. What the singer sings, what the listeners hear is the manifestation of lehan. Lehan itself is a sound so fine and subtle as to be produced and perceived only with the heart, not with the voice and ears—though these do become the vehicles by which we poor mortals might call into being and appreciate this perfection. Linked to the idea of lehan, then, Ayaz's layi-layi ki alaap becomes deeply mystical, something that he himself speaks of in other contexts as going beyond the dualities of even *had* and *anhad*—an echo here of Ramana Maharishi's statement that he has gone beyond the dualities of *dvaita* and *advaita*; an echo, too, of Siraj Aurangabadi's going beyond the dualities of reason and mad passion:

> Na khirad ki bakhiya gari rahi
> Na junoon ki jamadari rahi

Layi-layi, heard and understood this way, suggests to me Ayaz's sense of his work as so deeply mystical as to have gone beyond all known categories, all dualities, all ways of knowing the world.

What a wonderful gift does Ayaz give us then—music, his music as 'classical,' serious and so, refusing its more common description and classification as light/popular; of music as simultaneously playful, serious, calm, strong, rousing; and of music so deeply mystical as to go beyond all known categories, as the paradox of the universe—music as the manifestation of silence.

Along with the strong, rhythmic and playful alaap, Ayaz's singing also abounds in *rangeelapan*[3] and *shokhi*[4], qualities evident as he proceeds further in his singing. This quality is seen in some of his *bandish*es such as the charming 'Kanhaiya, yaad hai kuchh bhi hamari' and the very folksy yet deeply moving 'Mere banne ki baat na poochho.' Yet his singing does not display the delicacy of an almost Poorbi gayaki, a thumri-like quality found so deeply in the singing of two other qawwals—Ghous Mohammad Niazi of Pakistan and Jafar Husain Badayuni of India.

In fact, that this nom-tom/layi-layi ki alaap is very much a choice Ayaz is making is evident from the fact that another wonderful qawwali singer from Pakistan, the late Ghous Mohammad Niazi, sings in a style very close to that of Jafar Husain Badayuni (which I will describe later). This could just be a question of personalities and personal styles, but I am inclined to think not. I do think that Farid Ayaz's choices are saying something, and not just about music.

There are also other interesting aspects that one observes in Farid Ayaz's gayaki and in his remarks. Both Ayaz and Nasiruddin Sami, during their performances and in conversation, repeatedly stress that theirs is the true Dilli gharana; the ones who remained behind in India are not, they say, the true heirs to the tradition. On stage, in performance (and, in my experience, even in conversation), the khalifa of Dilli gharana in India, Iqbal Ahmed Khan, has neither refuted nor accepted this, maintaining a silence, at least in public forums, on this contentious issue. Again, I have to ask, what does this mean? And I wonder if, on the part of Ayaz and Sami, this is not really a claim for legitimacy of gharana status, a claim to be the true, the only heirs to the gharana. If this is so, then I need to ask further—why the need for singers like Ayaz and Sami to repeatedly emphasise this legitimacy of gharana status?

Is it because the wider and easier access to music (of all kinds) that India has managed to provide (despite bureaucracies, despite corporate preferences, despite the creation of a 'star' system, despite even the preferences accorded to certain styles and not to others) has made this need to claim true gharana status somewhat less important today? Gharana identity is marked by the singer's gayaki and knowledge of the repertoire, but especially with an understanding and assimilation of the gayaki. Many Indian singers today say that the proof of *shagirdi*[5] lies in a singer's gayaki, and not just the repertoire. Yet, while gharana remains important, a sign whereby we may 'recognise' a singer and understand, even judge his/her music (and, might I add, inner being), I think that in India, the desperate need today to prove legitimacy of gharana status is not as important as it has been earlier. This need has almost totally collapsed in some areas (and this might be in both India and

Pakistan), given the rise of different audiences and different spaces for music, and the blurring of the understanding of what defines a given musical form. Within the 'classical' tradition, certainly in India, while both singers and listeners are aware of the typical features of a gharana's gayaki, yet they are very willing to accept a mixing of styles, provided this is done appropriately, and from a space of deep *taleem*. Hence, the repeated emphasis on gharana status by some artists from Pakistan suggests to me a certain anxiety about musical identity. A caveat here—we need, however, to remember that movements across gharanas have always been possible. It is not just today that singers from different traditions have learnt from each other, formally and informally. And certainly this cross-fertilisation of stylistic techniques and repertoires only increased in the late-nineteenth and early-twentieth centuries.

Admittedly, Pakistan's Coke Studio, and even before that, Nusrat Fateh Ali Khan's bursting forth onto the world stage, and into fusion genres, has changed much in this area (of anxiety over gharana legitimacy) in Pakistan, and elsewhere in the subcontinent, blurring the lines between 'classical' and 'popular,' between forms and styles and interrogating somewhat the whole issue of legitimacy of musical lineage. Yet, despite this, I hear a sharper voice of anxiety about gharana legitimacy among Pakistan's singers than I do among India's. I sense, too, a greater and more ubiquitous need to constantly stress this notion of legitimacy, authenticity. And I also hear a greater need to 'showcase' *taiyyari*[6].

Might this be because the space of what we call classical music—khayal, dhrupad—is today a somewhat endangered, a somewhat shrunken space in Pakistan? And might this be both because of the uneven official patronage by the state (during Zia's time many forms, ways and venues of performance were banned; today, non-state terrorists go so far as to murder singers, merely because they sing)?

However problematic 'patronage' may be, whether state-sponsored, sponsored by corporate groups (or in an earlier time, an elite group), patronage has not dried up in India, nor is there any official negative perception of music. There have been other problems of course. Music is often co-opted into other agendas, whether of state, nationalist pride or even, slightly less problematically, 'good causes.' Patronage is always problematic—if one is not careful, it could encourage sycophancy, favouritism, the receiving and granting of favours, and sometimes, club-like groups. At its worst, it might involve patronage of, and catering to, the sensibilities of the lowest common denominator, thus lowering standards horrendously, deadening any aesthetic sensibility, making music mere entertainment rather than the life-transforming experience that it really is.

If patronage has not dried up in India, this is not to say that there are no problems at all with patronage. For years forms like qawwali and thumri were considered secondary, received little official patronage, and the traditional singers of these forms barely received any. The recasting of music, and culture in general, in the twentieth century was slanted towards seeing it as 'scientific,' 'spiritual,' 'serious,' and indeed in some cases as 'Hindu' music. Independent India inherited some of that slant, resulting in the meagre official patronage given, for the longest time, to forms like qawwali, thumri and ghazal, which did not qualify as 'serious' or which were perceived to have an association, even if 'spiritual,' with Islamic culture.

Similarly, across the border in Pakistan, patronage was uncertain, sometimes non-existent, and certainly only for forms that could be justified as properly fitting into an Islamic society—thus qawwali (though with the rise of Wahabi tendencies, even qawwali is seen as suspect). Might this lack of sustained patronage for forms such khayal, explain the tendency for almost all Pakistani artists of qawwali and ghazal to saturate their singing with virtuoso, complex tana passages, because the space for any other kind of music where such techniques might be more appropriately used is almost absent?

Despite some problems with patronage, it is important to remember that in India, music (of whatever kind) remains (so far) alive and well. As far as gharana legitimacy goes, many aspiring Indian singers are able and do now learn from many gurus from different gharanas, though as I said earlier, most people with any understanding of music will stress that a strong base in a single tradition is essential before one can move on to other styles. Nor is music any more such a closely guarded secret to be shared with only the chosen few of the family.

While music schools began to be set up well before Independence and Partition—the first Gandharva Mahavidyalaya was in fact established as early as 1904 in Lahore (that cultural capital of pre-Partition days)—after Independence this trend continued strongly in India, both by individuals and groups and by government bodies. As early as the 1950s, soon after Partition, music schools were set up where anyone could learn and where faculty included great musicians from a range of gharanas. That trend has only accelerated. Universities now include departments of music, and a university entirely devoted to music studies (Indira Kala Sangeet Vishwavidyalaya, Khairagarh) has also come into existence. Equally, many wonderful singers are noted for their styles that actually combine qualities of different gharanas—cases in point being Ulhas Kashalkar and Padma Talwalkar, among many others. Most Indian singers will emphatically say, as will their counterparts in Pakistan, that a strong base in a gharana's gayaki is essential before a student can move on to other gurus and styles. However, I wonder whether it might be that there is today, in India, less anxiety about gharana-based legitimacy? And maybe, because of the somewhat more difficult access to classical music in Pakistan, this anxiety remains and gets expressed thus? These are only questions I raise here.

Let me also say here that his comments apart, Nasiruddin Sami's performances have been among the most extraordinarily brilliant that I have ever heard—dazzling taiyyari matched by an extraordinary purity of swar, a meditative *thehrav*[7]. He is undoubtedly one of the finest singers of the subcontinent.

To return to Farid Ayaz, his repertoire includes many compositions—some of them khayal-like, others like *sadras*, which further underline a sense of what I might understand as his need to connect his singing with what are considered to be more 'classical' forms, and a need also, as demonstrated by his use of sargam in his qawwali, to display taiyyari. Regarding his use of the sadra, this form now associated with dhrupad gayaki, however, also suggests, as many believe, Sufic origins. Hence, although less-frequently heard today as part of qawwali performances, sadras are certainly not out of place here.

Equally, what is very striking and deeply moving is Ayaz's inclusion in his performances of bandishes such as 'Lanka charhyo Ram' in Raga Adana in jhaptala. This bandish describes Ram's victory over Lanka and the proclamation of that victory. It is a wonderful bandish—Adana's vitality and energy (*veer rasa*) matching the words of the bandish with its internal rhymes and rhythms, and the weightiness of the tala. It is deeply moving that Farid Ayaz (and presumably the entire Dilli gharana in Pakistan) have nurtured this bandish that would probably not find wide acceptance in Pakistan and where the possibilities of its performance might be limited. But it is also Farid Ayaz's almost inevitable choice of this bandish when he performs in India that interests me. Singers choose repertoires carefully for each performance keeping many factors in mind. His choice of this bandish to present at venues in Delhi (where I have had the good fortune to hear him) suggests both an acknowledgement and communicating of the syncretic nature of South Asian music and the consciousness that musicians have of this syncreticism to which they are heir, and that they represent and communicate. Along with this there is also possibly the sense of 'showcasing' the gharana's rare gems, and indeed its rich and syncretic traditions, and perhaps, a musical demonstration of his claim to true gharana status.

Apart from the opportunity to hear Farid Ayaz in concert, I have had the good fortune to meet him on many occasions, hear him at very small mehfils and even share the stage with him at some music festivals. I was fortunate to meet him through the Kabir project, with which both he and I have been involved. His work on the Kabir project presents yet other interesting facet of his gayaki and thinking. In Shabnam Virmani's film *Had Anhad*, Ayaz speaks with great elan of Kabir, and his own deep personal connection with Kabiri philosophy and music. Somewhere in this film he claims that Kabir is the only one, the only spiritual thinker/ teacher/poet who has gone beyond all boundaries, broken all rules. He quotes the verse:

Had had tape so Auliya, Anhad tape so Pir
Had Anhad dono tape, so vo hai das Kabir

Along with Shafi Faqir, another Pakistani singer interviewed and recorded for the Kabir project, Ayaz believes that music is beyond boundaries; lines drawn on a map mean nothing to music, to truth or to the inner being of seekers after truth. Nor even to ordinary people living their ordinary lives.

Listening to Farid Ayaz speak and sing, I realise that Partition has never been able to draw a line through the music of the subcontinent. And yet, Partition has created situations where musicians' lives, what they have to deal with on a day-to-day basis, how and what they will present at performances and how listeners respond to them and to their repertoires does change.

It is same on the Indian side of the border. And yet it is not the same.

I turn now to the singing of Jafar Husain Badayuni of India. Jafar Husain died, alas too soon—he never lived to see the 'Sufi music' craze that has brought qawwali to centre stage. On the other hand, with his gentle persona, and his softer style, who knows, he may still have remained somewhat in the shadows while other more flamboyant singers commanded the limelight.

If anything, this is something both India and Pakistan share— the current predominance, in many forums and among many audiences, of flamboyance, a focus on volume and visibility and a sometimes quite meaningless display of taiyyari, not necessarily always musical!

Indeed Jafar Husain's style is softer than what one has now come to associate with qawwali. Softness, delicacy—these are not qualities that one generally associates, especially today, with qawwali. But Jafar Husain's gayaki, while retaining the power, the trance-inducing quality typical of qawwali, yet has other facets.

My guru Naina Devi would often tell me that to understand the technique of *bol banao*[8]—a technique typical of thumri—one had only to listen to Jafar Husain Badayuni's singing. And indeed, I find this to be so.

I should add here that such a quality is also heard in the singing of another qawwal from Pakistan—Ghous Mohammed Niazi—so clearly, there are pockets of difference, spaces of choice. But Ghous Mohammed is certainly less well known than other qawwals of Pakistan. And again I suggest this could well be because of the delicacy of his style, which requires a different kind of listening.

This thumri-like quality that Ghous Mohammed and Jafar Husain bring to their singing is, I believe, not just an accident. The fragrance of thumri pervades the Dilli gharana's repertoire, being found in such, now rarely-heard, forms like *savela/sohela*. Both thumri and qawwali (especially of the Chistia *khanqas*) share an essential important characteristic. There is in both forms the centrality of the address and the intimacy of that address. And there is the technique used by both forms of *girah bandhna/girah lagana*—of framing and expanding a given bandish with verses from other sources. Many thumri singers have learnt bandishes and adapted bandishes learnt from qawwals; one example is Begum Akhtar's 'O nirmohi, sapnon me aaja,' a bandish that she learnt from Aziz Warsi (the well-known qawwal of Hyderabad). Similarly, the khayal singer Mushtaq Husain Khan composed a thumri (addressed to Krishna) which he offered as *hazri* at the Sufi shrine of Bareilly—'Laago mero dhyaam guiyaan saanvare salone se,' a moment that brought together musical forms and religious spaces.

Jafar Husain's singing also reminds us in other ways of the presence of thumri. His 'Man kunto Maula' shares with versions sung by other singers the strong rhythmic quality, the tarana elements, the typical qawwali throw of voice, and the largeness of the total sound. Yet along with this, Jafar Husain brings to this manqabat an extraordinary tenderness, a thumri-like intimacy of address. Much of qawwali poetry is couched in the female narrative voice, though this is not the case with 'Man kunto Maula.' Yet even here, despite the largeness of sound, despite the (imagined) vast-yet-intimate space of the dargah that qawwali inhabits and brings alive wherever it is sung, despite the presence on stage of the physical bodies of a group of men, Jafar Husain's style brings in a sense of the feminine, of intimacy, of the inner courtyard in a way that few other qawwali singers are able to do. I believe this becomes possible because of the quality of his improvisation, which is (and yet is not) thumri's bol banao. In Jafar Husain's singing genders, spaces and voices collide in a unique fashion. It is not just the text that makes us aware of the feminine; this would be too simplistic an analysis of Jafar Husain's gayaki, or indeed of any such gayaki. It is Jafar Husain's gayaki—not simply the narrative voice of the given text—that feminises qawwali and the word, while yet retaining its extremely male universe of the performing persona, space and even style. This is more than just a sense of the androgynous—I am not sure there is a word yet for this quality of going beyond everything: gender, space, time that Jafar Husain places before us through his singing.

Jafar Husain Badayuni belonged to the Rampur gharana and was a close relative of Mushtaq Husain Khan. His training was in the Rampur style. And as with the Dilli gharana, it would appear that while one branch of the gharana focused on khayal gayaki and the tradition of the darbari singers, another branch focused on the music of the dargah. This again leads us to remark upon the close links between khayal and the Sufic tradition, between khayal and the Qawwal Bacche gharana. Jafar Husain's gayaki reminds us too of that other element—the thumri and the feminine—that flits through these traditions, sometimes just an ephemeral fragrance, sometimes, a more full-bodied presence. It reminds us too that there has been a time when forms, though clearly different and understood to be so, were yet not so sharply separated. Thumri included *teentala* bandishes, complex ones at that, where virtuosity was supreme. (Many of these were documented and classified by Bhatkhande as *madhya laya khayal* bandishes.)

Traditionally (according to Naina Devi), the early training of thumri singers was in dhrupad rather than khayal. This seemingly odd fact is underlined for me by listening to Haveli Sangeet, which makes it so clear that both thumri and dhrupad, though apparently so different, seem to draw from this gayaki. Frequently the same bandish could be, and was, sung in different styles by different singers (according to their chosen genre) or differently even by the same singer for different performing contexts. Here, I recall two recorded versions of the lovely *bol bant ki bandish* in Raga Dhani, 'Krishna Murari' sung by Bal Gandharva. One version is clearly 'classical,' an interesting mix of khayal shot with thumri—a version sung for the mehfil/baithak. The other is so clearly a version meant for theatre, for singing as part of a play. In both versions the bandish, its poetry, its musical notations were absolutely the same. It was just Bal Gandharva's singing style, his different inflections that made the two recordings so very different.

So it is not altogether surprising that Jafar Husain chooses to bring this fragrance of a softer form through his sudden and unexpectedly thumri-like throw of voice (*gale ka nikaas*[9]/*swar ka nikaas*) that departs from the usual qawwali voice we are more accustomed to hearing, and also through his extremely skillful and moving use of the bol banao technique of elaboration.

As I myself participate in the Milad celebrations, reciting *hamd* and *naat* and *paidaish*, as I hear the women reciting the lovely paidaish texts (verses that are recited—sung actually—to celebrate the birth of the Prophet), I always recall Jafar Husain's deeply moving paidaish, 'Baro ghee ke diye na.' He sings it with such tenderness as to bring tears to one's eyes. And more to remind every woman who has ever held a new-born infant in her arms of that magical moment. Suddenly, in Jafar Saheb's singing, the world of religious rules, laws and pronouncements softens to just a mother's love and wonder at this miraculous moment of birth. The world of worship becomes just this—tenderness and love. In his singing every baby becomes Divine, the Divine becomes as beloved as a child. *Vatsalya bhav* at its best! Here again, it is not just the poetry, though much can be said about that wonderful bringing together in these verses of the world of Islam, the desert lands where it was born and that green world that lies between the Jamuna and the Ganga. It is Jafar

Husain's singing, the strangely delicate tonality, the fineness of bol banao, the haunting *pukar* that yet never detracts from the strength and rhythm of the basic quality of qawwali gayaki that brings alive this vatsalya, brings alive too that Ganga-Jamuni tehzeeb of which we can be justly proud.

There is too the fineness of his swar, its finely honed perfection; it is almost a thumri voice, and yet it is so clearly the voice of qawwali. And there is the brilliance of his gayaki, his own virtuosity, which again, thumri-like, never intrudes, never makes itself visible, allowing *bhav* to be foremost. I remember again Naina Devi's words that in thumri the listener should not respond with 'Waah!' but with 'Aah!'—a sigh, rather than an exclamation at virtuosity. Jafar Husain's singing was 'aah'-inducing. This is so whether it was his paidaish or his wonderful verses from Amir Khusrau, his playfully sweet 'Chhap tilak sab chheeni,' his soft and plaintive 'Eri sakhi,' his very dadra-like 'Dagar panghat ki,' or his exquisite rendering of ghazals in the style of qawwali.

As I write, I realise that Jafar Husain lived at a time (he passed away sometime in the 1990s) when the world was different. The nationalist project was, even then, with us no doubt, but not with quite the same stridency as it is now. Music was music, unencumbered by the need to see itself as a reflection of the nation-state, or at any rate, less encumbered by that need. But even at that time, in both India and Pakistan, forms and bandishes were being bled out of music. We owe a great debt to those singers in Pakistan who kept alive the traditions of ragas, bandishes and even gayakis that were anathema to an Islamic state, and to those singers in India who, despite a total lack of audience, continued to preserve these musical traditions that were severely neglected by a, no doubt, secular state, but one rapidly becoming majoritarian in nature. Irfan Zuberi shared with me about working with *gharanedar* musicians who dredged out and dusted for his hearing almost-forgotten khayal bandishes that spoke of Islamic traditions—of the Prophet, of the imams, of Husain and Hasan, of Ali and of the Panj-e-tan. Some of these bandishes had not been performed or even practiced in riaz for years; many had not been taught to the next generation—

after all, where was the audience who wished to listen to them anymore? What good then is a bandish that one might never be able to sing? This is so despite any articulated rule against such bandishes. Fortunately, we do still hear some bandishes that stem from the Islamic tradition—the exquisite 'Haan Pir more Auliya Nijamuddin,' 'Ab mori naiya paar kar de Hazrat Nizamuddin Auliya' or 'Nabi ke darbar.' Long may we hear them, and may we never forget them.

I want to end on a hopeful note. Change is inevitable. Time, distance, performance contexts, individual singers' temperaments, audience choices and certainly the political climate and both political and societal patronage, or lack thereof, influence the choices singers will make, the paths they will pursue.

But music is music, and when we hear someone who sings not just well, but with truth, we recognise that quality, and hear it as a reflection of our own path and being. That will never change, regardless of the number of lines drawn on the earth, despite the posturings of the powerful. We will always, Indians and Pakistanis, listen to each other, enjoy our shared traditions of music, and at that moment, recognise ourselves in the other.

Notes and References

1. *swar*: The musical note. In Indian music the position of the note is not according to the rational scale of Western music; it can therefore vary slightly depending on the raga being sung.
2. *swar ka nikaas*: The way the swar or note is sounded. Thus it might be approached with a slight hint of the previous (or following) note; it might be taken as a sliding *meend*, etc.
3. *rangeelapan*: A colourful, emotive, playful style.
4. *shokhi*: A mischievous, charming and playful quality; a slight flamboyance in the singing style.
5. *shagirdi*: Discipleship.
6. *taiyyari*: A state of musical 'readiness.' Musical accomplishment.
7. *thehrav*: The calm, poise and peace that comes through in the singing.
8. *bol banao*: Literally, making the words [come alive], a technique typical of thumri singing. A single word or phrase is repeated

over and over again in different ways to explore both the raga's structure and *chalan* [movement], and equally—and this is specific to thumri—to bring out different emotions and dramas hidden within the poetry.

9. *gale ka nikaas*: Literally, the path the voice takes [as it sings]. Largely a factor of gharana training, this refers to the singer's style of voice production.

Acknowledgements

My thanks to Tarun Saint for this opportunity to think about music in India and Pakistan, for his encouragement and immense patience with my many delays.

Thanks also to Rakhshanda Jalil for this opportunity to write for this volume, and also for the many Milads I have participated in at her home.

I am grateful to Irfan Zuberi for many discussions that helped me immensely in the writing of this essay, among them, about khayal bandishes with 'Islamic' themes, and on layi-layi ki alaap and lehan.

Yousuf Sayeed's film *Khayal Darpan* provided many insights into music in Pakistan.

To Amlan Das Gupta and the archives at Jadavpur University for many hours of listening pleasure and for so many enlightening conversations.

The archives at the National Centre for the Performing Arts, Bombay, were also a treasure trove of extraordinary recordings.

Above all to Jafar Husain Badayuni, Fariduddin Ayaz, Nasiruddin Sami, Ghous Mohammed Niazi and so many other wonderful singers whose music inspires us to recognise the truth about ourselves as inherently one with all living beings everywhere.

9

Scripting an Enclave's Marginal Lives
Selina Hossain's *Bhumi O Kusum*

DEBJANI SENGUPTA

> Depending on which side of this marking you may now be,
> you may or may not have an identity card, you may or may
> not need to take a fake name to enroll into a school, you may
> or may not be able to deliver your child with the real father's
> name in the neighbourhood hospital, you may or may not
> still be able to have electricity this evening even though the
> cable passes above your house, irrespective of the fact that
> your family may have lived here before countries were formed
> one night.
>
> —Extract from the booth text of an art installation
> on *chhitmahals* by Mumbai-based artist
> Shilpa Gupta, *Untitled*, 2013–14.

The Partition of India in 1947, to all intents and purposes, had the semblance of work well done in terms of population exchange or drawing up the new boundaries, particularly in the Punjab. On the Eastern part, the Partition's after-effects took a more messy turn. The international boundary in the East, drawn up with indifference to actual lives and geographical realities on the ground, was one of the many unfinished labours whose lines of vivisection echoed in the detritus of broken lives, families, habitations and the secret selves of the nations that came into being at the stroke of midnight. After numerous Boundary Commissions and high-level meetings between India and Pakistan, the porous borders between the two nations still contained anomalies and regularly hit the headlines because they extracted a price far beyond the imagination of the policymakers. Significantly, the price was mostly paid by border dwellers, people who lived on the edges of these nations, whose ties of trade and kinship often carried them across the invisible lines that demarcated citizenship and defined an alien. This paper looks at a pressing issue of boundary making (that has contributed to tensions in the subcontinent between the two neighbouring nations, India and Bangladesh, formerly East Pakistan) through the formation of enclaves in a novel by the well-known Bangladeshi novelist Selina Hossain called *Bhumi O Kusum*.

One of the fallouts of the drawing of boundaries between India and Pakistan in 1947 was the creation of 'enclaves' on the eastern border regions which were parcels of territories belonging to India while being surrounded by the territory of East Pakistan, or vice versa. In international law, states exercise legal and political sovereignty over their territories. Although rationally the territories should be contiguous or geographically adjacent, sometimes they are not. The Partition of 1947 throws us an example of geographically non-contiguous territories that yet constituted one state: Pakistan before 1971. This possibility of territories lacking geographical contiguity that yet form part of one state sometimes results in some parts being surrounded by the territory of another state. Such territories are termed enclaves. Locally known as *chhitmahal* in Bengali, where *chhit* means a fragment (something that is part of a whole but not unified to it), enclaves are pockets of India within Bangladesh, and vice versa. The reasons that lead to the birth of these anomalous geographical areas are obscure, but it is probable that the highly fertile lands belonging to the 'chhits' became bartering tools between the neighbouring rulers of the princely states of Cooch Behar and Rangpur when the former integrated into India, and the latter into Pakistan.

As per the joint verification carried out by the Indian and Bangladeshi governments in April 1997, there are 111 Indian enclaves in Bangladesh and 51 Bangladeshi enclaves in India, although these figures are disputable.[1] In India, these slices of Bangladesh can be found in the states of West Bengal, Assam,

Tripura and Meghalaya and point to the longstanding aspects of boundary challenges between the two nations, a direct fallout of the Partition of 1947. Enclaves, both Indian and Bangladeshi, cover thousands of acres of land where people live fragmented and makeshift lives. While enclaves have been crucial points of negotiations in Land Boundary Agreements (LBAs) between India and Bangladesh, a form of political expediency has prevented the two nations from seriously trying to resolve this longstanding problem until now. In a dramatic volte-face by the ruling Trinamul Congress in West Bengal, its supremo Mamata Banerjee has recently decided to support the BJP government's land boundary pact (this is a previous Land Boundary Agreement signed by the Manmohan Singh-led UPA government with Bangladesh that BJP now endorses) for a 'speedy solution to [the] enclave problem.'[2] The agreement with Bangladesh seeks to transfer certain portions of land along the border so that some of the major enclaves can be rationally merged with their mother countries. In spite of Banerjee's endorsement that has come because the LBA is of 'greater national interest,' the agreement has generated widespread protests, particularly in Assam where political parties have taken out rallies urging the government not to hand over an inch of Assam's land to Bangladesh.[3]

In the past, both India and Bangladesh have, from time to time, tried to address these issues politically, rationalising, for instance, the fact that 1000 kilometres of the Bengal border run through the meandering rivers of the lower Indo-Gangetic plain (an active delta region) and their shifting courses, and the sudden rise of *char* land or the silt banks and islands that have often been claimed by respective parties as their territory. By the Land Boundary Agreement of 1974 between the two countries, India and the newly independent Bangladesh decided to complete the demarcation of the land border between the two countries, and the question of the enclaves was taken up. The two countries listed fifteen sectors of the border that remained to be demarcated, and although the Bangladesh Parliament ratified this agreement, the Indian side did not. In the 2011 Protocol to the said Agreement, India and

Bangladesh again agreed to exchange these small parcels of land and to better demarcate the land boundaries between them. The borders of the Indian states of Assam, West Bengal, Meghalaya and Tripura would be affected to some extent by this exchange of territory; this Agreement has also not been implemented. The Constitution (One Hundred and Nineteenth) Amendment Bill, 2013, proposes to give effect to this proposed land exchange. This long overdue exchange will try to harmonise India's land boundaries and, more importantly, improve the lives of all those residents of the enclaves who, by an unfortunate twist of fate, have been living without a national identity and without enjoying or ever knowing the quality of life enjoyed by their neighbours. In August 2015, India and Bangladesh, in a landmark agreement, formally exchanged 162 enclaves, bringing to an end a process of exchange of land and citizens that had begun in the 1950s.

The people living in the enclaves are particularly vulnerable because they are virtually stateless persons who enjoy less legal rights than prisoners in any country. 'People who live in these enclaves are, even today, stateless people, without an identity, without documents, without any rights or privileges. They do not belong to anyone. India does not want to have anything to do with its citizens who live in chitmahals inside Bangladesh, and vice versa' as Butalia remarks.[4] The enclave dwellers possess no identity card (the fate of all those born in the enclaves), and that means the state's denial of basic civic amenities to them. There have been several contradictory population estimates, but it can be safely stated that more than half a million people live in these enclaves. As Willem van Schendel remarks in his book *The Bengal Borderland: Beyond State and Nation in South Asia,* 'understanding and unraveling the post-1947 realities of Partition requires an intimate knowledge of the borderlands that were created and permutations they experienced. The role of borderlands in the shaping of post-Partition societies, economies and states remain almost completely unexplored.'[5]

In Partition studies in South Asia, the terms 'resettlement' and 'migration' do not encompass some of these aspects of marginalisation that are faced by enclave dwellers, and a systematic study of life in the enclaves is yet to be undertaken. The unauthorised though sometimes inadvertent border crossings that are a reality of the Indo-Bangladesh borders epitomise and 'cement a deeply communal border and cross-border religious solidarities.'[6] Ties of informal trade, kinship and travel are sustained through the relative fluidity of this border and political persecution or natural disasters have added their share to make this an 'unstable landscape.'[7] The Indo-Bangladesh border is highly volatile and the border guards on both sides are often known to use excessive force on unarmed populace, which has led Schendel to name this a 'killer border' and illustrates again and again how border fencing shapes migrant bodies and how 'border maps' also become 'body maps.'[8] However, the newly created boundaries do not manage either to contain or keep out 'aliens' and the question of belonging has been a contested issue among the nations' religious minorities in both India and Bangladesh as well as for people who live in enclaves contiguous to the borders. The continued violence, both state-sponsored and tolerated, on those who are 'different' is a political reality of the subcontinent and has a profound effect on the social and cultural fabric of the two nations. The brutal separation of peoples through religion has been undone in Bangladesh in 1971; yet that nation continues to see unmitigated violence directed towards its religious minorities, as do both India and Pakistan. The reality of living either on the right or the wrong side of the border has created unbelievable hardships for thousands of people and destroyed their fundamental right to their land and homesteads. This existential marginalisation of a whole people, within and outside the nation states, has translated into living on the fringes of society with material deprivations and often, because of nationality and gender, to suffer a double marginaliation.

When India was partitioned, the reality of migration also encompassed those who did not leave: many Hindus from East Pakistan stayed back either for political reasons or because they thought that the division was temporary; some had ancestral property or jobs. Lower caste peasant communities like the Namasudras with strong ties to the land refused to move following the example of their leader Jogendra Nath Mandal, who stayed back.[9] Similarly, the Bihari Muslims came to East Pakistan to settle and later, under duress or willingly, joined the Pakistani army to perpetrate crimes against the Muktibahini and ordinary citizens. Many of them still live in large camps in Dhaka and Syedpur as stateless people as Pakistan has refused to accept them as citizens. Only recently has our historiography begun to pay attention to their stateless plight.[10] These recent Partition historiographies have made it clear that there are no linear, uni-dimensional histories of habitation and sojourn, and they are complicated by centripetal movements of people who move only to come back or who do not move at all. Often, the place of the 'home' where one chooses to stay on becomes a sacralised space that carries within it the markers of past struggles and future hopes—a way of reclaiming the land and language that had been shattered with 1947. The imperatives of the story of this attachment to the land nullifies and questions the ways in which the same land was divided and mutilated in the past. In many literary narratives, the landscape and the people living in them confer a web of meaning to the displacement or rupture of the Partition to give us a template of how land, both real and symbolic, imagines an identity implicated within and without the nation.

The struggles to be heard from the margins confer on the contingencies of Partition another set of images that articulate a different set of realities: not exile or refugee-hood but being the 'other' within the space of the nation. As cultural anthropology suggests, margins are not peripheral spaces but forms and practices through which the state is both experienced and undone; 'margins (are) sites that do not so much lie outside the state but rather, like rivers, run through its body.'[11] Agamben's theorisation of 'homo sacer' (1998) as 'not simple natural life, but life exposed to death (bare life or sacred life) is the originary political element' can be used to decipher and understand the life lived at the margins that yet 'exhibits an essential link with the terrain on which sovereign power (of the state) is founded.'[12] Therefore margins are spaces between bodies and states, and Agamben's bare bodies, when they live in the borders of nation states, become 'marginal and expendable' bodies that can be killed with impunity and sacrificed as pawns for nationalist causes. Partition's direct effect was to create borders where none existed and to give rise to categories of 'bare life': the 'refugee' and the 'minority,' the 'citizen' and the 'alien' that fed off each other. These examples of the 'bare life' proliferate in West Bengal's postcolonial political discourse as identities indicative of territoriality and sovereignty. As Gyanendra Pandey states in his exposition of the 'subaltern citizen,' the 'claim is rather about historical agency broadly defined, and about *belonging*—in a society and in its self-construction. That is to say, it is about the *living* of individual and collective lives, and the limitations on that living about the potential for life and creativity in given historical circumstances, and the restriction of that potential.'[13]

Enclave dwellers then come to stretch the semantic meanings of migration/settlement/resettlement and force us to see how geographical, historical and political boundaries reconstitute, consolidate and refashion marginalisation, subalternity and political violence that live at the heart of free nations. Literature has been more forthcoming to chart these dissonances just as recent art practices in the subcontinent have also done.[14] The enclave inhabitants, peripheral to the business of nations, attain newspaper space when they die in border security firings or remain obstinately lodged in no-man's land, refusing to move as prodded. From time to time these reports also tell us in a sub-text that the enclave dwellers are not passively awaiting their fate but actually intervening (though most times without success) to carve out their identities and their lives. However, an exploration of what it means to be an enclave dweller is beyond statistics or reportage. Literature seems to have recorded these seismic transformations in the borderlands most faithfully.

Selina Hossain's novel *Bhumi O Kusum* [Land and Flower, 2010][15] remains the only exploration of chhitmahals in Bengali literature and can be considered an important intervention in Partition studies where literature's role in constructing a society's sense of reality can be seen fully. As an investigator of the history and reality of enclaves, Hossain's novel charts out to do many things. Set in an enclave in Dohogram, the novel delineates the daily struggles of the inhabitants of the enclave to live lives of dignity. It also draws our attention to the way literature has portrayed cross-border actualities of the movement of people and goods that continue to accommodate and resist the realities of political boundaries. Depicting Bangladesh's citizens who live surrounded by Indian territories, the novel explores the lineaments of citizenship (that emerged after the Partition) that radically transform or mutate the longing for a human subject to live and work peacefully and to *belong* to a land that may be constructed as *home*. The everyday language of habitation and affect used in the novel reinstates the enclave dwellers as inhabitants of a history that they sometimes feel powerless against, yet in which they actively try to intercede. This representation of enclave lives thus creates forms of knowledge that may challenge our notions of habitations and belonging.

Before she began her novel, Hossain had visited the enclave of Dohogram-Angarpota a number of times to get to know the inhabitants and to research their lives. In her own words, the idea of the novel came to her when she realised that,

> the chhitmahals were a creation of Partition. Those who live here are controlled by international relations....Dohogram-Angarpota belongs to Bangladesh but is surrounded and controlled by India. People have no freedom to go anywhere. This crisis of the human subject moved me immensely.[16]

Hossain knew that there were hardly any narratives based on the history of enclaves and her novel would, in that sense, be a pioneering work that would address issues of belonging and violence that were often hidden in governmental statistics.[17] *Bhumi O Kusum* brings chhitmahal dwellers and their 'divided lives' lived on the margins center-stage of her text just as it lays bare their relationship to a land where they live and labour.

> Golam Ali could not explain the intricacies of the chhitmahal. He will have to call another meeting another day. Everything will have to be explained to people. If they did not recognize their own land, they will not be able to make flowers bloom in that soil....If the blooming of flowers was not done properly

then the earth would turn fallow: life would not take root there.[18]

Golam Ali's realisation that he is like 'a man who did not have a country to belong to' because the Partition has made him an enclave dweller at once severs him and Monjila and others like them from the land where they had lived, their memories of childhood and growing up, and livelihoods that spanned over communities and spaces. They can no longer travel to see their kin in distant villages because they are now enclave dwellers.

Peopled with a wide range of characters both Hindu and Muslim, the novel's narrative timeline begins with the formation of the chhitmahal called Dohogram that is surrounded by India (although the land belonged to East Pakistan) and ends with the formation of independent Bangladesh. The Hindu inhabitants of the enclave feel like 'proxy citizens' of the new state of Pakistan, while in India they would be termed 'refugees.' In one lifetime, that encompasses a range of marginalities.[19] The Muslims are not real citizens either because they enjoy nothing of the benefits that citizenship brings. Citizenship, that often expresses an implicit and explicit appropriation of the state's resources and an enjoyment of certain privileges, is totally destabilised within the enclaves. So although on paper the enclave dwellers are citizens, they enjoy no rights and no responsibilities of being one. Their disenfranchisement is complete when we realise that they own no official documents (like an identity card) that allow them any access to the state's resources. In every sense of their being, they lead forgotten and marginal lives. As Golam Ali looks on at Aghor Mandal and his wife, who are planning to leave for India, he realises, 'Their two faces had turned to two maps of the countries, India and Pakistan. They shatter to form chhitmahals, the breaking of the banks of the river Teesta. Humans make the country, the country is its people.'[20]

The novel, in keeping with its subject, has a fluid structure with episodic units tied together through a number of characters, although Golam Ali, Namita Bagdi, Monjila, her daughter Barnamala, and Bashar are the ones who influence the narrative flow. Hossain's novel abandons a linear narrative structure and an intricate plot. This loose episodic narration 'retains the sense of little histories' that give a panoramic view of enclave subjectivities.[21] In opposition to the daily constrictions and abjections faced by the enclave inhabitants, the novel is expansive and generous in setting out the existence of those who live on the edge. The small farmers and traders, their struggles, their loves and their friendships form the 'coda' of the novel. The daily skirmishes with the Indian Border Security Force, the midnight flights to other territories, the quiet lives lived with desperation and violence and yet encompassed within the cycles of nature are shown in meticulous detail. Violence is an integral part of the enclave dwellers' lives and it shapes their desires, dreams and ambitions: either to escape it or be identified with it.

The interlocutory discursive trope of the text is land and belonging; this in turn constructs the ideal of a 'home' that gathers within it both a goal and a method: the inhabitants of the chhitmahal unite to form a responsible society although they are denied citizen's rights just as they participate in the formation of their collective identity. Hossain effects a change in the paradigm of her political sensibilities in a way that is evolutionary; the novel celebrates the birth of Bangladesh but also suggests that it can be a nation only when it is truly inclusive: to deny citizenship to the enclave inhabitants is to construct a nation deeply flawed:

> We are Pakistani...inhabitants of the chhitmahal called Chandraghana. We are surrounded by India on all sides. Our flags are decorated with the moon and stars. We can see Pakistan when we look at that flag....Pakistan lives in every breadth that we take. But Pakistan is an absence in the vessel in which we cook rice.'[22]

Later on, Golam Ali describes the enclave inhabitants as 'the deaf-mute children of Pakistan.'[23] The text posits an important question regarding freedom. If the independence of a country is followed by the 'tearing of the rope of life' then 'how can freedom bring anything new?'[24] *Bhumi O Kusum* is a novel about the novelist's quest to 'work through' (to use Adorno's phrase) the subcontinent's past and its connections to the present, not only in the synchronic life of the nation but the diachronic inheritance of identities that live within an organic cycle of nature's seasons and in the shadow of the Partition. Hossain hopes to capture the world of the chhitmahal to subject it to the structure of her novel and give it a meaning that the chhitmahal inhabitants lack in the structure of a nation. Therefore her meticulous recordings of births and deaths, however trivial or fleeting, create a recognition and archiving of a history that has found no takers, and an acknowledgment of bare lives that have gone unrecorded.

One day, Dohogram's residents have to contend with the sudden presence of the state when all their lives the state had been a distant entity. Suddenly the state seems to be everywhere, as evidenced in the ubiquitous presence of the Indian security forces and the Pakistani officials who come to carry out a census. The inhabitants of the chhitmahal realise however marginal their existence may be, they now needed to reinvent themselves as citizens of a new state (twice over) and as inhabitants of a divided land. They need to be legible to the state. The state's attempt to restrict their movements across land they had historically considered their own and its interference in their livelihoods create tragic situations where the inhabitants of Dohogram realise the new impetus to their existence: to rebuild a social world where the older and newer inhabitants will have space to live peaceably yet constantly resisting and transforming their responses to the newly created borders. Their strategies of resistance, accommodation and innovation form the most important tropes of this text. As the Indian Border Forces fire on an unarmed crowd and abduct and rape Maloti, Golam Ali realises that the villagers' enclave existence is circumscribed by land: 'That was Teenbigha where the border post was, then a main road. After the road was Patgram, in Rangpur district. They could not cross to Patgram without the permission of the border force. By closing off the road to Teenbigha the enclave dwellers would be under their jurisdiction.'[25] Hossain's earlier novels *Japito Jiban* and *Gayatri Sandhya* both looked at the creation of Pakistan as necessary and right in the context of burgeoning Muslim nationality, and deplored the communalisation of that aspect within the larger forces of Indian nationalism. *Bhumi O Kusum* is to a large extent a movement away from Hossain's preoccupation with national level politics and the birth of Bangladesh that subverted notions of religious nationalism. Moving away from the centre, the novelist seems to be focusing attention on the border and the borderlands to ask important new questions about nation, identity and home that resonate through the post-Partition history of both India and Bangladesh.

Dohogram, situated next to the Teenbigha Corridor, is a small space packed with people of all faiths and creeds. Hossain's strategy of exploring this marginal community, in constant dialogue with hegemonic state structures, opens up a space that is between the factual and the metaphorical: the imagination of a 'home' is mediated through issues of territory and sovereignty; yet it is also something more than just land. Nitai the singer, who left his ancestral home in another 'chhit,' remembers his grandmother telling him: '*Jey bhitar swad bujhey na, taar jibon andhaar*' [Someone who does not understand the taste of home lives a dark life.] Nitai ruminates: 'Now there will be another turn and another life will start: another kind of soil, another kind of grass, trees and plants. Birds and bird calls. Humans and the way they turn their heads to speak, the way they look at you; a sigh and a long life that calls out for love. The glance of love and a naughtiness in its depth. To make a path and then to find a path again. And again—.'[26] The passage points to a 'third dimension' working within temporal markers of the idea of home: a home that is beyond the factual or metaphorical but consistent with the journey of humans through the earth, at once real and sublime. If the novel has been taken as 'the form of transcendental homelessness,' then Hossain's novel performs an extremely important task in its suggestiveness.[27] The novel's meandering structure seems to create a bridge between contesting ideas of everyday territoriality and human lives lived within cross-border movements and migrations where borders are not forgotten national frontiers but formative spaces of post-national identity formation. The aggressive margins of postcolonial borders constrict lives; yet they also enhance a desire to translate the loss and grief of these lives, however marginal, into the larger questions of diversity of moving, settling and living in the otherwise ever compiling migration data of nation states in the subcontinent.

Barnamala, whose name means the (Bangla) alphabet, scripts this new language of living and loving. The day she gets married to Ajmal, she watches the soft light spread over the chhit under whose benediction the huts, the grass, the wild bushes, the mud track and the rice fields look ever new. Ajmal tells her that in the soil of the chhitmahal, Barnamala is the best flower to bloom. Like the changes in Barnamala's life, the political fortunes of the chhit change, too: East Pakistan becomes independent Bangladesh, and Ajmal dies fighting for it. The political fate of Dohogram however does not change: India has to relinquish some territory for it to merge with Bangladesh, and that decision is forever postponed. The inhabitants of the chhitmahal realise that, 'they had been prisoners earlier and they remain so. They have not been freed. The country has been freed, the name of it has changed, the flag has changed, but the enclave has remained an enclave. Nothing has changed inside the chhit.'[28] Barnamala, at the end of the novel, possesses the self-consciousness of someone who has historically evolved—through living and through suffering the contingencies of borders. Imprisoned within the territoriality of the enclave, Barnamala tries to enter Bangladesh to pay obeisance to her dead husband; as the sentries stop her, she cries out, 'I want the people of the chhit to be free. You cannot keep us prisoners forever.' In her last cry, the geo-bio identity of the citizen is effaced and Barnamala, 'a citizen with no rights, in permanent deferral' refuses to be the 'living dead.'[29] Her cry tears into the silence that surrounds her: she enters a perennial language of protest with her demand to be free. Like her mother, Barnamala, too, finds herself at the border, trying to make sense of all that those invisible lines mean to many like her. But her cry for freedom is greeted with silence all around—a metaphor for how the larger events in political history lock into the lives of ordinary people. If we take Agamben's idea that only the bare life is authentically political, then Barnamala's cry to be free is the way in which she writes herself back into the body of the nation. Her cry is shot through with the 'uncanny' for it reappears after the nation state has been formed and freedom has been proclaimed. It is a reminder of how the postcolonial realities of border conflicts remain markers of the enclave dwellers' life circumstances. The uneasy confluence of state repression and border porosity that had made Barnamala a 'divided body' now asserts its right to be free, not just from the prison of legality, but in the momentum set off by her grieving and dying.

Notes and References

1. Shilpa Gupta, *Untitled*, 2014. However, Willem van Schendel gives the figure of 197 enclaves: 74 Bangladeshi and 123 Indian ones. See Schendel, *The Bengal Borderland: Beyond State and Nation in South Asia* (London: Anthem Press, 2005), 80, n54. Urvashi Butalia in her essay 'The Nowhere People,' *Seminar* (New Delhi: 2002), gives 128 Indian enclaves and 95 Bangladeshi ones.
2. *The Indian Express*, 5 December 2014.
3. Ibid.
4. Urvashi Butalia, 'The Nowhere People,' *Seminar* (New Delhi: 2002), accessed 18 February 2015. http://www.india-seminar.com/2002/510/510%20urvashi%20butalia.htm
5. Schendel, *The Bengal Borderland*, 31.
6. Malini Sur, 'Divided Bodies: Crossing the India-Bangladesh Border,' *EPW* (29 March 2014), 32.
7. Ibid.
8. Ibid.
9. Anwesha Sengupta, '"Preserving" an Identity: Schedule Caste Politics in East Pakistan 1947–1952,' paper presented at the International Students Conference, Centre for Historical Studies, Jawaharlal Nehru University (April 2012).
10. Papiya Ghosh, *Community and Nation: Essays on Identity and Politics in Eastern India* (New Delhi: Oxford University Press, 2008) remains the best study of the political fate of the Bihari Muslim community in Bangladesh. For a West Pakistani account of the Bihari predicament, see Abdul Rahman Siddiqi, *Partition and the Making of the Mohajir Mindset* (Karachi: Oxford University Press, 2008), 106–118.

11. Veena Das and Deborah Poole eds. *Anthropology in the Margins of the State* (Santa Fe: School of American Research Press, 2004), 13.

12. Agamben contends that the bare life can be killed but cannot be sacrificed (as in Roman law), but in the states of marginalisation that we find modern-day refugees and minorities, they can be killed and sacrificed for the sake of polity and nationalist stakes of 'belonging'. Giorgio Agamben, *Homo Sacer: Sovereign Power and Bare Life* (Stanford: Stanford University Press, 1998), 88–100.

13. Gyanendra Pandey, *Subaltern Citizens and Their Histories: Investigations from India and USA* (London: Routledge, 2010), 5.

14. Contemporary Indian artist Shilpa Gupta has engaged with the realities of the border in her last installation at the Dhaka Art Summit 2014. Also, Vishwajyoti Ghosh curated anthology of graphic narratives, *This Side That Side: Restorying Partition* (New Delhi: Yoda Press, 2013).

15. Selina Hossain, *Bhumi O Kusum* (Dhaka: Ityadi Grantha Prakash, 2010). All translations from this text are mine.

16. An interview of Selina Hossain done by me over email, 6 April 2014.

17. Ibid.

18. Hossain, *Bhumi O Kusum*, 32.

19. Ibid., 156.

20. Ibid., 157.

21. Rashmi Doraiswamy, 'The Panoramic Vision and the Descent of Darkness', in *Narratives of Indian Cinema*, ed. Manju Jain (New Delhi: Primus Books, 2009), 77.

22. Hossain, *Bhumi O Kusum*, 251.

23. Ibid., 270.

24. Ibid., 290.

25. Ibid., 130. The tiny Bangladeshi enclave of Dohogram, situated in North Bengal next to the river Teesta, is encircled by a ring of eleven Indian check-posts and seventeen observation towers erected by the Border Security Force. See Schendel, *The Bengal Borderland*, 110.

26. Ibid., 273.

27. Walter Benjamin, *Illuminations* (New York: Schoken Books, 1969), 99, where Benjamin discusses Lukács' idea in the context of Leskov's storytelling.

28. Hossain, *Bhumi O Kusum*, 399.

29. Paul Virilio, 'The Politics of Disappearance', in *Negative Horizons: An Essay in Dromoscopy* (London: Continuum, 2005), 170.

10   The Absent Presence
The Partition in Modern Urdu Poetry

RAKHSHANDA JALIL

Politics and history are said to be interwoven, but not commensurate. But then so are politics and literature. Recent studies have shown that, given the close relationship between social reality and literary texts, it is important to re-examine and revisit the literature produced during times of great social and political upheaval. Doing so can provide a far more nuanced understanding of historical events than a mere perusal of historical records or documents. The events of 1947 were witnessed by some of the finest Urdu writers, who saw and commented on what they had experienced, in many cases, at first hand. While there is a great deal of Urdu fiction dealing with the Partition, there is comparatively little in Urdu poetry that directly addresses the *taqseem* or partition. There is of course Faiz Ahmed Faiz's 'Subh-e-Azadi' [The Dawn of Freedom] and Ahmad Nadeem Qasmi's 'Phir Bhayanak Teergi Mein Aa Gae' [Once Again We have Come into a Terrible Darkness], but given the huge corpus in prose, these seem like slender pickings. What is more, when one goes looking for something specifically on the Partition by Indian Urdu poets, while one is met with a great deal on *azadi* or freedom and, in fact, several poems entitled 'Pandrah Agust' (Fifteenth August), one finds it difficult to find something that addresses the issue of Partition in the same gory detail as, for instance, the short stories of Saadat Hasan Manto or Krishan Chander or Rajinder Singh Bedi. It is enough to set one thinking. Partition marked the coming of age of the Urdu short story writer; it all but numbed the Urdu poet. Why was that? Is the Urdu poet more squeamish than the Urdu short story writer? Or is it the very nature of poetry that clothes itself in the indirect, the oblique, the allusive? Is the difference in output merely due to the inherent difference between poetry and prose? Perhaps.

It must be noted that politics and poetry have been inextricably linked in the Urdu tradition. In fact, the poet was quicker to take note of the turbulence of the times—long before Urdu prose began to record social and political upheavals. At a time when the prose writer was still immersed in the somewhat escapist *dastan* and *qissa-kahani* tradition, Nazir Akbarabadi (1735–1830) had emerged as the earliest poet of protest.[1] A people's poet in the true sense of the word, he wrote songs and ballads about real people facing real problems in *Banjara Nama* [The Chronicle of the Nomad], *Roti Nama* [The Chronicle of Bread], *Aadmi Nama* [The Chronicle of Man], among others. Nazir was an *ibn-ul waqt*, a man of his time and age in every sense of the word: he wrote of everyday struggles, sufferings and failures without resorting to sentimentality or subterfuge. Then there were the poets—scores upon scores of them, some known and remembered, others unknown and forgotten—who wrote a kind of elegiac, dirge-like poetry but nonetheless with a sharp political undercurrent known as *shehr ashob*, meaning 'lament of the city'. Flashes of political insight, dollops of humour and satire, witticisms on the age and the rulers made the shehr ashob[2] a precursor to the poetry of the progressives, the *taraqqui-pasand*, who wrote anthems of resistance and sang jubilant songs about the coming revolution. Some of the greatest exponents of this genre were the poets Hatim, Sauda and Mir who pulled Urdu poetry out of the thrall of romanticism— all the while retaining its high classical register and continuing to write in the tautly-woven ghazal, *qasidah* and *marsiya* style—and made it speak of newer concerns.

Poets dominated the cultural and intellectual landscape of most big cities across the length and breadth of undivided India: Delhi, Lucknow, Hyderabad and Lahore. In Delhi, which was the beating heart of the Great Revolt of 1857, everybody—from Emperor Bahadur Shah Zafar down to the beggar singing in the street—was smitten with poetry. Altaf Husain Hali (1837–1914) likened poetry to a 'magic lantern' that shines ever more brightly when the room, or the age, darkens.[3] Others too have noted how poetry flourishes when all else withers. When, in the words of William Butler Yeats (1865–1939), 'the centre does not hold,' when political chaos mars the even tenor of daily life, when violence tears the social fabric, it is usually the poet's finest hour. And we have seen in the history of Urdu literature, it was indeed so in the last years of Mughal rule in India. The decline and dismantling of the Mughal Empire was accompanied by calamitous events, each more tragic than the other—such as the rape and pillage of Delhi by Nadir Shah (9 March 1739); the repeated attacks by Ahmed Shah Abdali, the Marathas and the Rohillas upon poor hapless Delhi; the killing of Nawab Siraj ud-Daulah by the British in the Battle of Plassey in 1757; the establishment of British control in Delhi in 1803; the annexation of Awadh in 1856; and then the final nail in the coffin, the Revolt of 1857 that is now referred to as the First War of Independence.

The Urdu poets took note of the disarray, mismanagement and decline and wrote about specific incidents. If anything, with each fresh catastrophe, they evolved a vocabulary to express their angst, clothing their sorrow in a time-honoured repertoire of images and metaphors. Some favourite synonyms for the beloved traditionally used in classical Urdu poetry—*but* [idol], *sitamgar* [tyrant], *kafir* [infidel], *yaar* [friend]—began to be used mockingly for the British. Poets deployed traditional images such as the *gul-o-bulbul* [the rose and the nightingale]—popular tropes in classical Persian poetry—to decry the wilderness that their lives had become, the desolation in Shahjahanabad after the plunder and lootings, the lawlessness on the streets, the shabbiness of the once-handsome houses.[4] Several poets were actively involved in the Uprising, such as Munir Shikohabadi, Fazl-e Haq Khairabadi and Emperor Bahadur Shah Zafar himself.

And so the Urdu poet continued in this vein, drawing sustenance from the burst of political energy that was released from the events of 1857, donning the mantle of the reformer and activist, speaking in the voice of a political commentator and a social analyst, and evolving a new understanding of *wataniyat* [nationalism]. Gopichand Narang makes an important point regarding the poets' proximity to power and privilege; as the royal courts and the nobility became weaker and steadily more unable to extend any form of patronage, the poets' pen became increasingly freer.[5] Narang cites a range of literary commentaries, compilations of shehr ashob, volumes such as *Fughan-e Dehli* [The Lament of Delhi] and goes on to build an argument that it was only with the dawn of a new century that *hubb-e watani* [love for the nation], as we understand it today, could be seen as a literary phenomenon.

The poets who had chosen to stay silent immediately after the *ghadar* began to spread their wings, and a range of new emotions can be found in the poetry of the late-nineteenth and early-twentieth century—from overt expressions of hostility to British rule to sarcastic references to the presence of a tyrannical alien in one's midst. The prose writings of Maulvi Zakaullah (1832–1910), Nazir Ahmed (1836–1912), Muhammad Husain Azad (1830–1910) aided and abetted this change and served as a bridge between the old and the new. Altaf Husain Hali deserves a special mention for it is in his writings—inspired as he is by his mentor Sir Syed Ahmad Khan, the founder of MAO College at Aligarh—that we see the beginnings of modernism. In Hali's epic poem 'Musaddas: Madd-o Jazr-e Islam' [The Ebb and Flow of Islam], he shows how it is entirely possible to be both a Muslim and a nationalist, and a modern one at that, as he urges his fellow Musalman:

> No one wishes your religion and faith ill
> No one is hostile to the traditions and the Quran[6]

Another poet, using an altogether different idiom, with his tongue firmly in his cheek, was also busy decrying the contradictions of his age. This was the satirical, doubting voice of Akbar Illahabadi

(1846–1921). The genie, he believed, was firmly out of the bottle after 1857, and there was no putting it back:

> The minstrel and the music—both have changed
> Our sleep has changed, the tale we told has changed.[7]

Illahabadi wrote on a range of issues—the coming of the railway, telegraph, *Pioneer* newspaper, Pears soap, and a host of British-made consumer goods—and gave vent to an implacable mistrust of the British. Scornful of those Indians who wished to ape the British and adopt Western ways, he wrote:

> They became votaries of the Time
> And adopted the style of the West
> In their ardent desire for a second birth
> They committed suicide.[8]

From Akbar Illahabadi we move on to Urdu poetry's most problematic figure, Muhammad Iqbal (1877–1938)—problematic because of the dualities inherent in his more overtly political poetry. The pen that wrote the 'Tarana-e Hind' [Ode to Hind] in 1904 also produced the 'Tarana-e Milli' [Ode to the Religious Community, in this case the Muslim community] a short six years later. But there is much in his poetry that would provide rich nourishment to a later generation of poets who chose to address the nationalist cause without the trappings of religion. Here is a sampling of Iqbal's rousing poetry, exhorting his readers to break the shackles of colonialism in poems such as 'Gila' [Reproach]:

> Enslaved to Britain you have kissed the rod
> It is not Britain I reproach but you

With the coming of Gandhi and the first non-cooperation movement, something changed in the Urdu poet's psyche. Cries for revolution became more robust and the sense of nationhood grew stronger. Brij Narain Chakbast in 'Awaz-e Qaum' [The Call of the Nation] is speaking for an entire generation when he declares:

> From the ground to the skies there are cries of Home Rule
> And the youthfulness of nationalism and the urge for Home
> Rule.

In a poem written long before the Partition, 'Inquilab' [Revolution], Asrar-ul Haq Majaz, the romantic-turned-revolutionary poet predicts a bloody end to imperial rule long before 1947:

> *Khatm ho jaane ko hai sarmayadaron ka nizam*
> *Rang lane ko hai mazdooron ka josh-e inteqam*
> *Khoon ki boo le ke jangal se haiwan aayeinge*
> *Khoon hi khoon hoga nigahein jis taraf ko jayeingi*
> *Jhopdiyon mein mahal mein khoon, shabistanon mein khoon*
> *Dasht mein khoon wadiyon mein khoon*
> *Kohsaraon ki taraf se surkh aandhi aayegi*
> *Jaabaja aabadiyon mein aagsi lag jayegi...*
> *Aur is rang-e shafaq mein ba- hazaara anaab-o tab*
> *Jagmagayega watan ki hurriyat ka aaftab*

The rule of the capitalists is about to end
The labourer's passion for vengeance is finally coming true
From the jungles beasts shall come with the stench of blood
There shall be blood, only blood wherever the eyes turn
Blood in the huts and the palaces and bedchambers
Blood in the plains, blood in the valleys
A red storm shall come from the mountains
Setting the settlements on fire
And on the horizon, amidst a thousand tumults,
Shall rise the sun of our land's freedom

A study of the proscribed poetry of this period will reveal a strong unabashedly revolutionary, almost seditious, content: Hasrat Mohani is scathing about the so-called reforms introduced by the British as mere sops in a poem called 'Montagu Reforms'; Zafar Ali Khan is mocking the excesses of colonial rule and the brutality of men like General Dwyer in 'Mazalim-e Punjab' [The Victims of Punjab]; Hashar Kashmiri is writing a sarcastic ode to Europe 'Shukriya Europe' [Thank you, Europe]; Ehsan Danish is penning a rousing anthem of revolt 'Tarana-e Jihad' [The Anthem of Jihad] and so on.[9]

Taken chronologically, these poems begin to reveal a certain pattern. Each successive milestone of brutality, suppression, inequality, unfairness—the Rowlatt Act, the Jallianwala massacre, routine proscriptions and banning as well as imprisonments of poets and politicians alike—is producing voluminous poetry, polemics and posters in Urdu. The poets and publicists of the age are working in tandem: Urdu newspapers, journals and prose writers are echoing the call of the poets, and vice-versa. The firebrand Josh Malihabadi (1898–1982), poet and editor of the influential *Kaleem*, jailed for his revolutionary poetry, is declaring:

> *Kaam hai mera taghiar, naam hai mera shabab*
> *Mera naam inquilab o inquilab o inquilab*
>
> My work is change, my name is youth
> My cry is revolution, revolution, revolution

As we inch towards Partition, when the possibility of freedom becomes clearer, poets like Sahir Ludhianvi begin to seize the immense possibilities of social transformation that an event like freedom from the imperial yoke presents:

> *In kali sadiyon ke sar se jab raat ka aanchal dhalkega*
> *Jab dukh ke badal pighlenge, jab sukh ka sagar chhalkega*
> *Jab ambar jhoom ke nachega, jab dharti naghme gayegi*
> *Woh subha kabhi to aayegi*
>
> When the veil of night will slip from the brow of these dark centuries
> When the clouds of sorrow will melt and the goblet of joy will brim over
> When the skies will dance with delight, when the earth will sing songs
> Surely that morning will dawn some day

All through the 1940s, several members of the Progressive Writers' Movement had been writing songs of freedom that linked the anti-colonial struggle with the freedom movement. So there was Majaz, the Keats of Urdu poetry, expressing his longing for a better, more humane world, a world that will arise phoenix-like from the ashes of upheaval and change, in a poem called 'Rail' using the metaphor of a train hurtling through the darkness where the train becomes a metaphor for change and rebellion:

Going ahead fearlessly with a typhoon-like thunder
A rebellion in each motion
Singing songs of mankind's greatness.[10]

And even in a seemingly soft romantic poem such as 'Nazr-e Dil'
[To My Heart], Majaz cannot hide the yearning of his subversive
heart:

Let us together bring about a new revolution
Spread ourselves over the world so that all eyes are on us

There was little doubt in the mind of most Urdu poets, especially
the progressives, that the dawn that was awaited was going to be a
red one. And so, there was Makhdoom Mohiuddin, the poet from
Hyderabad writing in 'Jang-e Azadi' [War of Independence]:

Lo surkh savera aata hai, azadi ka, azadi ka
Gulnar tarana gata hai, azadi ka, azadi ka
Dekho parcham lehrata hai, azadi ka, azadi ka

Look, the red dawn comes, the red dawn of freedom
Singing the red anthem of freedom, freedom, freedom
Look, the flag is waving—the flag of independence, liberty
and freedom

And there is Kaifi Azmi writing an ode to the new woman who
must walk hand in hand with her mate, in 'Aurat':

Arise, my love, for now you must march with me
Flames of war are ablaze in our world today...
You must burn in the fire of freedom with me

But as we shall see in the poetry being written *after* the Partition,
the red storm that Majaz had predicted became the red tide of
blood—not revolution—as the country plunged into a horrific
bloodbath, and the dawn of freedom became a night-bitten dawn.
By far the most famous comment on the Partition is contained in
'Subah-e Azadi' by Faiz:

Yeh daagh daagh ujala yeh shab-gazida sehr
Woh intezar thha jiska yeh woh sehr to nahi

This patchy light, this night-bitten dawn
This is not the dawn we had been waiting for

Persistent and sustained readings within the narrow definition
one had set for oneself—Partition poetry, that is poetry on and
about the Partition—eventually revealed certain poems by Josh
Malihabadi, the firebrand revolutionary, the *Shair-e Inquilab* as
he was called, by Akhtarul Iman, by Jagannath Azad, by Sahir
Ludhianvi, and Sardar Jafri. These, I believe, need to be retrieved
and read once again. For the progressive poets, especially those who
were members of the Communist Party, the freedom that came in
the wake of Partition was a 'false freedom.' Taking the Party's line,
many poets too spoke of the sense of inadequacy, the squandering
of dreams that the dawn of freedom brought in.

Josh Malihabadi, in a poem called 'Maatam-e Azadi' [The
Lament for Freedom] written in 1948, strikes a sombre note:

Ai ham nafas! Fasana e Hindustan na poochh
Apna gala kharosh-e tarranum se phat gaya
Talwar se bacha, to rag-e gul se kat gaya

O friend, don't ask me for the tale of Hindustan
Our throats were torn by the scratching of our songs
When we escaped the sword, we were beheaded by the veins
of the rose

Majaz too had lost some of his youthful ebullience by 1948 when
he writes:

Hindu Muslim Sikh Eesai aman ke moti ro lenge
Khoon ki holi khel chuke hain rang ke dhabbe dho lenge

Hindu Muslim Sikh and Christian will shed tears of Peace
Having played Holi with blood, they will now wash off these
stains

By the time India celebrates its first Republic Day, Sahir Ludhianvi's
disenchantment with the new republic is already palpable. In a
poem titled 'Chhabbees Janwary' [Twenty-sixth January], Sahir
invokes the beautiful dreams the nation had seen, dreams of a
better tomorrow, and asks:

Come, let us ponder on this question
What happened to all those beautiful dreams we had dreamt?
... The helpless cannot even afford a shroud to cover
their nakedness
What happened to those promises of silks and brocades?

Then there is 'Pandrah Agust' [Fifteenth August] by Akhtarul
Iman, which I think deserves to be reproduced in full here:

Yahi din hai jiske liye maine kati thhi in ankhon mein raatein
Yahi seeli aab-e baqa, chasma noor hai, jalwa-e toor hai?
Isi ke liye woh suhane, madhur, rasbhare geet gaye thhe maine?
Yahi mahwash nisa, husn se choor, bhar poor, makhmoor hai
woh?
Suna thha nigahon pe woh qaid-e aadab-e mehfil nahi ab
Woh pabandiyan deedah-o dil pe jo thhin uthhti ja rahin hain
Woh majburiyan uthh gayin, walwale rah pane lagey, muskurane
lagey ab
Muhabbat kathin raaston se guzarkar lahakti mahakti hui aa
rahi hai
Wohi kasma pursi, wohi behisi aaj bhi hartaraf kyon hai taari?
Mujhe aisa mehsoos hota hai yeh meri muhabbat ka haasil nahi
hai
Abhi toh wohi rang-e mehfil, wohi jabr hai, hartaraf zakhm
khurda hai insaan
Jahan tum mujhe le ke aaye ho yeh wadi-e rang bhi meri manzil
nahi hai
Shahidon ka khoon is hasina ke chehre ka ghaaza nahi hai
Jise tum uthhaye liye ja rahe ho yeh shab ka janaza nahi hai

Was it for this day that I had spent so many sleepless nights?
For this damp water of eternity, this stream of light, this
mountain of miracles?
Was it for this I had sung all those sweet, melodious songs? ...
The blood of martyrs is not the rouge to paint the face of this
beauty
That which you carry on your shoulders is not the corpse of
the night

Not content with this dawn of freedom, Ali Sardar Jafri in 'Subh-e
Farda' [The Morning of Tomorrow] speaks of standing on the
border waiting for a new morning, the morning of tomorrow:

Yeh sarhad khoon ki, ashqon ki, aahon ki, shararon ki
Isi sarhad pe kal dooba thha sooraj ho ke do tukde
Isi sarhad pe kal zakhmi hui thhi subh-e azadi
Jahan boi thhi nafrat aur talwarein ugayin thhi
Yeh sarhad jo lahoo peeti hai aur sholay ugalti hai
Hamari khaak ke seene pe nagin ban ke chalti hai
Saja kar jung ke hathiyar maidan mein nikalti hai

On this border of blood, tears, sighs and sparks
On this border the sun had set yesterday, broken in two
On this border the dawn of freedom was wounded yesterday
Where hatred was sown and swords were grown
This border that drinks blood and spits embers
It slithers on the bosom of our soil like a serpent
It enters the battleground bedecked with the armaments of war

The wounds of Partition were revived after every war with Pakistan. Each time, the poet cautioned against war. Sahir, the most vocal pacifist says in a *nazm* called 'Ai Sharif Insanon' [O Civilised People]:

Jung to khud hi ek masla hai
Jang kyon maslon ka hal degi?
Aag aur khoon aaj bakhshegi
Bhookh aur ehtiyaj kal degi

War itself is the problem
How can it then provide the solution?
Today it will give fire and blood
Tomorrow it will bring hunger and beggary

It is interesting to see how nationalism increasingly became a leitmotif in the years immediately after Partition in Urdu poetry. There was the jingoistic hypernationalism that came in the wake of the Indo-Pak wars (some from the pen of progressive poet-lyricists who oscillated between being pacifists and ardently militant in songs for films such as 'Hindustan Hamara Hai' [India is Ours]) and more nuanced acknowledgements for the need for peace and harmony. From Partition came the wars, and the subsequent need for dialogue and *bhaichara*, maintaining brotherhood and amity. I will rest my case with 'Guftagu' [Conversation] by Ali Sardar:

Let us keep the conversation going
One word leading to another,
The evening meeting lasting till dawn,
The star-filled night laughing down as it moves with us
Even though our words are like stones of abuse on our lips,
Brimming with taunts we raise goblets brimful with poison
Even if we gaze at each other with hurtful eyes, none of this
matters.
Though we are helpless, let us just keep our hearts warm and
beating
Let our words not be stifled by the chains of helplessness
Let our words not be murdered

And here is Sardar Jafri on the communal riots, which, for many
poets, were the most abhorrent yet painful legacy of the Partition:

Ai watan, khake watan, woh bhi tujhe de denge
Bach raha hai jo lahoo ab ke fasaddat ke baad

O nation, dust of my country, I will give you
What blood is left in me after this latest riot

And lastly, there is 'Dushman Kaun?' [Who is the Enemy?], also by
Sardar Jafri:

You were slaves till yesterday, so were we.
And then came the season of freedom bathed in showers of
blood...
Between you and us rage rivers of fire
Tall frowning barriers of hate
With a mere glance, however, we can tear them down;
We can forget, forgive the cruel part;
And again embrace you, yes we can.
But first you will have to break your swords,
And cleanse these bloodied garments;
After that we shall be strangers no more.
You bring us flowers from the gardens of Lahore,
We will bring you light from the dawns of Benares,
Freshness of the Himalayan breeze;
And thereafter we shall ask each other:
Who is the enemy?

The poet, it is said, is a visionary too—he can see what others cannot. Perhaps that is why Ibadat Barelwi was voicing the worse that lay in store after the euphoria of freedom:

> Yes, the bitterness among the people will increase, still more
> Yes, the perpetrators of cruelty will keep struggling against cruelty

Even a traditionalist such as Jigar Moradabadi, seldom one to take up a political position, had not shied away from voicing his disappointment with an independent but truncated India:

> The gardeners still have time to mend their ways
> And still the spring they angered might return

But the 'angered spring' never quite returns, or at least never quite in the same way. Or perhaps no spring ever returns in the same way. Perhaps Partition chroniclers must take heart from a verse written by Mir Taqi Mir nearly 200 years before the actual fact of Partition:

> Is ahad ko na jaane agla sa ahad, Mir
> Woh daur ab nahin, woh zameen aasman nahin

> Do not think this age to be like the age before
> The times have changed, the earth and the sky have changed.

Notes and References

1. For a detailed study of Nazir Akbarabadi, see Ali Jawad Zaidi, *A History of Urdu Literature* (New Delhi: Sahitya Akademi, 1993); M. Sadiq, *A History of Urdu Literature* (New Delhi: Oxford University Press, 1984). And in Urdu, see the detailed introduction by Makhmoor Akbarabadi in his edited volume *Rooh-e Nazir* (Lucknow: Uttar Pradesh Urdu Akademi, 2003).
2. The first recognised shehr ashob is said to have been written by Mir Jafar Zatalli during the Mughal emperor Farrukhsiyar's reign. The early shehr ashob had elements of satire and humour, but with time the lighter elements leached out and what remained was a somewhat romanticised, pathos-laden, poignant poetry about the decline of the city the poet lived in.

3. Hali quoted in Frances Pritchett, *Nets of Awareness: Urdu Poetry and its Critics* (Berkeley and Los Angeles: University of California Press, 1994), 146.

4. For a detailed study of the poetry of the years leading up to 1857, see Rakhshanda Jalil, 'Reflections of 1857 in Contemporary Urdu Poetry', in *Mutiny at the Margins: New Perspectives on the Indian Uprising of 1857*, ed. Crispin Bates (New Delhi: Sage, 2013).

5. Gopichand Narang, '*Tehreek-e Azadi aur Urdu Shairi*' [The Movement for Independence and Urdu Poetry], in *Jang-e Azadi ke Awaalin Mujahideen aur Bahadur Shah Zafar*, ed. Vidya Sagar Anand (New Delhi: Modern Publishing House, 2007).

6. Christopher Shackle and Javed Majeed eds., *Hali's Musaddas: The Ebb and Flow of Islam* (New Delhi: Oxford University Press, 1997), 203.

7. Ralph Russell, *Hidden in the Lute: An Anthology of Two Centuries of Urdu Literature* (New Delhi: Viking, 1995), 201.

8. Shamsur Rahman Faruqi, 'The Power Politics of Culture: Akbar Ilahabadi and the Changing Order of Things', Fourteenth Zakir Husain Memorial Lecture, Zakir Husain College, New Delhi (January 2002), 5.

9. For details, see Rakhshanda Jalil, *Liking Progress, Loving Change: History of the Progressive Writers' Movement in Urdu* (New Delhi: Oxford University Press, 2014).

10. Translation by Carlo Coppola ed., in *Marxist Influences and South Asian Literature* (East Lansing: Michigan State University, 1974), 43.

11 Spaced

Notes Towards An Exhibition

SALIMA HASHMI

One evening, a phone call out of the blue, from Delhi. Lekha Poddar and Feroze Gujral on the line. Suggest an exhibition on Partition, to coincide with the Delhi Art Fair, less than three months away. Utterly impossible, so unthinkingly I say, 'Yes.'

———

I remember things in snatches. I was four and half years old. Srinagar, Eid day, my red taffeta *gharara*. Some shouting and drums. Soon my mother is packing; she keeps repeating, 'It's the last bus.'

———

So, this exhibition is about something that happened so long ago, when I was wearing my red taffeta gharara? I do some quick research; I can only think of Satish Gujral's well-known works on Partition. All the while Amrita Pritam's lines entreating Waris Shah to speak from the grave run through my mind. Nayyara Noor has sung that stanza so exquisitely. It is a plea to the poet to bear witness to the fate of the daughters of Punjab, a million of them, not just one 'Heer,' beloved of Ranjha.

———

I go back in memory. My hand in my mother's, a refugee camp on Egerton Road. A *Bait-ul Maal*—frenzied hands reaching out for blankets. I cling to my mother. Another snapshot. Children peering from windows, searching for a face. Families looking for children, also searching for a face. But this is only the stuff of memory, not an exhibition.

——

That other poem keeps coming back. '*Subh-e-Azadi*' [Dawn of Freedom], also known as 'Fourteenth August 1947' written that same week. It was not well received by all accounts. '*This is not the one—the long awaited dawn.*' It was just not good enough for the glory that was Independence.

——

Dr. Aftab Ahmad, a close associate of the poet, recalled how Faiz recited the poem in Srinagar in the presence of a few close friends. He was aware the poem pleased no one. In Lahore, he barely escaped being lynched by a mob, thanks to a sympathiser who informed him just in time.

——

But how would the poem read now, almost seventy years later, as the manifesto for an exhibition? Would it provide a framework for images and works not specifically addressing the '*batwara?*' Could one revisit memory and trauma through the prism of words—making memory vivid, infusing colour?

——

I began my search. So many constraints. Access to works, the knife-edge of time. Some artists came to mind immediately. Zarina

Hashmi, and loss of home. Nalini Malani's *'Toba Tek Singh.'* But they were too familiar to audiences. No surprises here.

———

I contemplate my objectives: to break new ground, widen the context and probe sensibilities which may surprise the artists themselves. The poem slowly fills out with images provided by the artists, and the Devi Art Foundation collection.

———

An image, seen months ago in Karachi in another show, returns to me with ferocity. Roohi Ahmed's hands, pierced with needle and thread rest firmly in the context of Faiz's poem. As does Anita Dube's *'Blood Wedding,'* which suggests its own companion-in-space, Imran Ahmed's *'Implode.'*

———

Amar Kanwar found his father's house in Beadon Road, Lahore. Partition is palpable, the wound still fresh. Amar must be in the show, but he is busy. I bring Faiz into the equation to plead with Amar. Faiz recites, *'Yeh dagh dagh ujala,'* and Amar listens.

———

'And the heart still aches and the eye still seeks and will not be still.'
For Risham Syed it was her grandmother's kurta, a bridal outfit, in the latest fashion in the Summer of '47. Pink and gold, fragile now, it claimed its place in her installation, *'vaila kee vaila,'* a signifier of the many heart aches and dreams put on hold.

———

A different pain. It was strange to invite Shilpa Gupta's installation into the space. It spoke of a different time and a later anguish, felt over and over again in these seven decades. The poem resonated once more: *'there was as yet no final rest for the anguished heart.'*

Gargi Raina had been to Lahore years earlier and went looking for family roots. She shared encounters and incidents with us, which eventually altered and informed her practice in unexpected ways. The haunting video in the show was as compelling as Sheba Chachi's remake of an earlier idea of cleavage and conjoinment.

I was determined the show should not only echo the poet's journey of sadness and loss, but also move gently through bereavement and grief, into what was literally a higher, lighter space. The uplifting of the spirit, as one moved upward in the building, needed to be achieved through nuanced work.

'... And the dark weight of night is not lifted yet
... And the heart and the eye have not found their rest
... Let us press on for the culmination is not yet'

So Faiza Butt's starry heavens perched on the stairway seemed an appropriate work to inspire hope, as did Imran Qureshi's floating, soaring gold leaves moving into space, lighting up the way, even when surrounded by darkness.

There was to be no curatorial essay. The effort of mounting *'This Night-Bitten Dawn'* had been draining. Viewers spoke of an emotional response to the show. For myself, it was deeper, cathartic, transformative.

11.1: From the series *Thin Cities*, 2013.
Plaster of Paris, hydrocal and paper residue
Approx. 13″ × 6″ × 4″

Courtesy: The artist, Unum Babar.

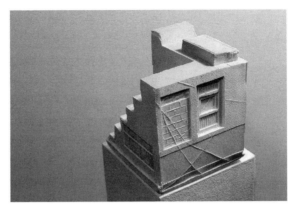

11.2: From the series *Thin Cities*, 2013.
Plaster of Paris, hydrocal and paper residue
Approx. 5″ × 5″ × 5″

Courtesy: The artist, Unum Babar.

11.3: From the series *Thin Cities*, 2013. Installation view at *The Night-Bitten Dawn*
2016. Variable dimensions

Courtesy: The artist, Unum Babar.

11.4: Installation view of *Thin Cities* at *The Night-Bitten Dawn*, 2016. Plaster of Paris, hydrocal and paper residue. Variable dimensions

Courtesy: The artist, Unum Babar.

11.5: *Letters from Home*, 2004.
Handmade Kozo paper mounted on Somerset paper
22″ × 15″

Courtesy: The artist, Zarina Hashmi.

11.6: Faiz Ahmad Faiz's letter to his wife Alys Faiz.

Courtesy: Salima Hashmi.

MEMOIRS

Maya Mirchandani
Fikr Taunsvi
Saibal Kumar Gupta
Manas Ray
Vishwajyoti Ghosh

12.1: Savitri and Sunderdas Mirchandani (Dadima and Dada) on their wedding
day, 20 December 1941.

Courtesy: Maya Mirchandani.

Overleaf photograph: Moyna Mazumdar

12 Inheriting the Hamam-Dasta and Its Stories

MAYA MIRCHANDANI

Sometimes, on Sundays especially, I like to cook. I pull out my old notebook of family recipes and take down a beaten brass mortar and pestle to pound the spices I need. Over the years and several conversations, I have written down recipes for signature Sindhi cuisine, with my grandmother's spectacularly revealing notes about how she conned us into eating stuff we didn't necessarily like as children—Sindhi *kadhi* (no yoghurt, and lots of kokum and lots of vegetables), *sai bhaji* (put in all the vegetables no one likes to eat, they will never know) or *sehal gosht* (the easiest mutton curry recipe ever—just toss everything in together and let it cook).

In my home, I don't think we have ever used the term mortar and pestle. We call it a *hamam-dasta*. And if it were a living thing, it would be the second oldest member of my family. Second only to my grandmother, Savitri, who arrived by ship to Bombay from Karachi in late October 1947 with two toddlers—my father who was two, and my aunt who turned one that month—one small suitcase of clothes and this hamam-dasta, packed for her without her knowledge by the lady who helped look after the children. So that even as a refugee fleeing the violence of Partition spreading to Sindh, she would be able to set up a kitchen no matter where she landed.

Dadima, as I call her, turned ninety-four in September 2016. She insists on living independently in her one-bedroom house in

New York in spite of entreaties by her children to move in with them. On Tuesdays she plays cards with a Sindhi friend she made there, about twenty years younger than her. Someone with whom she can speak in the language of her childhood, and what is still the language of her thoughts. If anyone drops in to see her, they will find her singularly engrossed in the rummy game. But her brood of children, grandchildren and great-grandchildren, who get their stubborn streak from her and insist on disrupting her game by walking through the front door unannounced, never tire of her stories.

Savitri Mirchandani (née Gidwani) was born in September 1922 in Hyderabad, Sindh, to a family of zamindars—the sixth of ten children. She moved to Karachi at the age of nineteen, as a young bride in December 1941. And there she lived with her husband, a police officer, his family and two very young children. Until one day six years later, around the end of October of 1947, when she was rushed out of the house overnight. She cannot remember the exact date, but does say that my aunt had her first birthday in Bombay— on the 19th of November.

Sindh, especially upper Sindh, and also the cities of Hyderabad and Karachi had stayed calm for some time after the bloody Partition of August 1947. Sindhi Hindus—for whom language and culture came first, and religion second—had no intention of leaving their homes and lands. After all, unlike Punjab or Bengal, Sindh was not divided, but went wholly to Pakistan, and while they were concerned about their new status as a minority community in a new Pakistan, the question of leaving hung in the air without a clear answer. But as a new Pakistan went about the business of nation-building, on the streets and in mixed neighbourhoods, anger simmered. It was only a matter of time before violence flared. As mobs began to loot Hindu homes, and her husband Sunder, was on duty round the clock, helping to maintain law and order, her safety and that of her two young children became paramount.

After having retired as one of the few Indian officials working for the British-run Karachi Port Trust, her father-in-law, Rewachand Mirchandani had become a card-carrying member of

Raja Ram Mohan Roy's Brahmo Samaj, working for social reform in the city. To him, Savitri was a daughter and given the same status and liberties as Mohini and Rukmini, her sisters-in law. He was liberal but strict—qualities Dada also inherited. But that day, there was no discussion; only an order. After assessing the danger, he came home with a ticket for a berth on a ship that was sailing a few hours later to Bombay, where Savitri's sister Sita lived.

I often tell Dadima that I consider all Sindhis Sufi. According to what I have learned from her over the years, in many families, the first son became a Sardar and many Amil Sindhis are Nanak Panthis, or followers of Guru Nanak, and follow many Sikh traditions, especially during weddings and funerals. My Dadima still recites from the *Granth Sahib* every day. My grandfather, on the other hand, pursued his father's Brahmo Samaj ideals and while he was superstitious about the stars and planets (he famously threw my grandmother's sapphire ring into the Indian Ocean when they lived in Colombo), he didn't believe in any religious ritual. In that regard, perhaps we are unlike many families, but in my mixed-up home (my mother is Telugu), Dadima ensured that my brother and I learned our prayers from the *Granth Sahib*, and even today we recite them anywhere and everywhere we feel like or in places of worship, irrespective of faith—at Gurudwaras of course, but also at dargahs and churches or at the most traditional Hindu temples.

Dadima recounts from memory the terror she felt that night. Like most days and nights at the time, my grandfather was at work. The Governor of Sindh had cancelled all leaves and rejected all resignations from police officers, irrespective of their religion. After a posting in Larkana, where he made local headlines for having killed a 'dacoit' in an encounter, my grandfather was finally back in Karachi. The city was burning and the Governor needed his men. Hindu neighbourhoods and their women were suddenly no longer safe, and her frantic arguments against leaving home, her pleas to stay, to contact my grandfather, all fell on deaf ears. Rewachand told her not to worry, Sunder would be told, but she simply could not stay.

Today Dadima loves to tell everyone that she travelled from Karachi to Bombay in the same ship and in the same cabin that Fatima Jinnah had made the reverse journey in. No one understands why she so has clung to this story. Perhaps because it allows her a chance to make sense of her hurried departure from Karachi— after all, others who had made Bombay their home were doing the same, in reverse. Sindh was part of the Bombay Presidency and the two were considered sister cities—bustling, cosmopolitan and wealthy. Telling us about the ship and of strangers tied together by a shared experience must make it easier for her to talk about it. I don't know about Ms. Jinnah—who left behind a thriving dental practice in Bombay—but I do know about Dadima. The thought of having left for good was somehow inconceivable to her. Maybe my grandmother's domestic help who packed her hamam-dasta without telling her knew better.

It wasn't until after some months later, during which there was absolutely no communication, when my grandfather was finally able to resign from his job and make the journey to India; Dadima says it was a little after Mahatma Gandhi was assassinated in January 1948. But there was an uncomfortable condition to his resignation, a final assignment. He had to escort a train-load of Hindus fleeing from Sindh—alive, wounded or dead—across the newly created border. His resignation letter was submitted and accepted only once the assignment was complete, at Khokrapar, on the border inside Rajasthan.

Dada—Sunderdas Rewachand Mirchandani—a lawyer by training and a policeman by profession, was a man of letters. Fluent in Farsi, nothing was more valuable to him than his books. He had some time to prepare before he left for Bombay and so he carried a few things he felt were important—a book of historical essays he had received as a prize in college, a wedding photograph and the front page of *The Sind Observer* with the lead story of Germany's unconditional surrender in World War II. And for Dadima he brought some jewelry and her wedding sari. A royal purple organza with bunches of grapes all over, woven in pure silver zari. So delicate that it is now frayed and split into pieces, one of which I still wear on rare occasions as a dupatta, to much admiration. Many Sindhis who arrived in similar ways to Bombay stayed on. The sea air, proximity to Karachi and the ability to speak in their own language with others from the community who arrived under the same circumstances made them feel close to the home they had left behind. In fact, Mumbai today has one of the largest Sindhi communities in the country and many of them have contributed significantly to the city's cultural and financial character. Their entrepreneurial spirit is legendary—often admired and reviled in the same breath. In fact, my grandfather's sister Mohini and her husband Gopal Sipahimalani (Sippy, for short) a practising lawyer in Karachi, who reinvented himself in Bombay as one of the most prominent film producers of his time, tried very hard to convince my grandfather to join them. But my Amil grandfather, who had no head for business and perhaps no stomach for painful nostalgia that gripped so many members of his family at that time, wanted to leave the lament of exile he heard all round.

For those who are unfamiliar with the class-based segregations in Sindhi Hindu society, the Amils (from the word Ámal in Farsi, meaning to administer) were well educated and mainly worked as accountants and lawyers. Some even held government positions— of the very few government positions that Indians were allowed during the Raj. Many Bhaibands—the other major Sindhi community of traders and businessmen—stayed back to protect their businesses as long as they could. But with relatively little in terms of trade and business interests to hold them back during the violence, most of the Amils fled, like so many others, across the Sindh province to India.

Days after he found Dadima in Bombay (not wanting to be a burden on anyone she had moved out of her sister's place by then), the reunited family left bag and baggage for Delhi and lived as refugees, crammed into a single room with another of my grandmother's sisters, Kalavati (Kala) and her family comprising a husband, Rochi and two children. In the Shershah Mess refugee camp, where the Delhi High Court now stands, Rochi uncle and my grandfather searched for work, joining the line every day to meet the government recruiters who came there. Ours is a family of civil servants and so, Sunderdas Rewachand Mirchandani decided he was going to do what he knew best—serve the new India in whatever capacity he could. Several weeks and many queues later, he was re-employed as a police officer, this time with the Gujarat cadre. Together, my grandparents and their three children (my father's youngest brother was born twelve years after Partition) travelled all over Gujarat, and then overseas, as my grandfather went up the ranks of the Indian Police Service.

In the winter of 2004, fifty-four years after she was forced to flee her home and her culture and thirty years after my grandfather died, I decided to make the journey back to Sindh with Dadima. I had heard several stories of Partition survivors breaking down and bending to kiss the earth upon arrival in their villages in modern-day Pakistan, so as a caveat, I must state that my grandmother is not a sentimental woman. In my lifetime, even though the stories are told and retold, sometimes with embellishment depending on the audience, I have never seen her express either extreme joy or extreme sadness. And so, armed with a walking stick, she wandered about Karachi as a curious tourist more than anything else. We drove around the city's formerly Hindu areas in circles—what were empty *maidans* once were now built-up colonies, old bungalows had given way to swanky new buildings, all but obscuring the streets and landmarks of the Karachi that she once knew.

But Hyderabad, the small dusty town of her birth two short hours north of Karachi, was different. The city had grown, but its core felt familiar to her. In the small narrow streets of Hirabad, the formerly Hindu neighbourhood where my grandmother spent so many of her early years, the old *havelis* still stood (at least twelve years ago, they did). Engraved in stone at the entrance were names of the families who had once lived there and the dates they were constructed—testaments to the affluence of the original inhabitants. It is hard to say what happened to the individual residents of each home, but in all likelihood their stories must be similar to that of my grandmother's. The journeys and histories of so many like my grandmother's family who left Sindh and suddenly found themselves landless, homeless and most importantly, stateless, is largely undocumented. While many of the Hindu families from upper Sindh moved south into the cities after these homes were vacated, the vacuum created by the sizeable community's departure was largely filled by Muslim refugees from India—the muhajirs, as they are called in Pakistan today. While the Muslims from Punjab settled mostly in and around Lahore, those who left Uttar Pradesh, Bihar, Bengal, Madhya Pradesh, settled in Sindh.

So it was a more than special surprise when, while searching for my grandmother's childhood home in Hyderabad, we were directed to an original resident in one of these havelis. For two complete strangers—my eighty-two-year old grandmother and eighty-eight-year old Dadi Leela at the time—their connection was almost immediate. In 2004, when they met, Leelawati Harchandani, better known to everyone as Dadi Leela (Dadi means older sister in Sindhi), was the oldest living Amil Sindhi in Hyderabad. Her memory was sharp, and her wit still dry. She told us the entire neighbourhood emptied out at the time of Partition, including members of her own family, but she couldn't bring herself to leave. When I asked her why, she replied: 'When I was a little girl, my headmaster told me I had three mothers. I remember getting very offended, as though he was saying things against my father. Then he explained to me who the three were. He said the first was my mother who gave me birth. The second was my mother tongue. And the third, my motherland. I never forgot that.'

My conversation with her was in Urdu; I understand Sindhi but unfortunately, cannot speak it. My grandmother and Dadi Leela, however, spoke in the language of their mothers, their childhood, and their hearts. And as I listened, half understanding their conversation—fast and furious with excitement and nostalgia—I couldn't help but reflect on the idea of home and the nature of identity. I watched as Dadima, elegant and cosmopolitan—she who called Delhi and New York home—transformed into Savitri, the young girl from Hyderabad, Sindh.

Dadi Leela was a singer. My grandmother has always urged me to learn Sindhi *kalams*—odes to the Lord written by Sindhi saints like Shah Abdul Latif Bhitai and Shahbaz Qalander, whose shrines in Bhit Shah and Sehwan are visited every day by thousands of people. As my grandmother sat down with her on the charpoy in the sunny courtyard where she spent winter afternoons, Dadi Leela pulled out her harmonium for us, and together she and my grandmother sang these kalams of their youth, and mine—I have heard these songs sung at Sindhi gatherings in Delhi and Bombay all my life. And at the end of our visit, she told us she used to know my grandmother's aunt, and directed us to the house she had lived in, almost next door. A family from Aligarh opened the door and their home to us and asked us to stay as long as we liked. Karachi, Pakistan's bustling commercial hub, may have been completely unfamiliar, but this short afternoon in Hyderabad, my grandmother's city made our entire trip worthwhile—as though we had found home.

Today, after over a decade since we went, the stories of that trip, rounded off with a visit to Panja Sahib Gurudwara in Hasan Abdal, have been added to Dadima's kitty of tales that make up our family history. Her travels in Sindh, like her memories of 1947, are told and retold to family and friends. At home in New York, where her self-taught English has become her first language, the only one who can speak in Sindhi with Dadima is her Tuesday afternoon Rummy companion, and the occasional extended family member who visits.

It wasn't always like this. When she first moved there in 1985, there were many like her—Sindhis of her generation who had lived all over the world and finally decided to create a home where their children had come to live and work. When they met, conversations were a happy, even if sentimental mix of nostalgia and entrepreneurship, of what home has come to mean for so many of them—where statelessness and exile were superimposed with discussions of new horizons and challenges. While Delhi and Mumbai particularly, followed by cities like Ajmer and Ahmedabad have sizeable Sindhi communities, the community has spread itself all over the world. From Japan to the Caribbean, from South America to Europe, and every place in between, Sindhis are running businesses, own real estate, and adopting new cultures and nations along the way. That is what happens when an entire 'nation,' in the ideological sense of the word, becomes stateless.

Dadima, like her few surviving friends, has learned to adapt to new cultures and identities, even within our family. While for some of them the adapting has been about new cities and cosmopolitanism, at home my Telugu mother has introduced the Mirchandani clan to a new cultural sensibility and cuisine; my brother is married to an American of Irish and Danish heritage. In that, I suppose we are not an oddity. Generation after generation, like with so many other cultures and communities, the 'Sindhi-ness,' as it were, is getting diluted. Today, even though she tells us not to disturb her concentration when we walk through the door, Dadima speaks our language and listens to our music.

I like to think, though, that the core of who we are as a culture, as a people, has not changed much. My grandmother's resilience, her perseverance in the face of adversity are to me singularly the most impressive and abiding traits of an entire community. She has held on to them for dear life and passed them on to her children, grandchildren, and great-grandchildren, despite our mixed identities and the many places we call home. We all still look forward to our Sunday lunch. In New York, her recipes—including her famous 'methi' fish curry—have found their way into the menu of my brother's Manhattan bistros. And in my kitchen in Delhi, I pound my spices fresh in that precious hamam-dasta, checking my recipe book as I cook lunch for my retinue of friends who walk through the door in much the same way as we walk into my grandmother's house—demanding our favourite food. As the sai bhaji simmers in its pot, the scents of my kitchen remind me of Dadima and the flavour of home she carries with her, and that will stay with me wherever I am.

13 The Sixth River

A Journal from the Time of the Partition of India*

FIKR TAUNSVI

Note by Fikr Taunsvi on 'The Sixth River'[1]

'T'he Sixth River' is the tale of that barbaric time when human civilisation was headed towards its acme with the help of science, philosophy, knowledge and literature; when nuclear man was breaking innumerable norms of tradition; and when two opposing religious traditions were colliding in India, leading to the bloodshed of millions of people.

Foreign rule had split the lively and verdant Punjab into two religious parts. Ten million people—having left their homes, fields, orchards, ploughshares, loves and hates—were dragging their feet, wandering, fighting, burnt, cut up, many only to bite the dust. Two-year-old innocent children were picked up on the points of spears and flung into the air so that these sons of snakes may not grow up to bite the other faith. Modest young girls were paraded naked by those sons of their mothers with the help of swords and lances so that these daughters of the Vedas, the Qur'an, and the Granth may nevermore give birth to man from their sacred wombs.

---

* Originally published in Urdu as 'Chhata Dariya: Taqseem-i-Hind ke Mauqe par Fasaadat se Mut'aliq Roznamcha' (1948), in *Fikr Taunsvi: Hayat aur Karname*, ed. Shama Afroz Zaidi (New Delhi: Biswi Sadi Publications, 1988), 232–270.

Therefore, man had reached that pinnacle of culture where he stood with his vain head held high at his own barbarity and bestiality. It is then that I wrote this story of blood and fire. The story revolves around those three months when—with the Partition of India, associated communal riots and the transfer of population—the greatest mistakes in history were committed one by one. I spent those three months in Lahore, that Lahore which was the centre of high culture and civilisation which, with a single imperial blow, had been turned into a river of blood and fire. This river had soon spread to all corners of the beautiful and prosperous Punjab. And then some religious brutes rode its waves to play such a game of terror that history was horrified, philosophy was choked, and the heart of science stopped beating.

In this diary you will also find characters that emerge at appropriate moments in keeping with their unique qualities. They retain a representative place in the historical tragedy. Here feature the conservatives, religious believers, non-partisan participants, progressives, gossip-mongers, beasts, innocents, masked men, and the main players of the time. If we look at them beyond their apparent personalities and locate them in their various social classes, then some confusion may be cleared and true meaning may be revealed.

June 1948

Mobbed by Darkness

11 August 1947[2]

After the sickening and soul-wearying curfew of twenty-four hours, I finally stepped out of my house today morning. All around, some languid, dull activity had begun. Layers of terror and fear had accumulated over the roads. People were stepping gingerly over these layers. Doubt and fear—fear and doubt! It felt as if everyone on the road was carrying a bomb or a knife and would bury it in the back of the enemy in the blink of an eye. All men kept turning around. Not men but enemies walked that road. Hundreds of scared and hesitant enemies had stepped out of their homes. There were no friends among them. Ambling around, I eventually started walking up the street leading to my office.

It stretched through a Muslim majority area, where there had been a bomb blast three days ago. Going through these parts was a habit for me. This habit was a part of my mental makeup. What else could I have done? Mental peril lay in going through the safer parts. By the time I reached my office, smoke and flames surrounded me. A grand building right next to the office was up in crackling flames. A large crowd was present. It was a curious mass—with Hindus and Muslims. Both were trying to douse the fire together. The fire had united two cultures, two religions. I welcome such a fire, I salute it. I am ready to sacrifice millions of philosophic, learned and literary opinions and views on such a fire that allowed Muslims and Hindus a common torment on 11 August.

The first floor of the building read Bishan Das Building. The ground floor of the building housed a book-binder's shop where scores of workers bound copies of the Qur'an daily. Both were burning—the Hindu building and the Muslim Qur'an. Some people were trying to recover the body of a seven or eight-year old boy buried under a girder on the first floor. Bishan Das' son was burning above as Muhammad's Qur'an burnt below. God's constitution was burning and Hindus and Muslims were dousing the fire together. A single sheath was taking in two swords.

I took great pleasure in the sight. Nowhere else in history had I found a reflection of such good taste. We were giving birth to a new history. I walked further. ...

14 August 1947[3]

Death, terrible death—in the lanes of Lahore, on the streets, in the bazars, at the corners, on windows, in Hindus, in Muslims, in Sikhs—stalks everywhere. But perhaps death's satanic eyes did not fall upon this skinny little poet. Or maybe he walks into the face of death, towards its eyes with such lack of care that death starts to blink its eyes. You? You? Who are you? Who are you? Do not come towards me like that. Those about to die do not come this way. Don't you know the ways to enter the company of death? Go away, go away. Get out of my sight. You fool, go! Saunter in the streets, ramble through the lanes. I cannot understand you. What is your name, what is your creed? People of your faith are not worthy of becoming victims of the bloody reign of this bestiality, barbarity and monstrosity. Go, whom do you seek here? Do you wish to meet Mumtaz.[4] Do you believe him? This Muslim? Has his Islamic honour and sense of community died that he won't stab you even once with his knife? A knife can kill twenty–twenty-five, thirty–forty people. A knife can show two hundred and forty million gods the way to redemption and peace. A knife can kill the awakened Islam of seventy million people. A knife can...You are a strange man.

Yes—seeing a strange man like me with his face turned up to the sky made Mumtaz tremble all over. Like the sharp edge of a sword, lines of sweat were making deep cuts on his forehead as they crawled along.

'Oh, it's you!'

'Yes, it's me,' I said nervously.

'Where are you going? Don't go! On the way, on the way is that terrible area where there was firing the whole night. Don't you go in the dark...'

15 August 1947

All of last night, the radio kept shouting: freedom, freedom, freedom! Today we are free of foreign rule. Mumtaz is happy that our politics has finally gotten off the fence and chosen a side. Early in the morning, I entered his room with an anguished look on my face: 'Do you know, Mumtaz, that we have been free from 12:01 last night, but firing still went on all night? Allah-ho Akbar, Har Har Mahadev, and Sat Sri Akal[5] are still in prison, and they have protested all night by shouting, echoing and jumping around, as if to say that we do not wish to be free, we wish to remain alive. We will die if we are freed.'

I do not know what had happened to me in that moment. It felt as if I had been diving into a pool of poison the whole night. Sarcasm, barbarity and hatred were erupting out of each of my body parts like sparks. And I was humming:

What place is this? Where have you stopped?

19 August 1947[6]

Radcliffe announced his award. Bengal's culture, art, dance and music were divided. Punjab's plough, farming, songs and romance were split. One aspect of this division was really curious, with which both Muslims and Hindus were dissatisfied. But what is the use of their dissatisfaction? This was an act of fate. And fate lay in the hands of Radcliffe. A few serious-minded people were calling this emotional dissatisfaction meaningless. Because the leaders had agreed to abide by the verdict even before it was ever taken. Mumtaz bought a map from the market. The map of Punjab. And while listening to the verdict on the radio he drew a line on the map. He was drawing a snake. A thousands-of-miles-long snake. And the snake had thrown his birthplace Batala into India. His face was livid. I could see millions of glowering faces in his flushed face. Faces that were protesting, shouting:

'Why was our birthplace not included in Pakistan?'
'Our birthplace should have been included in India!'

Millions of faces were livid, smarting, and disappointed. But the snake had been sent by Brahma. And Brahma was interested in neither Mumtaz nor Batala. He was only interested in obeying the will of God.

The artist's [Mumtaz's] veins had become taut. He was fidgety. Looking at his face, one perceived the touch of fear. And I was trying to think of the means to allay that fear. I wanted to pick him up from this small world and throw him into a cosmopolitan world. 'Here, here, Mumtaz; come out of the shell of your Batala. This is a common grief, not yours alone. You are an individualistic artist. But who cares about individuality anymore? The world is rapidly getting divided into two camps. The globe has come to a crossways in its perambulations. And the astrologers are keenly observing its path. They are trying to predict its revolutions. The division of Pakistan and India and their new existence are only one part of these revolutions. Who are you? What is your Islam? What is my Hinduism? Nothing. We are but pawns, my dear! The player keeps us where he wants. Nankana is kept in Pakistan, Batala in India. Both pawns are shouting: "We will overturn this game! We will not allow this game to continue. This is tyranny, this is injustice." But, Mumtaz, the game goes on. It will reach its conclusion. Look, look, do you see that spark?—that flame which grants the same light to Arabia and Himalaya, to China and Egypt, to Batala and Nankana; the same passion, the same pain! And look, look into that light, in the tangled darkness, in the growing dark, how we are being looted again.'

All of Punjab is burning. The flame has reached Achha's brow in Batala.[7] In Taunsa, my wife's sari is catching fire from the crackling blaze. I have reached my village. My daughter reaches the house of Ali Muhammed Butt as she plays. And Ali Muhammed has picked her up and thrown her on the ground with force. Her soft, delicate bones are broken into bits. Ali Muhammed is my childhood friend and companion. We used to play *gilli-danda*[8] together in the colony. He is a big landlord in the settlement now and writes letters full of affection to me. He has brought the body of my dead daughter to my house.

'Forgive me, my friend. I did not break this branch. A harsh and rapid gust of wind came, and she broke with a snap to fall into my yard.' His eyes are wet with tears. There is uproar in the village. Clack, clack, clack. Possibly, the Masudi clan had attacked the village once again. And Hindus and Muslims are combating them together. Maybe the Hindu-Sikh military has started gunning down the

Muslims, and the Muslims have started firing at the Hindus. My daughter lies dead on the ground. And Ali Muhammed is handing his six-year-old son to me: 'Fling him, brother Fikr, dash him hard on the ground, such that my sins may be forgiven! My heart may come to rest and I stand punished. Dash him, dash him, my friend!' I hugged the little, rose-like Rashid to my heart. 'Go away, go away, Ali Muhammed, you have gone mad. Why don't you get yourself treated? Go, go, I will not give Rashid to you. Rashid, my son!'

25 August 1947[9]

For the past four or five days, I feel as if I have been hung in mid air, like someone spending their life in a dream world. So many jolting, sombre and severe realities are presenting themselves from all sides. But I do not wake up from my sleep. Mumtaz has not met me for four days. I am straying in the dark. Mumtaz is straying in the dark. All creation is crashing around like whirlwinds in the overwhelming darkness of the abyss.

I try my best to focus myself on a single viewpoint, but everything is slipping through my fingers. I cannot grasp anything. If I had airplanes then I would drop bombs like rain on these goons who kill innocent people on trains. The bloodied trains then reach Lahore Station, and the platforms get covered with mounds of corpses. And then groups of Muslim mujahideen attack Hindu-Sikh trains passing through Pakistan to cover the platforms of Amritsar, Jalandhar, and Ludhiana in human blood, so that the people of India do not think of them as shameless cowards. What madness is this? Oh, why don't I wake up from my sleep? Why doesn't Mumtaz wake up? Why don't Jinnah and Jawahar bat an eyelid?

I went to Qateel's today in the evening.[10] There wasn't a line of worry on this romantic poet's forehead. His curly hair had a new sheen and glow. His face shone in waves of splendour. He told me that he had married his Hindu actress friend. The Maulvi sahib from the local mosque had married them for five rupees and had said that if any scoundrel still considered her a Hindu—despite her having recited the *kalimah*—and wanted to kill her, then Qateel should inform him and he will set them right. I said: 'Qateel, forget what the Maulvi sahib said; you have saved a life with five rupees. For me, the experience of this happiness is enough. And yes, tell me, what is the source of this splendid glow on your face?' 'The consummation of romance,' said Qateel, blowing smoke rings into the sky. He now needed a new house because the neighbours had told him he could not live there with a Hindu girl, or the goons will set it ablaze.

What Place is This?

8 September 1947[11]

There was a king in the bygone era called Muhammad Tughlaq whose job was to move his subjects from one city to another and to rule them. Today, my mind is on the India of four hundred years ago. Muhammad Tughlaq is travelling with his subjects, and thousands are dying every day with hunger, disease, and fatigue. Their lips are dry, no sign of water anywhere. But the king called Muhammad Tughlaq is fulfilling his ambition. He is the king, deputy of God.

And after four hundred years when the populace has still not been able to rid itself of the yoke of kingship, it is dying yet again with hunger, travel, and fatigue. On both sides, the kings are carrying their subjects around. The transfer of nine million people has been accepted. Nine million people are living in camps, leaving their ploughs and farms, their bullocks and their homes. I wonder if doing this was necessary. Many statesmen think that doing this was not only necessary but also natural. Why should anyone live as a slave in another's country? I am a fool. Arif's father is a fool, who considers Amritsar his native land and is not ready to step out of his house.[12]

What will happen now? Where are we going? What kind of rulers are these? What sort of subjects are these? What is this freedom? I am surrounded by innumerable questions yet again. A frightful storm of devastation and destruction rises from the border at Wagah. Hatred has assumed the shape of truth. And people are crossing this line from here to there and from there to here by dying, running, getting their legs chopped off, having their heads smashed, losing their children, getting their honour violated, shouting and screaming. On one side of the line, the tricolour flies, and a crowd shouts the slogan: 'Hindustan zindabad!' On the other side, the crescent flag flies, and the people gleefully shout out: 'Pakistan zindabad!' Man has created a curious game of life and death for man. A tamasha is being played out. There is death on one side of the line and life on the other—this side is death and that side is life. Is this line the standard of life and the touchstone of death?

15 September 1947[13]

Today when Qateel and Rahi returned empty-handed from Taunsa,[14] instead of despondency a new hope was born in my heart.[15] My in-laws were amazed as Qateel and Rahi were two Muslims, and how could Rani and Kailash[16] be expected to be sent with them! Qateel told me that Khwaja was also amazed that who is this person who cannot distinguish between Hindus and Muslims. What sort of a mind is this that believes that two Muslims would bring his Hindu wife safely back to him in these communal times?

I wonder about our times of social contradictions and absurdity. Crossing the treacherous distance of hundreds of miles, Qateel and Rahi reached Taunsa but returned empty-handed. I was feeling very embarrassed in front of them. But Qateel told me that there in Taunsa there is another foolish and embarrassed person such as you whose name is Khwaja Nizamuddin. He has taken on the responsibility of the life and property of all the Hindus of the district upon himself. He has declared that even if a single Hindu were murdered in his region, he will put a terrible curse upon the

Muslims. Khwaja is a great saint of our region.[17] Religion has thrown all of Punjab into the hell fires of Nimrod. And religion has also taken thousands of Hindus under its benevolent shade. I have picked up the dictionary to find the true meaning of religion.

Qateel tells me there was a ticket collector checking the roof of the train they were on, although not for tickets but for infidels. That man would be thrown off the moving train who hid infidelity in his dhoti or pajamas. Scores of guffaws would follow, and the ticket collector would resume his checking in all sincerity. I wonder why Khwaja Nizamuddin was not a ticket collector. Why has he kept those Hindus close to his bosom? Why is he disrespecting religious law? Does he not know the meaning of religion? Does he think that the Hindus and Muslims who have lived together for centuries have lost their religious souls? And are they each other's companions in times of grief and pain and can't be separated from each other? Can they not be thrown off the tops of trains? How foolish is this Khwaja? ... I salute his foolishness!

Come, Let Us Look for the Morning Again

17 October 1947[18]

Lahore has become twice as lively. It is laughing at the corpse of its old self, and with these guffaws it is giving birth to a new life. The historical gap that lay between the Hindu and Sikh emigration and the immigration of Muslim asylum seekers has been very quickly traversed. The noisy atmosphere of anarchy, fear, arson and stabbings seems to be dying. Lahore is now at peace. But the face of this peace matches neither autumn nor spring. There's remorse everywhere, and also the desire for creating a new life. But this creation is taking place in an extremely uncouth manner. People cross the Wagah border in the near-death stages of starvation. They wish to heave a sigh of relief in the heaven of Lahore. But Lahore's garden of heaven lies devastated. The leaves are scattered, the flowers have wilted. Thus, the refugees find no shelter. No respite is to be found. The waves of song rise in the heart only to die. With the ominous emotions of petulance, despair, and death, the refugees have started ceaselessly roaming the streets of Lahore. Large, lonely and helpless groups dressed in old rags sit staring at the skies from under the trees on the footpaths. These people are conquerors, and have won the battle of faith against infidelity. They have entered Lahore to celebrate their victory. They have come running from Ambala, Rohtak, Jalandhar, Kapurthala, Panipat, Delhi, and Saharanpur and celebrate the day of independence here. They have defeated the composite culture of Punjab with such aplomb in the battlefield that posterity will remember it.

24 October 1947[19]

The pressure on Kashmir is increasing. Conditions worsen day by day. A new chapter of hatred opens. This hatred has been started immediately after the first so that the continuum of hatred does not break. The blood of thousands of innocent Kashmiris is being spilt. Only because the British emperor had handed the fate of the people to the Maharajah when he was leaving and the Maharajah's hand was in the hand of the Indian dominion. Thus, the foundations of the Indian dominion and that of Pakistan were laid on hatred. And this hatred had not heaved a sigh yet when this hatred was tied up to the springs and gardens of Kashmir. Everything was clear. Our programme was fixed. The atmosphere was desperate. Emotional whirlwinds were flying on the streets and lanes of Lahore.

What will happen now?

3 November 1947[20]

My desire to leave Lahore has gotten stronger again. But there is no obstinacy and petulance at the back of this desire now, nor is there any anxiety or escapism. In fact, a shining ray of light has come piercing all these emotions. Every day I see trucks full of Hindu and Sikh refugees as I cross the Mall Road, and I feel as if they are all pulled towards the graveyard in the terrible shade of the night. I do not see a ray of life on anyone's face. These burnt out, sad, and depressed faces carrying a meagre vision of their futures in their hearts are piling into the trucks. I want to stop each one of these trucks and loudly ask these people to take me with them so that I can also watch them dragging their feet in their independent and prosperous country. Such that my eyes can look upon that sight where your little children, wives, mothers, sisters, and women shiver in the bitter cold to give up their lives at the doorstep of the goddess of freedom. I wish you knew that in the country of your religion you would have to deal with sodden and burnt farms, ruined houses, and bloodied and fiery streets. The arms that will open for you will not harbour the cool breezes of heaven, springs of honey, and the gurgling river of love and beauty. Because a few robbers control this embrace. And the robbers do not want you to be acquainted with the beautiful vision of a free life. You will be released like cattle into the dry and arid jungle of the camps. Instead of being able to shout and scream, and heading for a lush grazing field, you will have to cool the hell-fires of your stomach with dry and bitter grass. And you will be burnt in the flames of your own hell.

7 November 1947[21]

A short soldier stopped me: 'Hey, hey, where are you going? Who are you?'

Chowdhury, Arif, Rahi, and Sahir[22] looked at me with a smile. A tearful melody rose inside me: 'Life has come to a fork.'

The Gurkha soldier of D. A. V. camp, who was the protector of Hinduism, Hindu culture, Hindu rule, and Hindu atmosphere, was asking me: 'Who are you? This is a Hindu camp. Are you Hindu? If you are Hindu then what have you been doing in Lahore for so long? You should have come to this camp on 15 August. You should have...'

I bared my forearm to the Gurkha soldier, showing him the blue Om tattoo I have had since my childhood. The Gurkha soldier had got the proof of my Hinduism. He had approved my entry into the camp. And Sahir, Arif, Chowdhury, Jabir, and Rahi were left on the other side of the line of Hinduism and Hindutva. Those five Muslims could not step on my land. For the first time in my life, I felt intense hatred towards Hindu religion. Prior to this, I had never considered such a casual thing as religion worth the hallowed and grand sentiment of my hatred.

8 November 1947[23]

Hindustan zindabad!
Pakistan zindabad!
Jawaharlal Nehru zindabad!
Quaid-e-Azam[24] zindabad!

From the border of Wagah to Amritsar our trucks resounded with such slogans. These slogans turned into a large and continued stampede and bewilderment by the time we reached Khalsa camp. The camp was glittering with the light of lamps. But our hearts still carried a wretched darkness. Freedom's sweet and enthusiastic vision was being shattered. Where will we go now? What will we do now? In this independent nation, who will give us a place to sleep, bread to fill our stomachs, and cloth to cover our bodies? Who is he? Who is that person? Who told us that you are free now and are free to play romantic games with the moon and the stars? That their stellar assembly will gather? That the dawn's gleaming and invigorating splendour will rise up in your souls? That billows of the soft and sweet morning breeze will bring a beautiful and magical future to your life?
Where is that future?
Where is the morning?
Where is freedom?

Translated from the Urdu by **Maaz Bin Bilal.**

Notes and References

1. 'Chhata Dariya,' *Fikr Taunsvi*, 232.
2. Ibid., 237–8.
3. Ibid., 240.

4. Mumtaz Mufti (11 September 1905–27 October 1995) was born in Batala, now in Indian Punjab. He was in Lahore at the time of Partition and stayed on as a Pakistani citizen. He was a short story writer, and was initially inspired by liberal and European ideas such as that of Sigmund Freud before being attracted by Sufism. He published a number of short story collections and two autobiographies.

5. Referring to the three most commonly used slogans during communal riots by Muslims, Hindus and Sikhs, respectively.

6. 'Chhata Dariya,' *Fikr Taunsvi*, 244–5.

7. Achha is Mumtaz's son.

8. A game involving a wooden stub and a stick, a bit like tipcat.

9. 'Chhata Dariya,' *Fikr Taunsvi*, 245–6.

10. Qateel Shifai was the pen name of the Urdu poet Muhammed Aurangzeb (24 December 1919–11 July 2001). He published over twenty collections of verse and wrote over 2,500 film songs for Indian and Pakistani films. He died in Lahore, where he had once started out as an assistant editor of the monthly *Adab-e-Latif* and published his first poems.

11. 'Chhata Dariya,' *Fikr Taunsvi*, 251–2.

12. Arif is a friend of Fikr.

13. 'Chhata Dariya,' *Fikr Taunsvi*, 254.

14. Fikr Taunsvi derived his name from his ancestral home in Taunsa Sharif in the district of Dera Ghazi Khan in Punjab, now in Pakistan. 'Sharif' is added to its name as several Sufi saints are buried in Taunsa.

15. Rahi and Qateel were friends of Fikr Taunsvi.

16. Rani was Fikr Taunsvi's daughter and Kailash his wife.

17. *Pir* does not have an exact approximation in English; saint is used here.

18. 'Chhata Dariya,' *Fikr Taunsvi*, 260.

19. Ibid., 262.

20. Ibid., 264–5.

21. Ibid., 267–8.

22. Names of the friends of Fikr.

23. 'Chhata Dariya,' *Fikr Taunsvi*, 270.

24. Meaning 'Great leader,' this is how M. A. Jinnah came to be known in Pakistan.

14 Dandakaranya
Some Memories in Words*

SAIBAL KUMAR GUPTA

Author's Preface

The development of Dandakaranya was undertaken to solve an almost intractable human problem—the rehabilitation of a large number of refugees who were uprooted from their homeland in East Pakistan, victims of a political decision to divide the country in which they were not consulted. Vast numbers re-established themselves in West Bengal without help. A sizeable fraction did so, fully or partially, with such help as the Ministry of Rehabilitation was prepared to give.

Dandakaranya was expected to provide a home for the residuary refugee population in camps or elsewhere for whom there was supposed to be no more room in West Bengal. Crores of rupees were spent and further expenditures were in the offing, but

---

* Editor's note: Saibal Kumar Gupta wrote three articles on Dandakaranya that were first published in *The Economic Weekly* in three consecutive issues from 2 January to 16 January 1965. He also prepared a *Memorandum* on the Dandakaranya Project after he resigned as Chairman of the Dandakaranya Development Authority—a post he held from November 1963 to September 1964. Extracts from his memoir *Kichhu Smriti, Kichhu Katha* (Calcutta: M. C. Sarkar and Sons, 1994) and his *Memorandum* are compiled here in form of the Author's Preface, followed by an extract from the first of his articles on Dandakaranya. The English text is in the original.

barely seven thousand families were given rehabilitation of a sort in the course of five or six years.

What is the end result of all this expenditure of time and money? What are the prospects? It is time that a proper assessment was made and people saw Dandakaranya without any blinkers.

My ten months at Dandakaranya, of which four were largely preoccupied with the new influx at Mana, were not sufficient to allow me to know the facts as thoroughly as I would have liked to, because under the peculiar administrative arrangement of the Dandakaranya Development Authority [DDA], most matters were dealt with at a lower level and hardly reached the Chairman unless they were regarded as matters of high policy or unless the Chairman specially called for information. There were no annual reports, nor any collected body of statistical information covering all aspects of the project and its working up to date.

Even so, what I saw myself and learnt on further enquiry caused me profound disquiet. I have decided to share my disquiet with the public, not to cast reflections or start a polemic, but so that if things are what I believe [they] are, immediate action may be taken to set things right. Human distress on a large scale is much too serious a matter to be passed over in silence, either to feed official complacency or to save reputations. 'A willing suspension of disbelief' may be, as Coleridge thought, a necessary precondition of imaginative writing or literary appreciation, but for the administrator nothing could be more fatal. He must not pull the wool over his own eyes, nor over those of others.

Rehabilitation in the wider sense embraces all aspects of life. Here the word is used in the narrower sense of economic rehabilitation. The enquiry is confined to the different ways in which such economic rehabilitation had been sought to be effected, and whether they were adequate. Of these ways, agriculture, industries and employment and trade are the most important. The first essay in the series is about the agriculture followed by industries and [about] other relevant fields in the next ones. My comments relate specifically to the period of my Chairmanship (November 1963 to September 1964), not to the years following it.

My views on agricultural schemes and irrigation projects will be found in the first article of the series. I want only to emphasise that while the Expert-Team from the Ministry of Agriculture laid stress on small irrigation schemes by excavation of tanks, which would serve the dual purpose of irrigation and fishery, the DDA did exactly the opposite, going in for grandiose schemes whose benefit [to] refugee-occupied lands was minimal. [...] My latest information, which I have not been able to verify, is that even this small benefit was further whittled down after the administration of the Dam had been handed over on completion to the state government.

When I left Dandakaranya in September 1964, the completion of the scheme in Malkangiri zone was still a long way off, though I read in the papers that the Parliament was assured that it was just round the corner. Similarly, the costly Potteru scheme in the same zone was still in an embryonic stage.

What is important to notice is that with the possible exception of the minor Pakhanjore scheme in Paralkot zone, all these irrigation schemes, like the network of roads presently to be dealt with, rendered vastly greater benefit to the local people than to the refugees, though the refugee-rehabilitation budget footed the bill.

My comments on the industries in [the] Dandakaranya project will be found in the second article of the series. Judging by the two categories into which the Ministry classified the displaced persons, it seems that its imagination did not at first go beyond agriculture and small trade as the two alternative means for their economic rehabilitation. No sound economy can, however, be built upon agriculture alone, even under the best of conditions, and in Dandakaranya conditions were far from ideal. Trade, too, in the narrower sense, was not a sufficient alternative, for it could not play a significant role in a rural economy where thirty to fifty families in a village earned a precarious living from land while the nearest village was sometimes miles apart. Even in urban and semi-urban areas, its scope was limited because of strong competition from old established rivals.

The pattern of non-agricultural rehabilitation, which was limited to providing a loan for building a house with three months' grace within which to make good and be independent of aid, was, therefore, foredoomed to failure. Here and there someone with an instinct for business set up a shop, another opened a barber's salon close to a staff colony, a third started a confectionery or a bakery or an eating house near some urban concentration; but their number was small and the shop rooms built by the project were mostly vacant because of high rent and unsuitability of site. The majority failed in their venture, ate up the business loan and looked about for jobs.

Many non-agriculturists had only their skill as carpenter or weaver to offer and could find employment only if there was an entrepreneur to organise work, provide capital and take charge of marketing. The project authorities were thus gradually forced to start industries on their own with the twin objects of finding supplementary work for agricultural families and self-sufficient means of living for the non-agriculturists.

For the second purpose the tests of efficiency of an industry were whether it could be economically viable when the artificial crop of the Dandakaranya Development Authority was withdrawn, whether it could offer a living wage to the workers, and whether the volume and scope of employment bore a reasonable relation to the capital invested. Unfortunately, no commercial accounts have been kept and the figures supplied by the Industries Department are sometimes slightly discrepant. There are, however, three other sources from which helpful data are available.

A profit and loss account for most of these industries was drawn up from the start of the industries up to the end of March 1963 in a specially devised proforma at the instance and under the supervision of the Deputy Financial Adviser and Chief Accounts Officer of the DDA.

An Economic Investigation Team set up at my request by the Development Commissioner, Small Scale Industries, New Delhi, to explore the possibilities of small scale industries incidentally dealt in its report with the present state of some of the major industries run by the DDA and their working in March 1964.

Lastly, the Rehabilitation Industries Corporation lent me the services of its Chief Cost Accountant, who made a detailed scrutiny of the working of the industries during the three months from April to June 1964 and submitted a report in August which was quite illuminating.

All these materials have been made use of in the second essay on the industries of the Dandakaranya Project.

Apart from industries, the other possible means of earning a living in urban and semi-urban areas are private or co-operative trade, transport, contract work of all sorts, public service, and independent professional or consulting work. Of these, the last may be ruled out at once, for, displaced persons who moved to Dandakaranya lacked the necessary qualifications to set up as lawyers, doctors or consulting engineers.

What scope did the displaced persons have in the rest and what opportunities were created? A few odds and ends on this have been dealt with in the last essay of the series to bring the discussion to a close.

As regards education, my comments in the third article of the series may be seen. What I did not say then but what needs to be said is that in at least one state, the insistence of the government not only to compel the DDA to admit into its higher schools [a] large proportion of local people (non-refugee) but to provide for their teaching in their own mother tongue, and to insist on the local vernacular being compulsory for the refugees [had] a damping effect on refugee education in that place. The employment position has also been dealt with fairly fully in the third article of the series.

I have no present knowledge of what non-official social and cultural organisations are working in Dandakaranya. When I was there, the Bharat Sevasram Sangha and Mother Teresa's organisation did splendid work to relieve distress at the time of the great influx at Mana, only in 1964. Mrs. Asoka Gupta, who was a member of the Central Social Welfare Board, got the State Social Welfare Board interested and many *mohilasamities* sprang up in different areas to do construction work. A scouts and guides movement also sprang up and did good work. There might have been a few other organisations working to similar ends which I do not remember, nor do I know whether they still survive. I have no information about false propaganda by interested people. I consider it extremely unlikely that under satisfactory economic conditions refugees would run after a will-o-the-wisp merely because somebody raises a slogan, 'Bangla-Chalo.' Desertion due to economic plight is not a new feature in Dandakaranya. It has been going on every year, almost every quarter of the year, sometimes in a trickle and sometimes in a flood. The notes submitted by the Chief Administrator to the successive quarterly meetings of the DDA will confirm this.

Whether there has been discrimination against the refugees is a question to be decided on evidence, it is not a matter of opinion. The fact that even after long possession the refugee settlers have not acquired any title to the land or any documentary evidence of such title lends colour to the suggestion that there is discrimination.

This, again, is a question of fact, not of opinion and the best persons to answer the question are the refugees themselves.

There can be no question that if the refugees are to stay in Dandakaranya there should be cordial relations between them and the local tribes. I would go further that such relations should exist not only with tribals but with non-tribals also.

Only the refugees can say whether the incentives now offered by the Government of India are sufficiently attractive. I am afraid I have not seen the details to offer any opinion as to whether they are reasonable.

There is another intricate question in which opinion is bound to differ. But there is one thing which I think should be said. Since any discontent among Dandakaranya refugees is bound to read on the economy of West Bengal and since the people of West Bengal are, or at least should be, vitally interested in the fate of their kith and kin, which the refugees are, the Government of West Bengal should have a more controlling [hand] in the administration than it [h]as.

Saibal Kumar Gupta

Dandakaranya: The State of Agriculture

That the emphasis of the Dandakaranya Development Authority was largely, if not exclusively, on agriculture admits of no doubt. Prior to the influx which began in February 1964, there were approximately 7,500 families of displaced persons within Dandakaranya of which 7,261 were recorded as agriculturists and moved to village sites by the end of June 1964. By the end of the agricultural season of 1963–64 about 6,286 families had been allotted agricultural land at the rate of roughly 6.5 acres per family and half an acre for homestead and kitchen garden in four widely separated zones of Orissa and Madhya Pradesh, viz., Pharasgaon, Umarkot, Paralkot and Malkangiri. Seven acres were not an inconsiderable area for an agricultural holding [by] East Bengal standards and one would think that the settler would be fairly well-off. But the result of the experience of a few years belied any such facile optimism.

The fact of the matter was that it was not the quantity of land but its quality which, together with other factors, determined the yield on which rehabilitation depended. Among these factors, the most important were: (1) soil texture and topography, (2) climatic conditions, (3) water (or irrigation), (4) a suitable cropping pattern, (5) good farming practice with improved seeds and implements, and (6) the skill and energy of the individual farmer together with the man-power he could mobilise in his support. Almost all these factors were inter-connected. The soil texture might be good but if rainfall was low or of very short duration, seeds did not germinate or would wilt even if they did, unless there was irrigation. If the soil was porous, even heavy showers proved unavailing in retaining the quantity of moisture which the crops required for growth and maturity; and if the land was sloping, fertilisers were washed away along with the water. As for good farming practice, much depended upon how quickly, under new soil and climatic conditions, the age old habits of the cultivator and his preference for paddy could be changed in favour of a novel cropping pattern, which in its turn depended upon a good agricultural extension service designed to bring new knowledge and technique[s] to the notice of the cultivator.

The personal factor included man-power as well as the skill and energy of the individual farmer. One of the contributory factors for the latter was incentive which came from the prospect of a good yield in return for input as well as ready marketability of the produce at a reasonable price. Man-power shortage in Dandakaranya during the crucial period of cultivation was a by-word. There was no surplus labour waiting to be employed nor any season[al] influx of such labour. The ordinary settler family had usually only one adult male member for whom it was difficult not only to plough and sow all the 6.5 acres within the short period available but also to eliminate the fast-growing weeds, which were a characteristic feature of lands reclaimed out of the virgin forest during the first few years. Women who, in East Bengal, did not work in the fields had sometimes lent their hands in sowing and weeding, but their number was small as household work could not be completely neglected. There were undoubtedly a few slackers, especially among those who were not traditionally agriculturists, but by and large the cultivators were inherently hardworking when there was at all any prospect of wresting a fair yield even out of reluctant soil. But as the soil scientist of the Project observed in February 1962 with regard to Boregaon and Jugani, 'you can't expect anybody to go on working hard if the predictable result was a poor yield which would not pay for the cost, far less maintain a family.'

Poor Quality Land

The low quality of the soil in the areas released for the refugees was not a new complaint, but was noted by Sukumar Sen more than once and commented upon by the Agricultural Expert Team set up by the Food and Agriculture Ministry at his instance. In fact, the settlers had to make do with the worst lands, hitherto regarded as uncultivable. The local adibasis had, as one would expect, occupied all the fertile low-lying areas in the valleys enriched by silt and moisture. They had even cleared many up-land forests to carry on their peculiar '*padu*' cultivation in the slopes and burnt the forest undergrowth every year, which deprived the soil of the enrichment it might have received from the decaying forest litter in the course of [the] years. What remained was generally virgin forest land with little humus and with soil depth and texture varying from place to place.

In Boregaon and Jugani (Pharasgaon zone) the soil was generally shallow, sandy loam to loam in texture, acidic in reaction, poor to medium in nitrogen and organic content, and poor in phosphate as well as moisture-holding capacity. The soil scientist reported that 6 per cent of plots were basically unfit for agriculture, 32 per cent were poor and sub-marginal, 53 per cent could be of medium quality if their moisture retention capacity could be improved, and only 9 per cent were of good quality. In the Umarkot region (comprising Umarkot and Raigarh sub-zones) the soils were somewhat shallow in depth and [did] not show properties of moisture-retentivity adequate for paddy cultivation. They would have to be put under cultivation for several seasons—about 4 or 5 years as Dr. Govindarajan told me verbally—before moisture-retentivity would improve. The texture varied from sandy loam to loam and in some cases clay loam with heavy-textured soil underlying the surface at places. It was generally acidic in reaction with moderate to poor nitrogen and organic content and poor phosphate content. In 23 villages of the Umarkot sub-zone whose lands were subjected to a detailed soil analysis, the soil scientist observed on the basis of their topography and soil texture that out of 8,198 acres about 60 per cent was suitable for paddy while another 15 per cent could be added from the highlands by terracing and field-bunding, but that the remaining 25 per cent of light-textured highland would never be suitable and it would be foolish to persist with paddy cultivation in these lands instead of trying cash crops.

The soil of Paralkot was closely similar to that of Umarkot area and was expected to behave in the same way under cultivation. In fact, soil survey reports indicated that the soils were fairly deep, generally acidic in reaction, medium in nitrogen and organic content and poor in phosphate. The texture varied from sandy loam to clay loam with underlying heavy-textured soil in places and moisture-retentivity was not very satisfactory. The picture was different in Malkangiri where the soils varied a great deal in their profile, character and surface textural properties from that of Umarkot zone. In villages on either side of [the] Malkangiri-Motu road the surface texture varied from sand, loamy sand to loam with sub-surface texture becoming heavier. On such land, according to Govinda Rajan, the suitable crop was not paddy but groundnut, tobacco and 'mesta'. On [the] Malkangiri-Balimela road, however, the soil was darker, deeper and heavier and therefore suitable for paddy. All the lands for the tribal[s] had been taken from this region and none from the other.

The primary effect of climate was on rainfall, which was important because artificial irrigation was as yet non-existent. Apart from its quantity, the period over which rainfall was spread and the occurrence of occasional bright spells in between were important factors in paddy cultivation which was the staple crop on which the settlers' heart was set. Most of the annual rainfall of 50"–60" took place usually within a limited period of 100 to 110 days from mid-June to the end of September, starting and closing almost abruptly without pre- or post-monsoon showers. Because of this and the hardness of the soil for lack of moisture during the preceding dry months the settler could not start preparing the seed beds and sowing seed till after the monsoons started, and since these operations took a minimum period of 2 to 3 weeks the effective period of monsoons left for helping plant growth and formation of grain was barely 90 to 100 days. Under these conditions the paddy which could be grown here must be of the broadcast, rain-fed, short-duration variety since impounding of water was not possible on account of the light texture of the soil and its undulating contour, and there was no irrigation to supplement the rainfall and extend the period. But the shorter the duration of growth, the less the yield and the more the susceptibility to diseases like 'blast'. Application of fertilisers on a large scale without artificial irrigation did not help much in increasing the yield because the high nutrient content of the soil increased the period of vegetative growth of paddy plants, deferring the reproduction phase and making the plants more susceptible to damage for want of soil moisture at the most crucial grain-formation period of the plant life. Moreover, in a short-duration paddy, suitable for the agro-climatic conditions mentioned above, the heading stage came towards the end of September or early in October when vagaries of climate like heavy rains or storms or drought often damaged the prospect of a good harvest. Broadcast paddy required to be weeded at least twice, but if the sowing started after the commencement of the monsoons the appropriate time for weeding coincided with that phase of the monsoons when rainfall was heaviest and most continuous. [This] adversely affected weeding, even apart from man-power shortage in the family and lack of resources to employ hired labour.

The effect of the soil and the climatic conditions in those parts of Dandakaranya where refugees had been settled was that the lands were not ideally suitable for the production of a satisfactory paddy crop except where the soil was of a heavy texture and low in situation. According to the Director of Agriculture only about 20 per cent of the holdings had a yield of about 15 maunds per acre while 80 per cent had an average not exceeding 8 maunds. The Chief Administrator before me would not believe it and held that the yield must be higher, and an obliging subordinate officer of the Agricultural Department dutifully gave him a note in support, but the Director of Agriculture stuck to his view. To the Chief Administrator's statement that at least 60 per cent of the lands given to displaced persons must be yielding 10 maunds of paddy per acre if not more, he observed that: 'the lands would then be very good indeed and there would have been no scope for us to find hundreds of acres in the tract unutilised. My view which I had submitted to the Chief Administrator about the potentialities of paddy production still holds good.'

Detailed Analysis

A more detailed analysis of the condition of agricultural settlers and the yield from the lands will, therefore, be attempted for each of the four zones, though absence of reliable statistics is a great handicap. Selective crop-cutting experiments on a 5 per cent sample survey basis generally exaggerate the yield and are highly unreliable. Whether this was due to a natural desire on part of the agricultural extension officers to justify their existence or encourage complacency in an easily convinced top-level administration it is difficult to say, but most Zonal Administrators had been skeptical of crop-cutting figures and relied more on their own comprehensive estimates made by their *sevaks* by house-to-house surveys under the guidance of Assistant Administrative Officers after the crop was harvested. The difference in respect of some villages was indeed striking. In one Umarkot village, while crop-cutting showed an average of 8.26 maunds per acre, [the] house-to-house survey showed 3.16 maunds. In two others while crop-cutting showed a yield of 15.27 maunds and 14.8 maunds respectively per acre, the house-to-house survey showed 10 maunds. In another prosperous village the house-to-house survey estimate was 14 maunds against the crop-cutting result of 17.14 maunds. The Agricultural Development Officer's report for 1963–64 shows that only 439 families in Umarkot zone received 30 maunds of paddy or less, while the Zonal Administrator gives the number of such families as 768. It was because of these discrepancies and the insistence of some villagers that the actuals were even less than what was recorded in house-to-house surveys that I directed a simultaneous comprehensive verification of the entire stock of paddy in the settlers' houses to be completed by the end of December 1963 or the beginning of January 1964. The result was startling and will be referred to later in the course of this discussion. True, this verification showed the position three months after harvesting during which, apart from what was consumed, some paddy must have been sold, but the suggestion of the then Chief Administrator that the settlers concealed their paddy in adibasi houses was too absurd and had only to be stated to be disbelieved. It was a snap verification without notice, and in any case there was not so much mutual confidence between the settler and the adibasi as to league them together in a conspiracy of silence.

The figures should therefore be taken with some caution and in case of conflict the house-to-house survey figures should be preferred. It should be remembered that for the purpose of assessing the nature of rehabilitation correctly, averages are not a safe guide as they mask the condition of the economically weakest group. When the declared intention was to start each individual displaced family on the road to rehabilitation by giving all families identical advantages in the shape of equal quantities of land and equal loans or grants or services, [the] success of rehabilitation must be judged by the condition in the lowest bracket. One should ascertain how many people were unable in spite of honest effort to make ends meet from their agricultural land and other subsidiary pursuits carried on along with agriculture.

We must also have a clear idea as to how much paddy a family needed in order to make ends meet. A conservative estimate for a family of 4.5 persons puts it at 36 maunds for food, 7 maunds for seed, and 18 maunds for sale to meet his cash expenses—a total of a little over 60 maunds per year. Some supplementary items of food might probably be raised in the kitchen garden provided there was a well for watering the garden. Supplementary cottage or small-scale industries might also meet part of the need if favourable conditions for such employment were created. But if industrial employment was whole-time with little respite left for ploughing and sowing, as was the case with a substantial portion of people in Boregaon and Jugani, it was obviously a failure of agricultural rehabilitation.

Pharasgaon Zone

Pharasgaon zone comprised three villages: East Boregaon, West Boregaon and Jugani. This was the earliest settlement where 205 agricultural families and 46 non-agricultural small-trader families were moved in 1959. The latest figures suggest that the number of small-trader families came down to 30 or 34 in 1964.

In 1961 and the preceding years the yield of paddy was less than 5 maunds per acre while the district average was 10. In 1962 an experiment was made on 129 plots to improve the yield by the application of manures and fertilisers (ammonia sulphate, super phosphate, oil cake and green manure) and the conservation of water through proper field-bunding. The result, so far as yield was concerned, was encouraging with an average of 11.38 maunds per acre, though the Zonal Administrator does not put it higher than 10.5 maunds approximately. But the expenditure on manures, fertilisers, seed loan and labour was enormous, and there was no satisfactory supplementary crop. Only 'mesta' and 'til' grew well and 'urid' thrived when it was treated with super phosphate. Castor, niger, cotton, vegetables and spices did not do well while maize and 'arhar' suffered damage from cattle trespass. In 1963–64 when the experiment of manuring was not repeated and 93 per cent of the area was sown with paddy and 7 per cent with other crops, the yield was again poor, averaging 5.44 maunds per acre according to crop-cutting trials, and 3.37 maunds according to house-to-house surveys. The Zonal Administrator's report shows that out of 1,214 acres as much as 200 acres (32 plots) were unproductive, 131 plots (or families) received upto 30 maunds, 16 plots yielded between 31 and 40 maunds, 5 plots between 41 and 50 maunds, 10 plots between 51 and 60 maunds and 11 plots above 60 maunds.

15 Orality of Silence

MANAS RAY

One day, without notice, Pritikana came. We, brothers and sisters, did not know about her presence till she turned up that day along with her husband and their three-year old daughter. They started visiting us fairly regularly—initially once in every two weeks, then every week and more. The man was dark, very dark, had a chiseled nose and broad eyes. He was very lively. I remember him singing at times, sitting on the steps that led to the verandah—loud, unhesitant, full-throated, direct from the heart. The woman bore an eerie resemblance to my mother—the same height, the same face, the same complexion, the same voice, the same way of talking. She was, as if, what my mother must have been some twenty years back.

The child was about five years younger than me and, like any other child, soon became part of the family through her cries, tantrums and wonders. They all did; there was no way they couldn't: the man through his uninhibited manners and direct way of talking, a loud and clear voice, and she, my mother-surrogate, through her quick grasp of the family's folk history: the stock of gossip, the stories that circulated, the jokes, the memorable happenings of the past. She was affectionate and loving towards us, me and my siblings, and showed an ardent, even if ruffled, admiration and love for my parents.

Even then I did not know who exactly she was. I knew and also did not know. Information came in bits and pieces as I grew up. Her eerie resemblance to my mother bothered me. She became part of my childhood mystery, my sense of the unknown, unknowingly, clouded with a moral ambiguity I could not locate. Strangely enough, their presence brought a sense of jubilation too. I started hiding in that jubilation, always looking for something else than what was present, always uncertain, always cheerful.

The neighbourhood's reaction was complex. The happenings in our family were too mammoth for gossip, but also the source of infinite curiosity. If I ever drifted in course of play to someone's courtyard and found myself in the midst of the afternoon chatter of women, maybe the too curious among them would ask me about the new family who visited us so often, mentioning Pritikana, her husband Sunil, and the child Tukun by their names. The gesture was to demonstrate familiarity and perhaps a restrained acceptance. The touch of extra affection was clear. It was part of good manners for the neighbourhood not to discuss the visitors in our presence, as if their very mentioning threatened to crumble the nascent social order and solidarity on which the riot-ridden refugee colony's existence depended. But curiosity remained. Coping with collective anxiety, curiosity, moral dilemma and the sheer puzzle about pieces that refused to fall in place became part of the locality's protean journey towards urbanity. Perforce it introduced an element of detachment in a setup where no ontological differences existed in human experience between the relation of human groups with each other, with animals and plants, or with earthquakes and thunderstorms. Or, was detachment in-built into the patterns of involvement of these mostly rural people from East Bengal thrown into the social vortex of post-Partition Calcutta? Or, could it be that detachment and involvement depended on the position of the sun? The faces in the fading light, especially the older faces, looked distinctly detached, released as if for good from the claims of the everyday. The stories they recounted of a land now past became murmurs, barely audible, sighs. For the close relatives, who half knew about what happened to my mother a long time ago, Priti's arrival was a past calamity brought back to the present and quite unnecessarily. But in that way everyone was related to Priti just as we were—she was a niece, a cousin, a grand daughter and hence an object of affection.

My sister's sudden arrival in the family was also the cause for another kind of reshuffling. Anjali, the sister so long everybody knew as the eldest, was no more the eldest. Anjali was the centre that held the family together, the fountain of love and affection. She was also the first among the siblings to realise who Priti actually was—my parents' first child, born before they were wed. She never told us then.

What seemed to be one explanation, one answer, never remained one. In order for any answer to be an answer, it had to return to that elusive point of origin, seek sanction from a past veiled from public eye but immensely real, and be relayed back from there through the intervening years right up to the present. The trail takes me back to my father's involvement in the Independence movement, his early years in the terrorist outfit, Yugantar Party, his later conversion to Gandhism, his stints in the British prisons. Were they not actually married before Priti was born? Priti's foster mother, an ex-terrorist. Priti's ultra-modern, urbane but lonely upbringing in Calcutta (Priti played the *piano*—for a refugee boy on the outskirts of Calcutta, the ultimate sign of Europe). What happened when my parents returned to Dhaka, leaving Priti to the care of her foster mother? Under what circumstances did they get married, formally and perhaps for the second time? Was it the Partition that made the re-union possible? Was it the Partition and its impact on moral codes that made it possible for our neighbours to accept the happenings of our family silently? It all seemed like a kaleidoscope that gave a different picture with every turn. I was ardent in my need for a rational interpretation, a fine temporal scheme of things. Reason eluded; I allowed it to elude. I looked for half-truths. I could never ask my mother and settle the unyielding. Nobody in the family did. It is the riddle that constructed the family.

As things started settling down, there was another turn of events, and in a way more traumatic than the first. Towards the mid-60s, and for a long while, my father's salary from the school became irregular. The family gained some notoriety from a photograph that appeared in the newspaper, showing my father and his colleagues on hunger strike next to the locked gate of the school. Anjali had completed her B.A. degree by then and as one more enactment of the much-repeated refugee allegory, she took up a job as a junior stenographer in a government office. Marriage proposals were put on the backburner; her job came handy in stabilising the listing boat that was our family. On the day she joined work, Anjali—like many other womenfolk in our locality—in starched and pressed printed saris, purse strapped on her shoulder, was about to set off. Mother paused for a moment—she was prepared yet somewhat ungirded—blessed her thrice and went through the gesture of mock spitting once on her forehead, a ritual to ward off evil, reserved for special occasions. Father accompanied my sister to her office, a long red colonial building, Number 3 Government Place, in the city centre.

Anjali has been getting late coming back from office. Quite often it is fairly late and past bedtime. The home gets restless waiting for her to return through the burnt brick-chip-laid lane. The moment I hear her heels clack-clacking on the red cemented verandah, I turn the other way round in my bed and close my eyes. In the mornings when I wake up I find her doing the beds, humming absentmindedly, her face suffused with a hint of a smile and eyes lit up with love.

It was revealed that she was having an affair with Sunil, the husband of my eldest sister, Priti. This left everybody spellbound. My mother looked helpless in her agony. Brought up on the banks of Buri Ganga in interior East Bengal, she was not only not in tune with the world of Rabindra sangeet, her modes of persuasion too were thoroughly inadequate. The best she could plead with her: 'While you all along have chosen your sarees, your ornaments, now let me choose the man for you.' I have seen her sob in quiet corners of the house. Tears rolled down Anjali's cheeks too, but she grew more resolute in her love. Finally my parents agreed to their marriage. By then I was fifteen, about to leave school.

My family's claim to ordinariness must have been enormous, for despite everything, it seemed so ordinary, so utterly ordinary, so reassuring, so normal, like any other family. And this worried me, even annoyed me perhaps. I watched carefully the movement of the ants: in one row, each busy, each carrying something white in its mouth, the straggler falling behind, the dead one carried by others, a long procession of activities, a long chain of regularities. I watched the butterflies as they swung on our karamcha tree in one corner of our courtyard, the multiple, intricate patterns of their wings. I watched our betel nut tree, its soft, quiet, green pulp would remind me of Madhusree long after I left St Mary's. The red snake. I knew its movements from the rustle of dry leaves lying behind my room. I watched it as it raised its hood, gently swing in the autumn breeze and go back to hiding again. The red snake would at times return at night, track lazily towards the pond, the weight of moonlight, blue like a grasshopper's body, on its back. At play, I waited eagerly for the football to travel all the way, wrap itself mercilessly in the nets and for the waves it caused. Everywhere, in whatever I saw, I discovered a network of deception. And love, its ordinariness and regularity made me impatient.

I found in Calcutta's Maoist politics, by then waning, the expression of my adolescence, and a good place to be. It introduced me to a new world of narrow lanes, meetings in dark, damp chambers, whispers, new words, new mappings, new kinds of excitement, a new sense of importance. I wasn't convinced by what they called their 'theory', their programmes, charts, and hopes. But I liked the way the raw betel nut smell of my adolescence mingled with that of hand-made grenades to create strange shapes in my dreams; I liked the way Swadhinda, the one who preached, and Bhakat Bhai, the local rice-mill owner whom we targeted for 'action', met as pre-historic beings in the wrinkled womb of darkness as I slept. For once, the circle of deceit was not exactly ordinary. But I wanted to go through it quickly, always aiming at the interrogation cell at Lord Sinha Road, headquarters of the detective department of Calcutta Police. There, sitting next to a spotless, guiltless table, with a bright lamp as the unusually bright solitary witness that would at times be turned on my face, I get ready for the encounter, challenging, I thought, for the prospect of torture that loomed large, all the time thinking of the willowy ripples of the pond, the red snake, a particular scrawny bird that sat in the path of the snake, and what I took to be its faded wish. I played the game of deception well, as I knew I would. I felt vulnerable but was also released in a matter of days.

My father died. At twenty-three, I thought I stood exposed. The city would take its revenge on me, I would be lynched. Half way through the month, I stopped going to the advertising agency where I worked and one day headed towards Howrah Station, making my way to an unreserved compartment of a Delhi-bound train. As I squeezed into the crowd, the smell of *khaini* comforting, the train slowly started moving. I could make out I was hiding again.

What was once unspeakable is now a matter of writing. When I think of my mother these days, her past seems a fetish, the wrinkles on her face real.

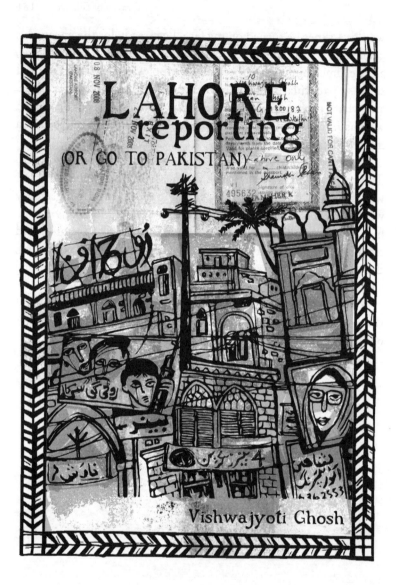

After 6 days of waiting, I received my visa on the 4ᵗʰ day of November, 2008. 'Lahore Only. Not valid for Cantt. Area.' A Reporting Visa. "No big deal", said the officer. "All you need to do is - go to the Police Station and report your entry within 24 hours of your arrival." Petty formalities of a larger dream. But who cares? A true Dilliwalah is never scared of such bureaucracies, leave alone a Police Station. For now it's Laaahorrre! Delhi smiled and talked to me politely. I was the city's original prince.

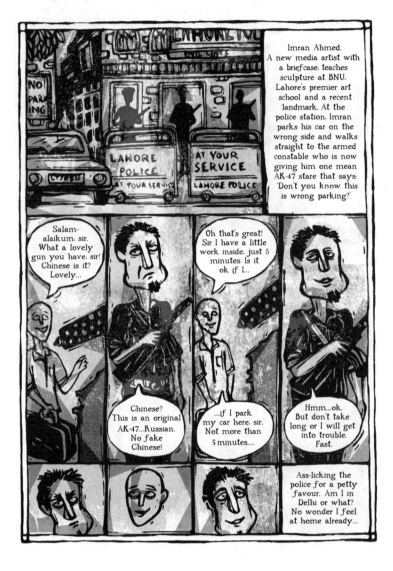

1947. The initial draft of the sub-continent's partition plan had Lahore marked for India. But since religion was the map maker for the two nations, the dividing line fell between Muslim and non-Muslim areas. Lahore and Amritsar. It was final. Lahore was to be in Pakistan. A loss that the people of Delhi never came to terms with. Once the 'Paris of the East', the romance was now a memory.

Like any other sub-continental city, Lahore too had moved from a classic to
a kitschy metropolis. The famous food street of Gawalmandi now serves a
platter of kababs with pro-biotic Nestle raita. On the other side were the
Boulevard, Gulberg, localities inhabited by the 'Burger classes'– a term
reserved for the English-speaking elite, used by the city's simpletons.

The longest 15 minutes finally got over when Inspector Rizwaan arrived. Black & white, technicolour, eastman colour, even neon images of Pakistani intelligence, ISI, Indian citizens in Pakistan, Breaking News, Intelligence goof-ups, interrogation, jail, prisoners of war -had all crossed my mind. I was now facing a middle-aged Inspector, who greeted me in a nasal voice, "Hello, hope you didn't have to wait for long."

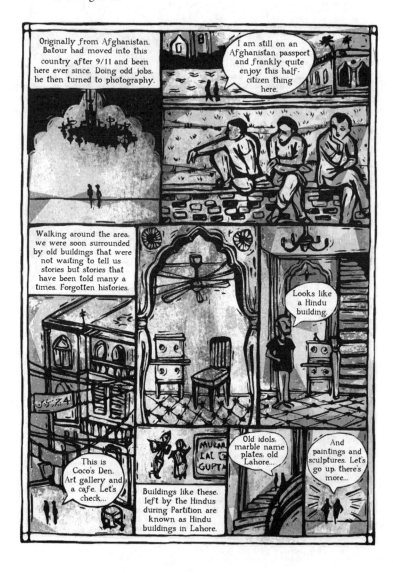

THANK YOU:

huma mulji
salina hashmi
imran ahmed
vasl/ goethe centre/ alhamra
hurmat-ul-ain
barat ali batour
mehreen murtaza
unum babar
sajna & raju
bani abidi
iqra & ehsaan
kyla pasha
umer butt
ayesha jatoi
haider ali jaan
adnan madni
rafay alam
&
inspector rizwaan

LIMITED RELEASE
NME: GHOSH/VISHWA
22NOV LHE BB63AE LHE417
PNR: 01/0012
DELHI
PK 270 DEL
0214 PK437196

FICTION

Anwar Ali
Gurmukh Singh Musafir
Meera Sikri
Syed Muhammad Ashraf
Zakia Mashhadi
Amena Nazli
Joya Mitra
Sunanda Bhattacharya
Jhumur Pandey
Selina Hossain

17   Of Lost Stories*

ANWAR ALI

Ieldganj was officially called Wilfriedganj. It is said that
at some point there was a house there that belonged to
Wilfried Sahib. No one really knew if he was English or
American. But he was definitely white. And because of the fear of
white men, thieves and robbers stayed away from his house. The
natives began to build their houses near his house. Land dealers
raised the price of land and before land became too expensive, many
people built many houses nearby. Noticing the increasing number
of new houses, the people from the committee moved their post
beyond the railway track, noting this place down in their accounts
as Wilfriedganj. The illiterate natives simplified this English name
into Fieldganj and they themselves became 'Fieldganjiye' or 'people
of Fieldganj.'

Fieldganj spread itself onto the other side of the canal. This
man-made canal generally remained dry throughout the year.
When it rained, the canal would collect water from various areas,
swaying into the old river. It would soon return to its earlier dryness.
There were graves on the other side of the canal. Some of these
had marble headstones but most were of plain earth. The earthen
ones had grass growing on them, fresh like new wheat. There were
many more graves behind these and many more behind those. This

*   Originally published in Punjabi as a novel titled *Gwacchiyyan Gallan*,
    meaning roughly 'lost stories,' (Pakistan Punjabi Adabi Board,
    October 1998). The extract chosen here is from Chapter 3, 11–17.

series of graves would have continued to spread had the railway track not interfered. Hindus and Sikhs lived on this side of the track. A colony of lepers lived behind the graves. God alone knew if the people of Fieldganj had erected these graves to bury corpses or to distance themselves from the lepers. And no one really knew if the lepers had always been there or if they had arrived and settled in the area later. But it was known that the lepers were definitely Muslims. They had their own well and their own mosques. They also had Muslim names: Deen Mohammad, Fazal Deen, Nazeer Hussain, Mohammad Sadiq and other such names. The people of Fieldganj would call them by their native variations: Deena (Deen Mohammad), Phajja (Fazal), Jeera (Nazeer). But they would call Sadiq by his name. 'Sadiq Korha' or 'Sadiq the leper.'

Even at his age, the signs of leprosy could not be detected on Sadiq's body. But the older lepers believed that the later the disease shows, the more intense the pain is; it renders the sufferer motionless. Sadiq did not look like a leper from any angle. Only his eyebrows gave away signs of his disease. Anyway, ordinary people often had receding eyebrows. And due to this fear—or maybe because someone would have rebuked him, 'You seem all right! Aren't you ashamed of begging?'—Sadiq had attached the word *korha* or leper to his name. This way, no one would be mistaken.

'Give alms to Sadiq Korha! Some flour please! May God fill the treasury of the kings. May he also give Sadiq Korha a half pice!'

He treated the people of Fieldganj like they were his relatives.

'Chachi Nooran, please put in a lump of jaggery. Sadiq Korha wants to have sweet rice today!'

The lepers would roam all over the city. Everyone would earn alms according to the intensity of their voices and illnesses. And Sadiq Korha would always have the heaviest bag. Once they returned from their rounds, the lepers would sell the extra flour to the shopkeepers of Fieldganj, who bought them at a cheaper rate from the lepers. Anyway, how would it matter to the customers where the produce came from! The egg-seller would buy eggs and chicken from the lepers. Whenever they had time, the lepers would visit a market to find out the prices of goods in the area.

The problem with chicken is that they often got stolen. This problem was faced only by those who kept chicken. Whenever someone among the lepers would lose a chicken, Sadiq Korha would come to Fieldganj complaining about it, collect some money through gaining sympathy and give it to the poor leper who had lost the chicken. When the theft of chicken among lepers became an everyday occurrence, Sadiq applied the strength of religion to his appeals: 'Brothers in Islam, Assalam aleikum. This is an appeal of Sadiq Korha. Please listen carefully! The lepers have lost a chicken. Some of its feathers are white, some black. Some blue and some yellow. Its crest is crimson. It is barefoot and its socks are yellow. Whoever finds it, return it to Sadiq Korha and earn your blessings. We lepers will bless him generously. And if it is not returned, we will still bless you. May the faith of the brothers in Islam remain intact!'

In every lane and corner of the city, Sadiq Korha would present his plea as the brothers in Islam laughed at him. 'Has a chicken-thief ever returned a stolen chicken?'

But the women of Fieldganj were terribly afraid of the curses of lepers. They believed the 'if it is not returned, we will still bless you' part of it to be no better than a curse. They would cover their children's heads with the ends of their dupattas and call out: 'Oye Sadiq! Take this money! Oye Sadiq! Come take some money!'

Collecting money from every lane and corner, Sadiq gathered more than the price of the chicken. He would keep the money for the chicken separate and use the extra cash to purchase and eat sugarcane and sesame candies. If he had two or three *annas*, he would go and play cards with the boys of Fieldganj.

There was no facility for games nor any entertainment for the lepers. Anyway, who would ask for game-money from those who asked for money from others? No juggler or trickster nor any magician ever veered towards their huts. The children played with small glass marbles, balls and sticks outside the huts. Or they would climb up and down the *sheesham* trees in the graveyard. They waited for leprosy to strike them so that they could then visit the city, begging for alms. The other event they waited for was the arrival of the *Meems*.[1]

Every fifteen days the Meems from the Mission would visit the slums of the lepers. These visits were like fairs for the lepers. Seeing them from a distance, a boy hanging from the sheesham trees would shout out: 'Here they are! The Meems have come!'

The children would swarm out from their huts and the older people would begin to look for their sticks.

'I had kept it here behind the door. God knows where it has gone now!'

'Here it is, still standing. Can't you see it? Come, let's go to the Meems.'

The Meems would always come in threes. Two black and one white. The black ones would be really black but their saris would be extremely white. Like milk. Their white shoes were made of cloth. One of them had a brown cloth bag in her hand. The other held a bundle of rolled photographs. The white one held a long stick in her hand. It was as tall as a man, with one fat end and the other sharpened. She would often ask one of the black Meems to hold this 'pastor':

'Here, hold my pastor.'

The white Meem was tall and well-built. She looked like a creature from another world, with a white solar hat on her head, a white coat with half sleeves, a white skirt, long white socks and a pair of brown, manly boots up till her knees. The lepers would come barefoot and surround them. They would put their weight on their sticks with both hands. The children would sit in front of them, elbowing each other. Some of them would draw images on the ground with their fingers.

'Assalam aleikum' the white Meem would say and the children would reply with a 'Waleikum salaam' so loud that the crows on the sheesham branches would fly away with loud cawing, and after making a few wide rounds in the sky, would come back and perch on the same branches again. The black Meems would nail some wooden pins on the wall of a hut and hang the unrolled pictures. The white Meem would select an image and tell its story. She would point at different places on these photos with the end of her stick. The stories would be about sheep and goats or about the Lord and Messiah Jesus. In these pictures, he was either bringing light back into someone's eyes or restoring the health of a sick person. Then the white Meem would close her eyes and, addressing her heavenly father, she would pray for the safe return of the lost herds and the health of those who are sick. After every prayer, the black Meems would say 'Ameen' and the children would repeat loudly after them. The Meems would wait for the children's voices to die down. When there was silence at last, the black Meems would open their cloth bag and take out worn and used frocks, skirts, blouses, waistcoats, pants and socks; the white Meem would go about distributing these among the lepers. The children were given cards from last Christmas. While leaving, the Meems would also leave some medicines and bandages for the lepers. They would take the bag and the roll of pictures along with them. Even the wooden nail would go. Since the time Fieldganj became a settlement and lepers began to live here, the missionaries began to arrive from foreign lands and the Meems came to the leper colony every fifteen days, showing pictures, telling stories, distributing medicines and used clothes and giving old cards to children.

But no leper had ever converted from Islam to Christianity. And this is how things remained till the end. Or till the creation of Pakistan at least. When Pakistan was created, the Muslims of Fieldganj left their colony and went away to Pakistan. No one asked the lepers if they would go to Pakistan. So no one knew what became of them.

When peace and security was regained, people got back to normalcy, and began remembering their lost homes. They started crossing the border to see their houses in the name of visiting shrines, temples and gurudwaras. The people of Fieldganj started doing the same. They met those Hindus and Sikhs who now stayed in these houses. They, in turn, began to remember and miss their former homes which they had left behind in Pakistan. The Hindus and Sikhs were very friendly and hospitable towards the people of Fieldganj. They even opened up their homes for them. On the other side of the canal now there were homes instead of graves. Those who stayed in these houses said, 'The living need homes more than the dead.' The lepers were still living in their slums. But their clothes and appearances had changed somewhat. They wrapped their dhotis in a different fashion and wore red loincloths. Sadiq Korha was now Ram Prakash but everyone called him 'Prakash'— only 'Prakash.' Not even 'Prakash Korha.' And now his entire face was a signboard of his leprosy. Prakash narrated his story to the people of Fieldganj who had come to visit from Pakistan, thus:

'When Fieldganj was attacked, we took shelter in our slums, hoping that you all will come to take us along. Then we realised that no one will come to take us, no one will let us sit in their vehicles. When the chants of Allah-o-Akbar ceased, we began to wait for the Hindus and the Sikhs. They did not come either. By then, all our supplies had become depleted and our children had started crying. Their mothers tried to distract them again and again, but they would not stop crying. Then the mothers clung to the children in their laps and joined them. And we left the huts to sit on the raised gravestones and continued to wait and reflect. And none of us spoke to each other. One night, all of us got together and consulted each other. Everyone spoke of what was in their hearts. We could not see each other's eyes in the darkness of the night and were not scared of revealing our hearts.

'Next day at dawn, we gathered near the railway tracks—all the lepers—those who could walk and those who could walk with the support of sticks. The mothers had picked up the crying children and were carrying them. When the six o'clock express passed us, we had crossed the railway tracks. A Hindu priestess, Mai Faujaan, was standing in front of us. She was holding a stick with a colourful variety of small flags attached to it. She said in a nasal tone, "Say the sacred word."

'And all of us, adults and children alike, began to repeat after her, "Ram Chandarji di jai!"[2]

'As we moved down the slope of the tracks, we began to walk towards the houses of the Hindus and Sikhs, who, on seeing us, went and hid in their houses, and continued to stare at us. We stopped at a distance from their houses and began to declare "Ram Chandarji di jai!" Our voices were affected by the leprosy and the children's whining cries were interrupting the chants. They did not understand what we were saying. Later, when they understood, they came out of their houses and bought some leftover food for us—some roti, rice and lentils. They left these for us in front of their houses and went back inside.

'The next day, they came across the railway tracks on their own and left some lentils, rice, rotis, jaggery, salt and chillies for us, along with some oil and soap. One day, along with these supplies, they also left a statue of their God—it was white as milk. We placed it in our mosque, mister. It would only have gathered dust and smoke if it had been left there on the tracks.'

Translated from the Punjabi to Urdu by **Julien Columeau,**
and translated from the Urdu by **Farha Noor.**

Notes and References

1. *Meem:* A Punjabi derivative of the native word, *mem*, an abbreviation of *memsahib*, which means the wife or woman of a sahib. Foreign women were, and are, referred to as 'mem' in North India, Pakistan and Bangladesh. There is a certain sense of detached respect and simultaneous mockery in the term that cannot be replicated in translation. For this purpose, the word has been retained in its original. In Punjabi, the singular is *Meem* and the plural, *Meemman.*
2. A popular chant among Hindus, meaning 'Victory to Ram Chandarji!'

18 People of God*

GURMUKH SINGH MUSAFIR

Respected Bhai Sahib,
     I don't know if this pain-wracked prayer will reach you or not. Savinder has been found. At first I was happy when I came to know about it, but almost immediately my happiness changed into deep sorrow and anxiety. You know that I regard Savinder as a daughter. Now I am facing a great dilemma. My daughter is in the clutches of strangers somewhere close by, and I am powerless to free her! How terribly frustrating it is! Oh, Asmaan Singh, how difficult it must be for you and Bharjai to be able to sleep a wink at night! What festering wound must gnaw at your bosoms! Your very insides must be writhing on thorns. But if someone were to ask me about what lies in my heart, brother, I too am lying on embers. My heart would have wept even if Savinder had been found in another neighbourhood, but not so much. Now this is a matter of extreme shame for me. I used to have a pretty cordial relationship with the Khan of the North-West Frontier—and he's not a bad man—but an evil breeze seems to be blowing. I have been pursuing him, but he's proved elusive so far. These people have other girls as well. The moment they sense any danger, they have them sent to Pakistan. The good and the bad are all in cahoots

---

* Originally published in Punjabi as 'Allah Wale' in *Aalney de Bote* (Delhi: Sikh Publishing House, 1955). The title literally means 'People of God,' but another meaning of the word *alla* is raw or unhealed; it could also be seen as a metaphor for those whose wounds have not healed.

with each other in this matter. But even then, brother, humanity has not been destroyed. God-fearing people are alive even in these times. I sent you a message earlier that Savinder is in the custody of the Khan of the North-West Frontier. But who knows whether any message from us reaches you or not. Anyway, with God's grace, I will surely send my niece to you, even at the cost of my own life.

You yourself are embroiled in so much difficulty; you wouldn't have got any news about the whereabouts of Hari Chand the goldsmith and Harnam Khatri, would you? Where must those poor wretches have gone? They left some belongings with me, and the weight on my heart won't lessen until I am able to return these to them. Who can tell about this heart, brother; as you yourself used to recite from the Guru's verses: this heart is not to be trusted. My salaam to my sister-in-law and my nephew; and please believe that I share your sorrow.

One doesn't know how this letter of Munshi Allah Baksh managed to reach Asmaan Singh in Delhi. The letter had been written in the Urdu script and did not carry a date. Savinder had disappeared during the Muzaffarabad attacks on 22 October 1947. Had Asmaan Singh and his wife been certain that she had been killed somewhere, they would have heaved a sigh and accepted their fate. They had lost all hopes of Savinder being alive because Asmaan Singh had searched for her among all the survivors in the refugee camps set up for those who had survived the attacks. He had counted all those who came to those camps—there were about fifteen thousand people. There were about thirty-five thousand Hindus and Sikhs in Hazara if one counted those who had escaped from Muzaffarabad. Asmaan Singh estimated that about twenty thousand people had been killed, and there was little likelihood of Savinder having survived. Asmaan Singh also knew that thousands of girls had jumped into the Kishan-Ganga and Jhelum rivers. Bahadur Khan, the Contractor from Raadewala, was well known for one thing—that he had Giani Rangeel Singh and several others killed at one go.

Despite all these incidents, however, one thing or the other would come to their notice, like this letter from Munshi Allah Baksh, and they would relive the turmoil all over again. Today, reading

Munshi Allah Baksh's letter, on the one hand he felt gratified at the loyalty of an old, close friend and on the other, serpents seemed to writhe over his heart. His blood began to boil. Asmaan Singh knew Khan of the North-West Frontier quite well, and his own home also fell in the district of Mansehra. Savinder was married in Naluchi, and her maternal grandparents also lived there. Naluchi and Muzaffarabad are one and the same place. After hearing stories of the destruction in Dhani-Pothohar and Sooyan, a large number of Hindus and Sikhs uprooted from Hazara had sought refuge in Muzaffarabad. When Asmaan Singh had learnt of this, he had sent Savinder to her in-laws' place. This was in August 1947. Lahore had been on the brink of being consumed in the flames of the riots. They had received Munshi Allah Baksh's letter after more than two years since then.

Dear Mataji,

I am saved! After listening to what the others have gone through, believe me, I am saved. In one place, the necklace around my neck saved me, in another, my bangles, and my earrings saved me in the third place. The ring I still have. Didn't know if I should carry my mother-in-law's young ones or take care of myself; there was so much chaos one lost track of days, weeks and place. When I jumped into the river the first time, one Pathan pulled me out by my hair, and when we reached the bridge I realised that this was the Jhelum bridge of our Naluchi gurudwara. The skin on my face and my scalp were raw. When I ran, shouting and screaming, another man said, 'Where are you off to? Not a single Sikh has been left alive.' I was wearing the iron kada on my left wrist. When one girl shouted, 'Military, military!', that man said, 'What military? The General himself has been killed.' We saw a large number of Sikh men and women come from the Bastaad side, and we all heaved a sigh of relief. As we ran towards them, a blow from a stick struck my forehead. When I regained consciousness, I was all alone. I couldn't make out where I was. I got up to walk but had no energy. I could hear the sound of bullets and of splashes in the water, which made me realise that we were still near the bridge. When I stood on my toes to peep over the edge, I could see the bridge. But this was a very big one; I couldn't

understand which one it was. Spinach leaves grew along the boundary...
or some other greens perhaps; don't know what leaves but they tasted
like spinach. I ate a great deal. I saw five–six men approaching, and I
ran towards the bridge. I must have gone about half a kilometre when
I realised that this was some other bridge. When I turned to look back,
I could not see anyone. By the time I reached the bridge, my feet were
swollen. Mataji, if anybody saw that terrifying scene even in a picture,
he would be frightened to death. Leap after leap was being made into the
Kishan-Ganga. I had myself jumped into the Jhelum, but now seeing
this, I felt dizzy. My feet were already swollen and I had no strength
left; I fell into the river in a swoon. The river was in spate; those who
were sucked away were sucked away. If anyone was pulled close to the
banks by its waves, those rogues would grab her. I came to know later
that my body and that of my fellow villager, Banso, had floated towards
the banks as soon as we had collapsed.

I had about forty wounds on my body. It took six months for them
to heal. Mataji, this turned out to be a boon. Now when I meet you,
you won't be able to recognise me at all. Chacha Allah Baksh could not
recognise me. As soon as my wounds healed, a high fever gripped my
body. By the time I was in a condition to walk again after three months,
Banso had an infant in her arms! How shall I write to you, Mataji,
please don't ever let Pitaji read my letter; it was really fortunate that my
condition was so bad. Sometime later I got to know from Banso that I
was going to be sold to a cobbler. I also got to know that Chacha Allah
Baksh was trying to find me; he even came to the northern belt with the
Indians once, but they all got to know about it. All the girls who were
here in the locality were sent to Pakistan. I have come to know only now
that Chacha Allah Baksh was under the mistaken impression that I
had also been sent to Pakistan. Actually, I was still here. I was supposed
to take care of Banso's child. No one noticed me. No one could recognise
me from my clothes at all, nor from my face. If you see me even you won't
recognise me; nor will he, my husband. Don't show my letter to Pitaji.
When Banso returned from Pakistan the second time, she told me that
the cobbler whom they wanted to sell me to wanted another girl, so the
deal could not be struck—that girl belongs to Bastaad. About me the
cobbler said that my face was not pretty. Mataji, you must be thinking

how shameless I am. You know about Parmeshwari from Bastaad, don't you; she used to come to Naluchi on Baisakhi. Here we were priced like cattle, Mataji. Finally I was sold, to Fajja the blacksmith of Shinkiari. He beat me black and blue and left me half dead. Indians were taking rounds on this side, but here all the good and bad had become one. The good people didn't speak up out of fear of the rogues, and moreover, the propaganda spread was that in this way, Islam was being propagated.

One day a rumour spread that people had come to get the Indian girls released; that day I was beaten mercilessly. Fajja said we had to go to the Qazi to get the nikah done. He said that he could not touch me without the nikah ceremony; 'I don't want to rot in hell' he said. He wanted to escape to Pakistan, taking me with him. The Indian search party entered the neighbourhood, so Fajja caught me and set off in the dark night. The pain in my feet started again; there was no proper path that we could follow, nor did we know how far we had to go. Barefoot, we walked on stony paths, and as soon as it was dawn, we got caught. Fajja only told me that the place was called Badal, and that Pakistan was six miles away. On the way he kept trying to persuade me to marry him as soon as we reached Pakistan. 'In any case, most probably the Sikhs would all have been killed by now; and even if they were alive, no one would accept me—neither my parents nor my in-laws,' he said. Is that true, Mataji? When I would not agree with Fajja, he would gnash his teeth and say, 'Once we are there I will call the Qazi and force you to marry me. I have paid money for you. Even if the Indians snatch you away from me, I'll make sure I send you off with a memento.' Mataji, don't let Pitaji read my letter. I thought he meant something else by 'memento,' but he meant something entirely different. The policemen who caught us were Pakistanis. They took Fajja to a neighbouring police station and locked him up there. One policeman looked at me from top to bottom, asked me some questions and brought me to the northern belt. There were three policemen and they stood apart to talk among themselves, and that scared me.

'Let this headache go, let this headache go'—these words kept falling upon my ears. Once we reached the northern belt, we came to know that the Indians who had come there to search had left. Handing me over to a woman in one house, the policemen went off to Khan's

house. Sometime late in the night, I was summoned to Khan's house.
There was no policeman there. Khan said to me:
  'You'll have to go with Fajja.'
  I said, 'But Fajja has been arrested.'
  'The man who can arrest Fajja hasn't been born yet!'
  I fell silent upon Khan's words. The very next morning I saw that
Fajja had also arrived there. Khan said to Fajja, 'Take her with you,
and tell me if she says no-nay; I have already taken enough tantrums
from her.' Fajja said in a very disheartened voice, 'This is a big headache.
Every other day the Indian rescue team comes looking for them. Today
our own police caught me; if you had not come and saved me, I would
still have been there. And this one refuses to marry me, so what's the
point in going on feeding her?' Fajja was saying all this in my presence
itself. Today I did not find Banso in the house, and later I got to know
that she had been sent to Pakistan again. Mataji, I had to return to
Shinkiari again with Fajja. On the way I managed to convince Fajja
to take me to Abbottabad, so that I could give a statement before the
district magistrate that I wanted to live in Pakistan of my own free will.
This way at least this daily uncertainty would come to an end. This
time even Banso said the same thing to Khan upon returning from
Pakistan—that rather than packing us off to Pakistan every other day,
it was better to take us to the district magistrate to have our statements
recorded. It so happened that by the time Fajja took me to Abbottabad,
Khan's men brought Banso there. Chacha Allah Baksh too got wind of
it. He was present in the courtroom. Banso was clad in a burqa. I ran to
Chacha Allah Baksh and clutched his waistcoat. He was taken aback,
and when I told him who I was, he said, 'Savinder, marjaaniye, I've
gone crazy looking for you.'
  The people in the court crowded all around us. They didn't let
me appear before any magistrate at all. Banso got frightened and
blurted out before the magistrate that she didn't want to go to India.
Half the people of the group that had come from India were present in
Abbottabad. After enquiring about my condition and circumstances, it
was announced that I should be sent to India. Enquiries are still afoot
regarding Banso. Till the time a decision is taken about her, both of us
have been entrusted to Chacha Allah Baksh's care. I don't know about

Banso, but who knows, I may reach you as soon as you get this letter. Banso is not very sure. She says, 'Who knows if my family will accept me after listening to all this or not.' She is in a quandary; moreover her case is different.

Yours
Savinder

When this letter was given to Asmaan Singh by a member of the rescue party, both husband and wife went to Lahore and camped there. They felt very disappointed when Savinder was not among the women who had arrived. Anyway, they immediately came to know that Savinder had been sent to the Kashmiri refugee camp. It took another three months. Finally the mother and father could get some consolation. Savinder's mother caressed her back and, wiping her tears, asked, 'Any news of your mother-in-law?'

Savinder said, 'I met her accidentally in the camp. Her sight has become very poor; as soon as she met me, she groped all around my neck, then felt my arms. I thought she's looking for signs of any wounds, but when she touched both my earlobes, I realised what she was looking for.'

Translated from the Punjabi by **Hina Nandrajog.**

19 Nothing but the Truth*

MEERA SIKRI

What was the point of ringing the bell, she thought, the Lohri fire will be lit on the roof anyway. Everyone must be there. She went up straight to the roof. For fifteen days she has been trying to come. But now that Shanti Behn has to return to Pakistan in a day or two, how could she stop herself. At last she would be able to meet her, she thought, at last see what Shanti Behn looks like now. The word 'looks' brought a smile to her face. She herself was nearing fifty. Shanti Behn must be at least ten–twelve years older. At this age why worry about looks. And anyhow, meeting in person was another matter.

She got out of breath as she reached the roof on the fourth floor. Music was playing and the children of the house and their friends were swaying to the beat. In the middle a fire was burning in a pit. If only there was a chair she could sit down. She felt dizzy. Without bothering about anyone, she sat down on the last step. Noticing her sit down all of a sudden, some child must have informed Golu, who came and asked her, 'What happened, Mausi?'

'It's nothing really. Bring me some water, beta.' After drinking the water she was able to steady herself; her breathlessness eased somewhat.

---

* Originally published in Hindi as 'Saccho Sach' in *Vibhajan: Bharatiya Bhashaon ki Kahaniyan*, Vol. I, ed. Narendra Mohan (New Delhi: Bharatiya Jnanpith, 2009), 298–303.

What was the need to climb up all the stairs in one breath? After all she is a middle-aged woman now, no longer a girl. It must have been the eagerness to meet Shanti Behn that made her forget herself. After collecting herself fully, she asked Golu, 'Where is Shanti Behnji?'

'They are all downstairs, Mausi. Shanti Behnji is really scared of fire. She won't come up. Can I take you downstairs?'

'No, it is fine. I can go by myself.' She sat for two minutes and then went downstairs. Their drawing room was on the first floor. She had to descend two floors, not as difficult as climbing up for sure.

Although the door to the drawing room was open, there was no one to be seen. She stepped inside, looked about carefully and then saw a woman sitting in a corner.

I have seen her somewhere, she thought. But where? And suddenly it flashed in her mind...

Arre, she was the one who had spoken the previous Sunday at the meeting of the Women Writers' Association on the 'Identity of Women.' She had arrived a little late at the meeting and had not heard the speaker's name. So was *this* indeed Shanti Behnji? She must be some fair-complexioned, overweight Muslim woman with a flabby figure, she had thought. Instead, she turned out to be this slender, graceful and self-absorbed woman. Her bearing was intellectual and she was attractive in a quiet sort of way. Seeing her now, she was brought to a halt in her stride.

The woman had also noticed her standing there, and said, 'Come, come in. Pushpa is probably in the kitchen. I am her cousin sister, Shanti.'

Hearing the name 'Shanti' it was as if she herself was stilled, as if her whole being was attuned just to hearing that name.

'At the Mahila Sangh, you...?' She left the sentence unfinished.

'Yes, it was me.'

'But your name did not feature on the invitation card?' She could remember two other names—Fahmida Riaz and Taslima Nasreen.

Shanti Behnji had sensed her curiosity. She said with utmost simplicity, 'S. Ahmad. There in Pakistan and in Lahore, that is who I am.'

'Shanti Behnji...!' she said, stepping forward, but contrary to her expectations, Behnji neither embraced her, nor, in the fashion of older Muslim women, addressed her as *'Meri jind, meri chann,'* my life, my moon. She simply took her hand in her own, and for a long while she sat like that, clasping her hand.

Years before, in an earlier life, on just such a day, grasping her hand, Shanti Behnji had taken her inside from the *chabutra*. She was the daughter of the owner of the biggest haveli in the street. Even though she did not quite understand what a widow meant, she knew that Shanti Behnji was a child widow.

The huge haveli was built of Makrana stone, the floors of which she polished with her own hands every day. She studied at the Government College perhaps. Clad in a sparkling white outfit, a lace dupatta over her head, she would pass through the street with a serious demeanour. Outside the street, the curtained tonga would be waiting; we would watch her going to college in that carriage. Although watching her gave us pleasure, we were afraid of going near the haveli. All the needy street dwellers would go to Taiji in the mornings for *lassi*. Often children would be sent to the haveli for this purpose, but she always hesitated to go.

She still remembers the day there were no vegetables in the house. Mother sent her to the haveli with the container to get some lassi to make *kadhi*. She made her way to the stairs leading up to the high platform by herself, but there was no one with her who might help her cross the threshold. Who knows how long she might have remained standing there if Shanti Behnji had not spotted her. She took her hand and led her indoors. Despite her protestation, 'We don't need the full bucket of lassi,' she filled it to the brim. And she introduced her to Pushpa. Pushpa was Shanti Behnji's mausi's daughter who had come with her mother from Gujarat, in Punjab, to spend the holidays there. Behnji asked her to come to the haveli every day to play with Pushpa. Pushpa was sent with her so that after taking the lassi home, the two could return to the haveli together.

In childhood how long does it take to become best friends? We used to play with marbles and with a ball. But we were scared of drawing lines with coal on their fine polished floor.

That is why we went to play *shatapu*[1] on the roof. It was there one day that we glimpsed 'him.' On the pretext of bringing back a book, he would approach the parapet around the haveli. Shanti Behnji would often stand us on the raised platform on the stairs, give us things to eat, draw naughts and crosses on our copies and say, 'Play—I will see who wins most often.' It was while we were playing on the roof that we saw 'him'—he had taken Shanti Behnji's hand in his own. She saw us watching her. But after that day she stopped keeping us out of sight or hiding from us. Without her telling us, it must have been our intuitive sense that what had happened near the parapet should not travel downstairs to Taiji.

That day when we went down, we got a harsh scolding from Taiji and Mausiji, '*Moi marjaniyan,*[2] where were you? And where has Shano gone to? We had sent her to find you. In these times of riots, fires are raging everywhere, and you accursed ones have to go upstairs!'

That day Taiji herself dropped me to my house. It was a hot summer day of that year 1947, perhaps May or June.

In our Bajajonwali *gali*[3] Hindu-Muslim riots had spread like wildfire. At that age we were truly terrified but we did not realise the gravity of the situation. Yes, this much I do remember that all the men had gone to the meeting at the gurudwara and had taken the decision—before another riot took place, everyone should leave for Amritsar, Delhi or any other place where they had relations.

A telegram was sent to summon Pushpa's father. No one had any idea who went in which direction. It was only years later that she had met Pushpa in college. She had recently got a job and had enthusiastically given her name for the admissions committee. Pushpa had come there to get her younger sister admitted, and that was how she had found out from her—that her father had tried his best to persuade Taiji that she should not leave mother and daughter behind during such terrifying riots. But Shanti was not ready to come along. Bearing father's anger in mind, Taiji began to pack some ornaments, valuables and essential belongings. When nobody was watching, Shanti Behnji vanished even as a fire suddenly broke out at the back of the haveli. Pushpa's family insists that it was Shanti who lit the fire. If she was hiding somewhere, no one was able to find her. Having no desire to be burnt to ashes in the fire, Shanti's crying mother was forcibly taken away. They only discovered much later that Shanti Behnji was alive and had settled there.

Pushpa's arrival applied brakes to the dappled journey of light and shade that she had embarked upon, holding Shanti Behnji's hand, in that corner of the drawing room. 'Arre Ninna, you've arrived. That's good—otherwise you would not have met her. Behnji is leaving by the morning flight at 4:55 a.m. We will leave the house at 3 a.m. Phone home... we can drop you off on the way back... let us have our meal at once... then the three of us can chit-chat ... Who knows when we might meet again?'

Pushpa was right; this was not the time for long-winded introductions—we were long past the age of hesitation. But simple human curiosity had not yet been overcome.

'Shanti Behnji, in our memory, we still see you framed by "rooftops," "parapets" and fires. Won't you tell us about the crossing of that wall?' said Pushpa.

Perhaps it was the Lohri atmosphere, or perhaps because these were the last few minutes in which she could share her joys and sorrows with those she considered close to her. Shanti Behnji began her story.

'There is a saying in our Punjab: *Kisi nu mah badi, kisi nu naroye*. It is a relativist philosophy. In other words, it is common experience that for some, black lentils induce indigestion, and for others they are delicious and edible. In the same way, the fires that were consuming humanity in those days came like Diwali for me. You people must believe that to win Ahmad I must have lit the fire myself—no, that's not how it was. I don't know how the fire started, though it was the leaping flames that caused me to rise from mother's side. But I will not deny that those leaping flames lit a festive lamp in my life. Ahmad had probably come to the roof to douse the rising flames which he had seen—seeing him there, overcome by passion and without further thought, I crossed the parapet and went over to him, and then we forgot about the fire and hid under Ahmad's staircase for some time. When the commotion died down, we were in Ahmad's house. In those days it was considered a matter of pride to bring Hindu girls to a Muslim household. I have no hesitation in telling you that I had no desire to live the barren life of a widow. My family must have assumed that I had been burnt to ashes in the fire, while I had actually stepped over the wall of fire to freedom. The India-Pakistan Partition had given me freedom as well—I had become free of mores binding mind and body. I had been liberated from false and rigid *samskaras*. One is hemmed in by one's society—the society I called my own was gone, and what I received instead was a new being, a new life, and a new home after marriage to Ahmad. While Ahmad was already married to his father's sister's daughter, there was nothing unusual about a second marriage among his people. But Ahmad felt a deep shame until his dying day on account of a sense of guilt, that in his own estimation, he was not able to give himself to me fully—perhaps it was as a consequence of this guilt that we never had a child. I did change my name from Shanti to Shan Ahmad; but to give me my own space, Ahmad took help from his family to ensure that I could stay in the Government College hostel and complete my B. A. and M. A.. I did an M. A. in English literature, and because of my interest in literature I studied Urdu and Persian literature and undertook comparative research; I became a professor there. Today, it occurs to me that if I had come along with you people, I might have become a victim of an atrocity like rape, living a bewildered, barren, insane life. Instead, by staying back there, I found my identity, and the meaning of being a woman. In my eyes, the nation India did not make sense—even so, I kept remembering mother. Indeed, if the writer's guild had not invited me here, I had no particular desire to meet you people. You feel the absence of those with whom you have had a deep and long relationship. Your world is to be found in your small home—it is your sensibility that connects you to the wider world. You may find this to be a contradiction, but for me this is life's greatest truth. Do not feel offended, it is such a pleasure to meet you, but it was Ahmad who gave me my space, my sense of self, and an independent mind. Today Ahmad is no longer there, but Ahmad's home is there—it is my home, and now I am impatient to get back home.'

Shanti Behnji had stopped speaking. All three of us were quiet. Pushpa broke the silence.

'Behnji, whether you remember us or not, we never forgot you—you were our childhood *heroine*. What difference does it make to us if your name is Shanti Mehra or Shan Ahmad. Look at me, the illiterate one, *sandwiched*[4] between two professors! The two of you, here as well as there, are leading a life of grandeur and dignity—poor me got left behind!' Laughing, Pushpa went on to say, 'My life molders between the oil-press of children's needs and obeying men's commands. See how the time of parting nears—I'm such a simpleton, unable even to hide my tears. Sitting with you, I had begun to feel special, I too had become important.' Then turning her tears into laughter, she got up and said, 'Just you see, I'll bring such steaming hot tea for you—we have to see you off on time after all!'

As Pushpa was going towards the kitchen, both of them observed at the same time that the clock was showing a quarter past two, and Shanti Behnji had once again clasped her hand in her own.

Translated from the Hindi by **Tarun K. Saint**, *with crucial inputs from* Chand Kishore Saint, Ravikant *and* Meera Sikri.

Notes and References

1. Hopscotch.
2. May you perish!
3. Street of cloth sellers.
4. The words 'heroine' and 'sandwiched' are in English in the original.

20 The Other Shore*

SYED MUHAMMAD ASHRAF

The gold-tipped waves gilded by the yellow rays of the setting sun dipping in the northern end of the Arabian Sea crashed upon the shore of Clifton Beach in the city of Karachi, their foam speckled the dun-coloured rocks and slid wetly away.

Even if it wasn't time for the sun to set, and even if the rays were not yellow, the waves rolling in from that direction would have been golden—as bright as molten gold. Because the water that comes to the Clifton Beach from the Arabian Sea is always golden now.

So I thought.

And recognising the envy lurking behind this thought, I was also somewhat abashed. I gave her a quick sideways glance.

She wrenched her gaze away from the waves that were coming and receding from the shore. The blue eyes peeping from behind the strands of dense black hair looked at me. What if she were to read my thoughts? The thought made me suddenly free of fear. I too looked closely at her. She was wearing a long, loose green-coloured garment.

I asked her, 'Are you Sabz Pari, the Green Fairy from the Caucasian Mountain[1]?'

She looked at me incredulously, let out a peal of laughter and said, 'No, I live in the city of Karachi, on Kashmir Road. My name is Uzma and I study in the eighth standard.'

* Originally published in Urdu as 'Doosra Kinara' in *Daar se Bichhre* (New Delhi: Tahleeqkar Publishers, 1994).

Saying this, she smiled in a way people smile when they come across small everyday joys. And I thought that this little Green Fairy was not so little after all that she could follow those small little jokes, nor was she old enough that I could not share such jokes with her.

And so, with great confidence, I asked her, 'If you are not the Green Fairy, why do you look so nice?'

She held my hand, smiled and said, 'Everyone is like this in our family. Come, I will introduce you to all of them. You haven't seen my Papa; it seems as though a radiance is bursting out of his forehead.'

I asked, 'In the land I come from, a radiance bursts from the foreheads of gods. Is your father a deity?'

'No, no, brother, we don't have deities in our country. You people have them,' she smiled but also spoke with some irritation. Then she said, 'Papa will be returning from Multan the day after tomorrow; you can see for yourself,' and fell silent.

I looked at a ray of sunshine returning into the sea and thought, when I had set out from India I had no clear idea about my relatives, especially the youth and children. All I had imagined then was that all the children would sit around me and the young people would stand near me. And all the elderly people would embrace me and ask, 'How are all those people that we had left behind all those years ago? Are they alive, or are they buried in the ruins of the past? And, in that neighbourhood, that ...' And the young people would ask, 'Why do people fight so much in your country? And do you people get admissions in universities easily? And do you people have to go to a lot of trouble to find jobs and do you...'

And the children would ask, 'Have you really seen the Taj Mahal and Qutub Minar that we have seen in photographs? How far is Bombay from where you live? And have you ever seen a shooting of an Amitabh Bachchan film and do you...'

The voice of Sabz Pari called me back to the seashore. She spoke softly, almost secretively in a tone of great affection, 'You have come for ever, haven't you? You are not going to go back, are you?'

I was surprised by her question. 'Bibi, I shall return in fifteen days. I have to join my duty as soon as I reach home.'

'*Arrey...*' is all that she could say.

I saw the colours of amazement flashing across her face, her eyelashes blinking rapidly as she watched me.

'But Arshad Bhai had torn up his passport as soon as he reached here. And now he is in Dubai. And Qaiser Bhai and...'

'No, I will go back.'

Her young mind tried to read my face. But, because I was clever, she could not succeed. Then she spoke suddenly as though she had just discovered a lost weapon, 'The other day we had heard on the radio that there are many ... thousands ... innocent... and last Tuesday they were saying on television that—what is that city called—anyway, forget that... Papa himself was reading out from the paper and telling us that—forget everything else—when we ourselves tuned into All India Radio to hear the songs, we heard the news that once again there has been a...'

I put my hand on her mouth. She removed my hand and said, 'Is everyone else except you lying?'

Then I thought that how certain unimportant moments can be so ferocious. And that is when I also thought what a weak creature I am compared to the television, radio, newspaper, and books. And because I could not answer, I stayed quiet. And because I was quiet, I kept looking at the white-crested waves in the steadily darkening sea.

She too fell silent when she saw that I was quiet. Then she spoke as though she was trying to divert my attention, 'Brother, when you go back to India you must tell your people how many different types of cars you saw. We have come to Clifton in a car. This is a Santro; the other is a Toyota. Then there is the Impala. The most expensive one is a Mercedes; it comes in different sizes. It has six doors. I will show you all these cars. All our relatives have these cars. All of Papa's friends have at least two cars each—really big ones! You people don't have such cars, do you?'

Once again, I was amazed. I stayed quiet. I kept looking at her.

She came close to me and said, 'Brother, why have you fallen silent? Are you remembering your mother and father? Tell me, are you thinking of them?'

I looked at her innocent face. Then I looked towards the sea and the darkening sky and turned back to cross the Sindh desert and, crossing the lush green fields of the Punjab, I reached the *doab* region that falls between the Ganga and Jamuna rivers and saw my quiet little settlement asleep amidst dense mango orchards—my home where I would reach fifteen days from now. When I get off the train at the railway station and take the dirt track, I shall see the moss-encrusted domes from far away. A large gateway will appear after the *dargah sharif*. A courtyard will appear just as one enters the gateway. A haveli-like large house set on a high platform will be immediately visible. When I enter through the main door of this house, as soon as I cross the threshold, I will spot him across the wide courtyard—standing in a verandah with broken niches. I will see the radiance bursting from his forehead. The monsoon rains must be lashing my settlement right now. My father must be standing in one of the alcoves in the verandah and reciting the *'Alhamdo sharif*[2] and blowing it towards the skies. He must be inviting the monsoon to come down to his home so that the fields in his village yield gold and mounds of pearls are stocked in his barns.

I was reminded of him when Sabz Pari asked about my father. Had she taken some other name, I would have been instantly reminded of that because at this moment she held the reins of my mind.

I consoled myself with the thought that even children have begun to make the distinction after hearing the radio and reading the newspapers and school textbooks and watching the television: that this happens in our country and that happens in your country. However, one thing remains undistinguished: our joys and sorrows are the same. Our functions and festivals are the same. Our ways of being happy are the same. Or, at the very least, there is a consciousness that our traditions and ways are still shared.

Sabz Pari changed the direction of my thoughts.

'People come out for a stroll here in the evenings. They get in their cars and zip across to Clifton. You can't see the sea after sunset and so they stop their cars at the edge of the sea but keep their headlights on. The water glimmers for miles in the lights from the cars.'

Once again I was surprised. Once again, I turned to see my father. After the Isha[3] prayer he switches off the big light and switches on the small light. Then, for a long time, he lies on his bed and listens to the news on the radio. God knows which thoughts he is lost in at that time. Then, he recites the Ayat-ul Kursi[4] and claps his hands. Then he asks for safety from Him Who Gives Protection, who gives friendship to friends and enmity to enemies, and then, giving thanks to Allah, lies down to sleep a dreamless sleep. For tomorrow he must rise to face the harsh sun.

A car horn blew somewhere at the back. A Santro or Toyota or Impala or Mercedes came to a standstill but its headlights remained switched on. Our long shadows stretched across the dark and noisome sea and appeared to tremble in the moving waters.

Then, another car came and stopped. Two fat parallel lines from its headlights entered the sea and we could see two brightly lit passages across the water.

Sabz Pari danced with delight.

'Look, brother, look!...Look at how the water is glittering in the light of the car that has just come!'

'Sabz Pari,' I called out to her softly. But my voice sounded strange to my ears. So I fell silent. I couldn't tell her, 'Sabz Pari, you can see the glittering water in the light of the second car, but, if you look a little further, see how our shadows are trembling and swaying in the dark sea.'

God knows why I was surprised by Sabz Pari's happiness. Perhaps this surprise was the remedy for my wound.

'You have become so quiet, brother. Day after tomorrow... you are listening, aren't you... it is Seema's Roza Kushai.[5] You must come. You have to come, or else...'

She said this and fell silent.

We were standing by the rampart. The strong sea breeze was whipping our clothes into disarray.

Trying to holding on to her green dress, she presented a pretty sight. I consoled my heart with the thought that I was right: there is still much between you and us that is common—our rites and traditions, our ways of living, our festivals, our Eids, our *roze*. Dear girl, I will certainly come for the Roza Kushai. Yes, there is still a shore left on which you and I can still stand together.

Patting her hair into place, she came and stood close beside me and spoke with great affection as though trying to explain something to me: 'You must come for the Roza Kushai on Friday or else when you go back home, you won't even be able to tell our family that...'

A strong gust of damp air rose from the sea. It ruffled her hair. She struggled to hold her wildly flying hair and could not complete her sentence.

I looked at her and said, 'Yes, yes, tell me Sabz Pari... what won't I be able to tell?'

Then she answered me with the utmost confidence and conviction, 'You won't even be able to tell people what is a Roza Kushai.'

From somewhere far in the dark sea, a ferocious wave came hurtling through, making a path for itself. It came and crashed near my feet with such force that my entire being seemed to tremble, and I felt as though the shore on which she and I stood would be washed away.

And she was saying, 'You see, brother, what happens is that when a child keeps the *roza* for the very first time, all the friends and family are informed and on that day a lot of guests...'

I kept my hand on her lips and looked into her blue eyes. She was talking to me as though telling me the truth. There wasn't the trace of falsehood in her eyes. There was only belief, utter belief.

Now I could only do one thing—which I did. I patted her wildly flying hair into place. I cupped her bright face in my hands and kissed her softly on her forehead and became silent, and sad.

This time I was not surprised. It was not possible to heal such a large wound with surprise.

Translated from the Urdu by **Rakhshanda Jalil.**

Notes and References

1. The Green Fairy (*Sabz Pari*) is a popular figure in fairy tales told to children. '*Koh-kaaf ki Pari*' is a popular expression for an incredibly beautiful girl. The region of *Koh-kaaf* is said to roughly correspond with a strip of land between the Black Sea and the Caspian Sea, a land where, even today, extremely good looking people are to be found.
2. Also known as the *Surah Fatiha*, it is the first chapter or *surah* of the holy Quran. Its seven verses are a prayer for the guidance, lordship and mercy of Allah. This chapter has an essential role in Islamic prayer; it also serves as an opening for many functions in everyday Islamic life and is used to invoke Allah's blessings.
3. The last of the five daily prayers prescribed for Muslims.
4. Verse 255 of the second chapter, *Surah al-Baqarah* of the Holy Quran, is known as *Ayat-ul Kursi* or the 'Throne Verse.' It is one of the most often recited verses from the Holy Book. In the text here, after reciting the *Ayat-ul Kursi*, the gesture of clapping the hands once (*dastak dena*, as it is referred to in Urdu) is an affirmation that Allah's protection is all around.
5. The first time a child keeps a fast during the month of Ramzan, a dinner is organised for family and friends. The occasion is known as Roza Kushai. *Roza* is the singular for a fast and *roze* is the plural.

21   The Echo*

ZAKIA MASHHADI

Like a tragedy that swallows an entire family, the mammoth truck swallowed all that was in their house.

Wiping her tears with the edge of her shroud, Chachi Amma broke a green leafy twig from the neem tree that stood in a corner of the spacious courtyard. Sniffing noisily she said, 'The fragrance of our neem is so sweet and the breeze passing through its branches so cool.' Then, fanning herself with the sweet-smelling twig of her neem, she returned quietly to her grave.

'Come on, begin in the name of Allah, the All Merciful and Kind,' said Ali Miyan, the property dealer who was distantly related to them. Then he jumped onto the furniture piled up in the truck. The immense vehicle made a great noise, rolled back a little and then surged forward. Soon it disappeared from Meraj's sight.

Babu Pyare Lal's wife appeared from out of the blue. Weeping silently, she dabbed her eyes with the end of her sari. She was Chachi Amma's contemporary.

For some time now, Meraj had become part of a scene which he had never himself witnessed; he had only heard about it from his elders: a big, spacious courtyard, a neem tree standing in a corner with its massive canopy, white cows and black buffaloes tethered in the barn, a pond nearby full of algae, vines of water chestnut and large *rohu* fish. Dark brown little boys swimming along with

---

* Originally published in Urdu as 'Sada-e Baazgasht' in *Sada-e Baazgasht* (New Delhi: Educational Publishing House, 2002).

ducks, splashing water, getting entangled among the vines and disentangling themselves to break water chestnuts.

Whenever Meraj's elders stole some moments of togetherness, this scene was written and re-written upon the susurrating winds. Chachi Amma and Babu Pyare Lal's wife who had come to see off Chachi Amma and had brought some traditional items on a flat winnowing basket to wish her good luck. Sniffling incessantly, Babuji's wife waved the basket around her friend's head in a gesture of warding off ill luck and smiled through her tears. 'One should not wish good bye weeping; it is a bad omen,' she said and started crying all over again.

Many such scenes were painted by Meraj's older relatives. Meraj had not witnessed them first hand, but they had been repeated so many times that they had become a part of his psyche; he had virtually grown up with them. Besides, though he had not seen Pyare Lal's wife crying, he had certainly seen his mother wiping her eyes quietly on many occasions, telling stories that still haunted her.

'You were not even born then, and your elder sister was just two months old,' went one of the stories. 'I was still weak after a complicated delivery. Times were such that even the rustle of leaves made people prick their ears. And in those uncertain times our street was rocked by stomping feet and loud voices that shouted aggressive slogans. Shopkeepers downed their shutters, people ran helter-skelter and women started wailing inside their houses, worrying about those who were out in the open.'

'What happened then, Amma?'

'I decided that I could not bear the sight of my children being slaughtered mercilessly. I would push all three of them into the well in our courtyard and then jump in myself. Your grandmother was alive then; she agreed.'

Meraj was thoroughly confused. Children were strictly forbidden to go near the well. If any of them was ever spotted in its vicinity, people started shouting and ordering them to immediately move away. And here, the same ever-watchful Amma was saying that she was going to throw her children into the well—all three of them. And Dadi had agreed!

'Why were the times like that, Amma?'

'I never found the answer to this question. Perhaps you will when you grow up,' she said ruefully.

(Meraj could not figure out a satisfactory answer even when he grew up and became a lawyer. In fact, no one did. The volumes of books that tried to solve this puzzle also failed.)

'What happened next, Amma? Obviously, we were not thrown into the well.'

'Just then someone brought the news that all was well; it was just a fight between two groups of contesting wrestlers. Ordinary citizens were not involved. Though tense moments were not infrequent, our little town was one of those fortunate places where, by and large, peace prevailed.'

'And then?'

'The town expanded, engulfing the farm lands and parts of the jungle around. Some industries were established; a couple of hotels came up. The intermediate college became a degree college; the town got the status of a district but...' Amma grew quiet; her face betrayed the anguish that always gnawed at her heart. After a pause she picked up the conversation again.

'But they never returned.' This time her voice betrayed the tears, tears that welled up from somewhere deep inside her.

'*Who* never returned, Amma?'

'Your Nana, that is my father, my brother and his family, your paternal uncle, his wife and children, and so many of our clan. We were left alone to bear the brunt of events we never wanted.'

Meraj had no concept of a nana since he had never known one. His father's father he knew well as he had lived till Meraj was old enough. But of course, a nana figured in the ditty that his Dada's friend Babu Pyare Lal used to sing to Meraj:

Nana, Nana, bhookh lagi; Khalo beta moongphali
Moongphali mein dana nahin; tum hamare nana nahin

Nana, Nana, I am hungry; Have some peanuts sonny,
Peanuts have no nuts inside; you are not our Nana, right?

For Meraj, a nana was like one of those characters he came across in tales like Alladin in 'Alladin and his Lamp' or 'Sindbad the Sailor' or a gnome in fairy tales. He recited the ditties with relish. But one day when he was reciting one of them, the roti Amma was baking on the hot girdle burnt to a cinder as she, forgetting the roti, had buried her head between her knees and started crying. Shamael, Meraj's father, was very angry with Chacha Pyare Lal. Once Amma's family had also lived in the same town, just a few miles away in the suburbs. They would often come to meet Amma and her in-laws. Amma's brother Wassey and Shamael were friends. But after Partition, Dada, realising that Amma's family was thinking of opting for Pakistan, had become wary of their visits, especially Wassey's. He thought Wassey may influence his son Shamael to migrate with his family. The very idea sent a chill down the septuagenarian's spine.

One day his patience reached the brim. Without mincing words Dada said to Wassey, 'Look, son, you should not come to your married sister's house so often. It is not seemly. Besides, I doubt your intentions. Listen carefully: I am dead against this two-nation theory of Jinnah and some of the deviant Congresswalas. I am one of those millions of Muslims who consider India to be their home. I will die and be buried here. Shamael, his children and their children's children will come to my grave to say *fatiha* over it. So don't you dare try brainwashing Shamael and your sister.'

'But Chacha,' perhaps Wassey Mamu was also in the mood for a showdown, 'Shamael Bhai is my brother-in-law, my own sister's husband; his future is very much my concern. I want his family to be safe. And for that matter, you too. So I am only making him see the light.'

'Only the future will tell how *enlightening* this "light" of yours will be. You better mind your own business. Just let us know when you are leaving; we will come to say good bye.' Dada turned his back on him, muttering, 'God only knows how many millions will be carried away by this unfortunate high tide.' His voice betrayed his anguish.

Wassey Mamu's family, whom Mamu had shepherded to safety in 1948, came back to India in 1971—devastated, sans all their belongings...and Wassey Mamu. They were now foreigners in India, which had once been their homeland. Like a bullet that has been shot or words that have been spoken, they could not be taken back. After initial sympathies and help from relatives, they were sent to Karachi.

Wassey Mamu's body could never be recovered. This time Amma's anguish was beyond recovery. A permanent depression took over her.

So many times history has committed blunders, blunders that could not be reverted. But can't people let the past be past and start afresh to minimise the painful aftermath? Hundreds and thousands of right-thinking people tried to find an answer to the question but failed; peace still evaded the subcontinent. Time flew by.

A major portion of the joint property of the four brothers was taken over by the Government. Children grew up without knowing many of their first cousins, uncles and aunts. Meraj, too, grew up and studied law to fulfill the wishes of his father and grandfather, married, had children and shifted to a big city nearby as there were greater opportunities for his career.

One day an elderly gentleman came to see Meraj. He had gone to Pakistan to visit some relatives. Meraj's cousin, Huma, had sent some photographs and gifts for his children. When the children were shuffling the photographs and asking about their unseen relatives, Meraj told them, laughing, 'Huma could have been your mother as Mamu wanted me to marry her.'

The teenagers were quite amused, though their mother gave them a stern look.

'Then? What happened then?' they asked mischievously.

Meraj grew serious. 'Abba and Dada both blew their tops. They were dead against Mamu opting for Pakistan. So they abhorred the idea of having any matrimonial alliance with his family. It was not only for personal reasons; relations between the two countries were never predictable. Besides, these family elders, along with many others, were against the principle of partition. They could never buy the two-nation theory. Though they had never joined active politics, they were die-hard supporters of Nehru and Gandhi.'

'And yet those humiliating slogans were written on the walls of our house,' said Meraj's daughter ruefully.

'And when Pakistan won a cricket match, the boys in my school said that for me it was time to celebrate. I was dumbfounded; I could not even understand why,' said her brother.

'Now you know the reason,' the girl said bitterly.

'Papa, you know,' she continued, 'This time there was a tie between two girls contesting for the Miss India title. Judges asked a question as a tie-breaker: "Given the power, which tragedy in the history of India would you like to avert?" One of the girls answered, "Indira Gandhi's assassination," and she won. If I were in her place I would have said, "Partition of the country".'

Meraj gave her an intent look. There was pain on her face.

If the country was not divided, perhaps the situation which gave rise to the murder of Indira Gandhi would not have arisen, and perhaps Babri mosque, too, would not have been demolished, and had the Babri mosque not been demolished...!

A riot had broken out in the city and though the area was some distance away from Meraj's house, the tension in the air was palpable. So when someone pounded the door, the entire family was terror-stricken. But just then they heard Meraj's friend, Jaiprakash, calling, 'Come on, Meraj, open the door! The rioters are coming to our area. Hurry, I have come to take you out...!' In a flash of a second a shadow of doubt crossed Meraj's wife's mind. The elders of the family had often mentioned that during the Bihar Sharif riots, it was neighbours, close friends and domestics of long standing who had betrayed people, leading to large-scale killings and destruction. But Meraj opened the door. An exasperated

Jaiprakash instructed them to quickly pick up some cash, jewelry and clothes and leave immediately. He, then, huddled them into his car and brought them to the safety of his house. Before leaving he removed Meraj's name plate.

After millennia of evolution the world had become highly complicated. Religion, class, caste, region, avarice, lust for power dominated. The showroom of the local rich cloth merchant was looted, not so much for rendering a Musalman pauper as for possessing a good warm coat.

Jaiprakash was receiving threats for giving protection to Meraj's family. Ram Nath Tiwari, too, was intimidated though he had not given protection to anyone; he had simply formed a peace committee to help restore normalcy.

Once the riots abated, Meraj returned, but Jaiprakash advised him to shift to some other place. 'I am not worried about my own safety; they won't kill me,' he said. 'But I may become helpless should some fresh trouble erupt. Won't it be better for you to shift to a neighbourhood of your own?'

'...A neighbourhood of your own,' the words pierced his heart like an arrow. More than half a century ago Pyare Lal Chacha had advised Meraj's grandfather to shift at least his son Shamael and his family across the border, to their 'own' land. 'Stay if you want to, but Shamael is still young; his whole life is ahead of him. Why do you want to put them to a disadvantage?' He had accepted Wassey Mamu's logic. Nobody could doubt his intentions; all this was said in good faith. But Dada was stung. Just like Meraj.

'Isn't this area my own? I have the right to live in this part of my country, in the house built with my own hard-earned money?'

Dada, perhaps, had uttered the same words albeit with much more anger and bitterness.

'Meraj, this area has suddenly become unsafe for you. There are only a couple of houses which belong to your community. When life is at risk, idealism takes a back seat. A property dealer told me that they are thinking of shifting. You, too, should think over it, my friend. You and your family are very dear to me,' Jaiprakash sounded genuinely concerned.

'Jaiprakash, could you tell me which place offers me foolproof security? What are the areas I can call exclusively my own? Some ghettos do exist, but do you really think I should shift to one of them? Can't I live where I want to in my own country?'

Jaiprakash scratched his head. It was almost a reflex action. Then he said, 'There may be better options if you look for them. But in your own area you will at least be saved from tensions which crop up every other day. It is so unfortunate that festivals like Durga Puja and Baqr Eid cause tension at times.'

Who is this person and who is he talking to? Is it Pyare Lal Chacha talking to Dada, or is it Jaiprakash talking to me, thought Meraj.

After weeks of sleepless nights, Meraj called Ali Miyan.

When the landlord was handing over the keys to Meraj, a man sipping tea at the nearby stall commented, 'This time the riots taught a good lesson to these sahibs living in posh colonies who have been riding their high horses all this while. They are now taking refuge in our humble neighbourhood.'

Meraj was stung by a strong feeling of guilt. No one could force his father or grandfather to leave though the times were more turbulent then. And here he was selling his beautiful house in that good locality, moving here, and facing such taunts. But then, is safety not above everything? Is Jaiprakash not right? Did his wife, Shahida, not agree to come here for the same reason?

And so after some running around involved in selling and buying of the property, the truck arrived and swallowed all their belongings like a tragedy that swallows a family, a community or even a whole region.

With tearful eyes both families said goodbye to each other. 'Hope you will come soon to visit us in our new house,' Shahida said.

'We will keep visiting each other whenever we have time. You don't have to say it, Bhabhi,' Jaiprakash said with a lump in his throat.

'I hope there won't be any risk involved if we go to that area.'

Though they had almost gotten into the car, Meraj's wife overheard Sudha whispering into her husband's ear. A shadow of anguish flit across her face. Quietly she wiped her tears as the car lurched forward and followed the truck.

Translated from the Urdu by **Zakia Mashhadi.**

22　Allah-ho Akbar*

AMENA NAZLI

'A llah-ho Akbar! Allah-ho Akbar!'
It was after a long time today that I could hear the
sound of the *Fajr* calls for prayers!

And after all, why not? This was our own land and it was for
the sake of this land that we had allowed our children and women
to be thrown into the oil press, crushed and destroyed.

Rubbing my eyes I hurried towards the mosque, which was
close to the station.

'Imam Sahib!' I called out.

Huddled in blankets, he was calling for prayers from his bed!

'Yes, yes...' He hurriedly got up from bed, baring his teeth and
straightening his lungi.

'Look here, *hazrat*, is this the way for calling out the *azan*?' I
asked, glaring at him.

'Heh heh. Don't be angry, sir! I swear upon you, this has
become my habit that I call out for azan during my sleep. If you
ask me, it is now over an hour for the time of the azan.' He yawned,
opening his mouth wide.

'So when will the congregation be ready for offering prayers?'

'Sir, in just two minutes!' he said while trying to straighten out
his beard with both hands.

'But there is no one here!' I said, looking past the door.

---

* Originally published in Urdu as 'Allah-ho Akbar' in *Bare Feet*
(Karachi: Ismat Book Depot, 1969).

'You and me,' he replied, quickly placing the cap on his head, and started mumbling his prayers.

It was getting close to the time for my train. But I still offered two *nafil* in gratitude.

'O sherwani-walah! Are you blind?' a passenger shouted at me with a hand on his bundle of dried lentils.

'Just move this bundle to the side, please! It will be very kind of you!' I looked at the train compartment filled to the brim and tried to appease him.

'No, I will not move it aside. *You* keep away—keep out!' He bristled with anger.

'Why are you all coming out of your country?' said an old woman, looking at me as if she would eat me alive.

'Traitors! They are all traitors. Don't give them any space!' An old man with round eyes glared at me as if I would snatch everything belonging to him.

'All right, don't give any space!' In despair, I stood by the compartment door.

There was a mad rush at the railway platform. Scratched and torn old women, weary and aged men and loudly wailing children who were hardy enough to have survived. Having survived, who knows what sort of ticks and fleas they must be carrying.

Close by, a Pathan stood next to a Kashmiri girl, twirling his moustaches, and a frail-looking babu was asking him, 'Khan, what will you do with her?'

'I will do nothing with her,' the Khan replied with indifference.

'Then why not sell her? Tell me how much will you take for her?' the babu asked hesitatingly.

'No, never! What do you know! I had to go through so much trouble to get her, this progeny of the *kafirs*. After all, so many of our women they took away, the sons of pigs. Now I will get her married to my eldest son. He is a strapping young man!'

The Khan's bloodshot eyes were filled with revenge.

'But Khan, she says that she has done her BA. How can she keep house for your son?' The babu was trying to coax him.

'But my son is educated, too, mister! I swear by God that he can read the Holy Quran. The Holy Quran!' the Khan retorted, puffing up with pride.

I had reached the largest city of my country, the one with the most hustle and bustle.

'Are you looking for a hotel?' a gentleman asked me.

'Yes; is there a decent one?' I asked looking at the flourishing market area.

'An excellent one, sir! Look there!' he said, pointing towards a tall and imposing building. 'Right in the centre of the city! And there is a ball room, too, sahib. A fine one. It will make you happy.'

'Is that so?'

I started climbing the staircase quickly.

'Look here, sir, do you like this room?' he asked me, standing at the entrance of a room.

'Yes, yes. It is all right,' I said hurriedly.

'Why don't you see it first?' The man was looking at me in surprise.

'Yes, I have seen it,' I said keeping my handbag on the table.

'And look, the room on your left, a great *maulana* is staying here. Oh what fiery speeches he delivers, sir! His voice can bring tears to his listeners' eyes. Only yesterday he gave a speech in the park next door!'

'What was the topic?' I asked.

'Oh, the same topic of abducted women. He has entranced many young men. Would you like to meet him?'

'Why not! Certainly.' I displayed my eagerness to meet him.

'Would you like to take a bath, sir?' a servant entered the room and asked me.

'No, tea ... get me some tea first.'

'Very well, sir!' he said and went out of the room.

There was a great hustle and bustle in the market place. I pulled my chair close to the window. A number of couples were rushing ahead, arm in arm.

'Don't let anyone grab. Hold firmly!'

An idle young man pressed his friend's shoulder and shouted, 'See the one in the *gharara*!'

'And that *shalwar*! Soft as a snakeskin!'

'But where have their braids gone?' the first man asked in amazement.

'The sahibs took them away!' the second one replied.

'And look at that burqa, like the moon peeping out!'

'You are right. She has done a marvelous job of painting herself. She must be about forty. But very attractive.'

'You are a perfect owl! Can a woman of forty years have such firmness?'

In hot pursuit of a young girl, both of them turned into the alley up ahead.

'The food is good in this hotel!'

I was chewing the gritty leg bone of a partridge.

'Do you want anything else, sir?' The hotel boy stood behind me with folded hands.

'Anything else...' I began to think.

'Yes, we have all kinds available.'

'What?' I asked looking at him intently.

'The government has put up the prohibition law, but we have old ones and fine ones, all kinds available.' He poured water from the jug and placed it in front of me.

'So how does one obtain it?' I asked him in surprise.

'With a bit of give and take. From the black market. It fetches high prices, sahib. But what to do? For the sake of our guests. Just let me know, what would you like?'

'But I don't want any.'

I lit a cigarette and lay down on the bed.

'Sahib, the dance has begun. It's Saturday today. The golden night! We have a better gathering here today than all other hotels. Would you like to dance?' A frail and uniformed worker of the hotel was trying to tempt me.

'Ye...yes—all right!'

I changed and walked towards the ball room.

The enchanting sounds of the piano reverberated in the large room. Reflected in the coloured lights there was abundant youth and slippery steps! Just like several pairs of water fowl swimming together.

I sat on a table close to the verandah. The whole place was fragrant with beautiful smells. And if on such an occasion some cheapskate opened up bottles of *henna* or amber, how repulsive that would be! I rested my head on the back of the chair.

'Why have you walked out, my friend? Dance some more with that girl!' Two young men were talking at the table next to me.

'No, my friend! You are set to insult me!' the other one replied.

'You are no less than anybody in dancing. This I declare!' The first one tried to boost him up.

'But her dancing is wonderful. She even ticked off a number of Americans while dancing!' he replied, his spirit flagging.

'I swear by God, if only I knew a little bit of dance, I would crash into her!' said the first one.

'Why are you dying for her?' the second one asked scratching his head.

'You don't know, my friend. She is from the same place where I come from. She is the daughter of a distinguished family from my own city. After all there is something called love for one's place!' He sighed.

'Do you know her then?' He stared at his friend in surprise.

'Yes—she's the youngest daughter of the seniormost imam! He was a tremendously learned scholar, and Englishmen would shiver when facing him! Silvery, flowing beard, milk and honey complexion glowing in the black dress he wore. He had an air of dignity. That is why there is only one like her in the entire hall.'

'Look, another person is turning towards her—that dark one—fatso!' He pointed out.

A delicate waist swinging in the gharara was in the hands of a fat Christian.

A lizard stuck to the black column. Waves of nausea passed through my entire body in quick succession.

'Sahib, should I get somebody to serve you?' A servant who looked like a pimp stopped me on my way.

'What do you mean?' I looked him over from head to toe.

'Huzoor, they are badly afflicted, but are gentle folk! She comes from your own country, recovered and refugee! They come from very respectable families, sahib! In these times, it will be like aid for them.'

'Aid?' My whole body began to tremble.

'Yes, and all arrangements for them are made with utmost care. Nailing the mouths of higher-ups... You must have heard that our government has prohibited prostitution. This is why...!'

'This is something good which the government has done...' My eyes had a questioning look.

'Some good, huzoor! You should ask us! They have all moved out to live in neighbourhoods where the gentle folks live. They have started living like housewives, and in days like these, which gentleman will be able to make them out?'

Yes, who will be able to make them out, I wondered as I lay tossing and turning on my bed.

'Maulana Sahib, from among the women recovered ... that girl is stunningly beautiful.' Somebody was speaking in the next room.

'You are right, my dear. Ever since I have seen her, I have been greatly moved.'

'So what do you think then?' asked the first voice.

'About what?' said the second heavier voice.

'In my opinion, you should set up your house, Maulana Sahib.'

'What do you mean?' The Maulana pretended not to understand.

'Sahib, you must get married to that girl. This will make your position very strong. People will literally start worshipping you! And day before yesterday, so many young men were entranced by your speech!'

'But my dear, I am not a novice player!' The Maulana's voice was dignified.

'But Maulana Sahib, she is the prettiest of the lot. You will be distinguished in high society.'

'What to say?' (There was a pause.) 'My heart does not go towards her—a kind of revulsion—but do bring her over some day! Perhaps I can aid her a little. But after nine o'clock!' The Maulana cleared his throat.

Why can't I fall asleep today? I turned violently towards the other side of the bed—some dark shadows crept outside and that pimp-like person was talking in a hushed tone.

'This is the hell everybody has to feed.'

I took out two analgesics from my bag and swallowed them.

The partridge was really delicious today. Slowly and gradually my eyelids began to get heavy.

Translated from the Urdu by **Asif Aslam Farrukhi.**

23   A Face to Hate*

JOYA MITRA

For the last two days a problem was pestering me, one that had to be solved at the earliest. There were problems every day, one couldn't avoid them, but most of them were common ones, like a family member sick or the children's studies or jobs or some misunderstanding with loved ones. These one had to negotiate. It was all in the game. Some of these even had to remain unresolved. What more could ordinary people like us do?

In fact, I wonder if there was any end to problems in life. They were with us even before we were properly aware of things. My earliest memory of that was in Khulna. The 'Independence Day' jubilation in school. I was perhaps in class two. A flag hoisting, the headmaster's speech of which everything was Greek, small packets of sweetmeat that I brought back for Buli at home. She was too small to go out. And the stronger memory of the next day, or it might have been a couple of days later. It was just the opposite of 'Independence Day.' Everyone going around with grim faces, Didu sobbing, strangers in the house! A hushed atmosphere while Ma packed things. For a while, I was happy because packing meant going out to places. But there was something in the air that told me nothing good was going to happen. Later we knew that at the time of Partition, Khulna had been allotted to India for the first

* Originally published in Bangla as 'Ghrinar Samasya' [The Problem of Hate] in *Kal Porshur Dharabahik* (Calcutta: Karuna Prakashani, 1990/91).

two days, and then the decision was reversed. How absurd it all had been! Just like someone playing cards, shuffling the pack this way or the other. And it was about a whole country, nothing less. Uprooting millions of people from one place and throwing them away somewhere else. No question of rehabilitation even on the smallest scale.

I do not remember other details of the time. Only the bullock carts coming in the evening. Leaving home with Baba and our whole family, Didu, uncles and all. It was dark all around. Memories of the time came like snapshots taken in the olden cameras. Only they were different shots without any continuity. I remember crossing a river by boat, both Buli and me under the cover of Ma's shawl. It was pitch dark. The river was black. Only two quivering reflections of lights, like the two *zari* borders on Goddess Durga's saree during Durga Puja. Then, a heavily crowded train, and a strangely clear memory of Baba offering me a piece of papaya that looked like a soft yellow boat. That was about all. Later, when I tried to recall all of it, I just could not fathom how the elders must have felt then. Not only about going to a totally unknown destination in an unknown country, but leaving home, and the place where they had lived for generations. For good! I am yet to understand how far an individual was a product of nature and how far he or she was a product of his or her surroundings. You took away that surrounding, home and locality and all—wouldn't the person tumble down, too?

I knew this was what we would call politics. These policies were made and decisions taken by people in very high positions. Perhaps they did not care about these sentiments because they never had to face similar situations or perhaps they were often too busy for this 'motherland' type of emotion. Maybe this was why most of the displaced people turned against the sitting political party of that time. Though I wasn't sure how sincere the other parties were about addressing the people's plight, but most of us became members of Left parties after that.

Still, that was mainly about the men folk. Didu, Ma and others like them suffered in their own ways. I felt this more whenever I remembered Chacha-jan. Chacha-jan had been the owner of the house we were living in at Park Circus in Kolkata. Our 'properties' were exchanged. But of course, that was much later. After the crossover, we were first dumped in a place in Barasat. Then Baba managed a job, I didn't know how he did that, but a year or two later, he shifted us to a thatched house. I restarted my schooling at Barasat, Buli along with me. We shifted to Park Circus when I was in class seven and Buli in five. Dada was put into a boys' hostel for better studies for he was already in his final class before the school-leaving exams. That house was a better one, with more rooms and more space. This was the home of one Mr. Faijuddin who had a motor mechanic shop alongside his house. Baba's income was inadequate for a family of six. Yet Ma managed. It was Didu we heard lamenting at times, particularly when she noticed a lack of fish or milk in our diet.

'Back home we had such wonderful cows,' she would moan. 'Not one but two of them...we even used to give out milk to the neighbours' kids...'

Usually it was Ma who cut her short, 'What is gone is gone. No use crying over that, Ma. They will have to learn to live under the present conditions. Think how many had to face far worse.'

One day, Mr. Faijuddin came to our house, a house that was not long ago his family's residence. Just back from school, we came upon him, a stranger, sitting with Baba in the front room. Didu was with them. He left soon after our arrival to return the next morning. By that time we knew who he was. He had also told Baba that his son-in-law was in the Pakistani border security force, and had helped him cross over to visit his old home. Didu asked him so many questions about the small details of the house she had to leave behind! Questions about the house, the courtyard, the pond at the back, even the recesses in the walls! We were astounded to find Ma standing behind the door, listening intently. This was so unlike her. Baba was perhaps a bit embarrassed and suggested Didu should stop, but Mr. Faijuddin (on Baba's instructions, we were by then addressing him as Chacha-jan) requested Baba not to stop her.

'Bhaijan, we do not speak up because of etiquette. We cannot express openly what we feel in our hearts. Please don't prevent those who can. Your Bhabi over there is in the same state of mind as Amma here. Your place there, you know, is so big with the large courtyard, a pond, so many trees, and yet she pines bitterly for this place. I don't stop her. We too weep through their tears, you know.'

When he came the next year, he brought some mangoes from 'our trees' with him. Didu's eyes were full. Baba enquired about Chacha-jan's sons. By then his boy was studying in Daulatpur College. Baba had been a student of the same college. Chacha-jan took a long walk around the Park Circus Maidan before he left. It must have been his playground or a place where he had spent time with his friends, I wondered. Didu's health had visibly deteriorated in the last few years. She did not suffer any particular ailment or disease as such. She was just getting smaller day by day. Ma had difficulty in making her eat at all. With time, Didu spoke less and less. Mostly she used to lie in her bed. Her face, arms and legs were somewhat distended. The little that she spoke was mainly about Daulatpur. Returning from office, Baba would go and sit by her bed and would stay there until she went to sleep. At times Didu seemed to forget where she was. She would mumble about the trees in Daulatpur, the cowshed, and even call her 'Nayan Bou,' my mother, to ask if she had bolted the door to the backyard. Sometimes she would ask Ma to open the 'large wooden box' to spread the warm clothes in the courtyard sun. Ma would move away from Didu's bedside to wipe her brimming eyes.

That year Chacha-jan had come again. Even a quiet and composed person like him could not hold back tears when he saw Didu's condition. In all those years, that was the only night he stayed back at our place. He sat down to dinner with Baba after Didu fell asleep and said, 'If it had been within my powers, I would surely have taken Ammi-jan to her house, even if only for a day. The folks who live within these four walls, Bhaijan, it is they who turn these walls into a home. And how it hurts them to leave that home behind...'

As far as I can remember this was the only time we heard Baba talking on the issue. He said, 'Some people cut a living country into two simply because it suited their own interests, and couldn't have cared less about the bloodshed. The lives of thousands of people turned topsy-turvy in a day. Whether tempers ran high or love prevailed, we lived in unison at our own places. No one wished to abandon their homes or property to go and live among new people in an unknown country. The self-seekers added fuel to fire, and we paid for it. You paid for it. The leaders sat together so many times to finalise the partition of the country, but did not bother to ask people like us even once.' We had no idea that our cool and calm Baba hid such fiery thoughts within his slight form.

Didu passed away within a month of Chacha-jan's visit. After that he came only once. Hearing the news, he sat dumbly on the steps to the terrace, his head in his hands. This time he had brought many photographs of Daulatpur—of the house, the windows from outside, the road in front of the house, the college, the grocer's shop at the turn of the road. He left the photographs with Ma. He assured us that he would come again. He did not. We had heard that the border patrolling has been intensified after that year. It was 1964, the year of the India-Pakistan conflict. Everywhere, even in our locality, one would hear of the 'Pak paratroopers.' All of a sudden people had become enthusiastically patriotic. Zealous youths rounded up rag-pickers as 'Pakistani spies' many a times.

Everything around us was changing fast, like in a whirlwind. Baba was a broken man by then. Or was it since Didu's death that the ending began? Buli was married off and sent to Dhanbad. That made the house feel emptier than ever.

Dada had finished graduation and had landed a job at the Sen-Raleigh factory near Asansol. He left to live there. In spite of all the hardships our parents suffered, they had always been serene. They both battled their way forward bravely in their own ways. They never seemed upset or cross. Were they in low spirits sometimes? Yes. But disturbed and confused? No. At least we had never seen them like that.

I grew up to be a very ordinary person with an ordinary job. Tanu is now the only person I value in my life. But our family remained limited to just the two of us. We had managed well throughout our life, but for this one crisis of being childless. It hurt Tanu more than it hurt me. Up to a time, everyone had to say one or two words to her about how to get rid of the 'misfortune.' At times she insisted on seeing some holy man or the other, but I always declined. We saw doctors but that did not help. I repeatedly told her to accept what we could not alter. I knew that she tried to do that, but it was difficult for someone who spent most of her time indoors. In recent years, strangely, I found that her problems had returned in peculiar ways. She was often irritated with me, wanted me to abide by her in almost all matters. Even on small issues I found her to be quite different from what she used to be earlier. For example, the matter of Rathin's daughter's marriage! Oh no, not the marriage itself, it was only a proposal. Rathin and Meena rejected it because the horoscopes did not match. Their 'guru' said so! Rathin of all people! It was too much for me.

We had been friends for years. We were in the same school in the 'refugee colony,' as our neighbourhood was often described. We went to college together, courted together and married at around the same time. But his lot was not as plain sailing as mine. Rathin was from a high-born brahmin family and Meena's caste was lower. How could that be helped? Cupid hardly paid attention to horoscopes and castes. Great hullabaloo ensued. Breaking the caste barrier, going against the family norm of patriarchy, Rathin became our hero. When this Rathin cancelled his daughter's marriage proposal on some guru's word, I could not swallow it and jokingly remarked, 'Which horoscopes did you match when you were getting married?' To my astonishment, Rathin was deeply offended! He said that I was digging up his family scandals. Scandal? So he considered his own marriage to be a scandal now? When later I related the whole incident to Tanu, she blamed me. 'That is quite normal,' she said. 'Everyone is not like you. No adherence to any custom, not the least piety even at this age!' Tanu had changed, too. Had I? I didn't know. I understood Tanu's change. The void still hurt her. Hence, all the pujas and pledges. A couple of times I tried to argue with her, 'Why do you make these offerings to gods? Does your god seek bribes?' She was livid at my questions. She had calmed down with time but the wound was still there, only it did not show on the surface any more. Ma never said anything to her about being childless, but my brother's wife had taken an occasional dig at her. That resulted in a distance between Tanu and my sister-in-law. Finally, we had to move out of the family home. My posting in the LIC office helped, but this moving out from my parent's house was difficult. A man's first memory is, of course, with his parents and my memory was, no doubt, a bizarre one. Still, that day I tried to make light of the situation and quipped, 'Why do you say so? Which discipline of your household do I flout? Is that not adherence?'

'It is not that. Why do you always have to adopt a stance that is different from the others?'

'What do you mean others, Tanu? Instead of having a few words with you over tea when I come home from office, should I flop down in front of the TV?' Tanu was exasperated but laughed nonetheless. She did not forget, though.

But the problem that troubled me recently was not of this nature. In fact, it was different from anything I had faced in my life till now. The drawback appeared to be graver for it came from younger people whom one thought to be more progressive. It started off rather casually. The air in the country had been hot about truckloads of bricks with a god's name embossed on them found on different roads of the country! There was communal tension over the matter. Lunch hour was almost over in the office canteen but the place was alive with all kinds of discussions. Only last month we heard about curfew being clamped in Asansol and deployment of the army. We had reasons to feel concerned. Akhil's daughter lived in Asansol and the son-in-law was a building contractor. He had to go out at odd hours. But recently, Akhil's daughter came to visit her parents and, to our relief, said that nothing untoward took place in Asansol. The police were perfectly in control of the situation. The curfew was more as a security measure. This led our usual lunchtime small talk to the role of the police as reported in the Mumbai riots. Many newspapers commented that police personnel were inactive when *bastis* of particular communities were torched. Apparently the police were abiding by the local political parties rather than the administration. It was time to leave the canteen and proceed to our respective departments while I held forth that nothing in this country could function properly because of political interference. There were a few familiar young faces from the computer section sitting at the next table. We did not notice that they had stopped talking to get a drift of our conversation. Before I could finish my remark, one of them came up to us and said in an unusually aggressive tone, 'You have made it a habit to criticise your own country in any case, isn't it? Don't you ever notice the unity of the people in the other religion? The whole sect will stand by whatever their leader says. And look at us—no love for our own country. No faith in our own religion. The ones you were criticising, have they harmed you? They were only trying to protect their own co-religionists; was that so bad?'

I looked around to find only Akhil and myself at the table; the others had slipped off. These boys worked in our office. I had seen their faces so many times on my way in or out, but they seemed unfamiliar now. The insolence with which they were speaking, within office premises, to a colleague at least twenty-five years their senior was unimaginable. Most of the tables were vacant. Though some from the new business section men were seated at two tables near the cash counter, not a single eye turned towards us. They seemed oblivious of anything outside their own conversation. From behind my shoulders, Akhil muttered something like, 'Then I... leave ...the section...' So Akhil too was leaving. I took a look at the young men again. Expensive clothes. Not all of them were completely buttoned up. Coloured stone lockets on silver chains could be seen around the necks of two; a third sported a rudraksha bead. Five of them were standing around me as if ready to pounce. I suddenly felt creepy. At the same time, anger raged within me. One of them challenged, 'Why don't you say something?'

'What is there to say? This is one of the country's major industrial centres. People of different castes and creeds have always lived here peacefully. We can hardly afford to take a step that would disturb the poor people's livelihood here...'

'Poor people, indeed! They are breeding like house flies everywhere in this country. And when these poor people of yours go around tearing down hundreds of temples in their own country? Why do you keep mum then?'

'If that has really happened, it should surely be condemned, but it is also true that rumours spread easily. Moreover, is there any point in killing an innocent man just because somebody somewhere else is doing the same?'

By now the room was empty except for the boys and I. Satya, who ran the canteen, was looking this way from his counter. For a fleeting second our eyes met. I felt there was concern in his eyes. I gathered myself and stood up straight.

'Look, discussions on such issues cannot be finished off so easily. In my opinion, religion is a very personal issue that should not be dealt with by force. Riots are hardly any solutions to questions... Anyway, we can talk about it later. Now I have to go back to work. Lunchtime is long over, you know...' I moved away without waiting for an answer. As soon as I reached the door, a comment flew,

'Bloody bastard...' Something snapped in my mind. Should I go back and challenge them? Again I was unsure. Did they want to pick up a fight?

Back at my desk, I was restless and uncomfortable. Why was everyone looking at me that way? Did they already know about the incident in the canteen? But no one asked me anything when our eyes met; they all seemed busy with their files. Somehow I passed an hour. Then I went to the union room. Bipul and Chitresh were there. Chitresh was our branch secretary in the Union. He was also a member of the district committee of the Party. I asked him directly, 'What is happening in this office? Is this a place for propagating openly communal views? How could these youngsters behave the way they did with me in the canteen?' My voice was trembling. Not out of fear but a deep sense of indignity. Chitresh laughed, 'Come on, take a seat Dada. Why are you so excited? What happened?'

'What happened? You saw it with your own eyes, didn't you? You saw how those boys charged at me in the canteen, and they were making strongly communal and provocative statements... How can they do that in this office?'

'Oh, come on! You are taking things too seriously. Of course I was there in the canteen. I saw you talking with Saurangshu and his group. No one was abusive.'

'They were supporting the rioting hooligans as the protectors of race and nation and using very objectionable words.'

'Oh no, Bijoyda,' Chitresh shook his head. 'You are an old hand. Why did you start the discussion when the country is so fraught with adversity? This was not expected from you. Don't you know these debates create dissension, and that enemies cash in on the situation?'

All this while Bipul had not spoken a word. Now he said, 'Who supports whom is a personal matter. It is not right to scoff at anyone.' Bipul was waving his hand while speaking. I noticed three rings of three different coloured stones, like the astrologers recommend, on his right hand.

'Moreover Bijoyda,' Bipul went on, 'You have been around a long time, haven't you? Just about two more years for your retirement, right? Why do you get involved with these young chaps? They are quite different from our times. Let them do whatever they want. Times are changing, you know. You'll have to keep up with the times.' Chitresh and Bipul laughed heartily at their joke as I slowly walked out of the room.

I remembered that the sanction for this union room had not been easy. At that time, employees had gone on strike asserting their right to form a union in the office. They had adopted the 'pen down' method. Some fourteen people had been show-caused; I was one of them. I did not feel like using the elevator and took the stairs. In those days, quite a few big trees could be seen from the landing window. They had now vanished to make place for a supermarket. Right in front of our office there was a glittering Maruti showroom. How long was it since I last used the stairs? I had been using the lift for a long time. I felt a tightness in my chest as I began to climb the stairs. I stood clutching the railing at the second floor landing. I noticed a group standing near the water cooler in the passage. Were they the same boys from the canteen? I could not make out. It was probably them and a few others. Two or three came forward. Not towards me, they were looking outside the window. Now they were going down the stairs. Their voices were clearly audible, 'Goddamn tout, old rascal…Amazing! He does not feel the slightest bit of hatred towards those…' a filthy word came from a loud voice.

'Just a crack in the skull will let some wind in,' said another. Bursting into laughter, they noisily went down the stairs. I felt a sense of desolation engulf me. I shouldn't have come by the stairs. I needed some air. I couldn't breathe properly.

That was the day before yesterday. I did not tell Tanu about the incident. In the evening when she was offering her weekly puja to goddess Laxmi, strange thoughts occupied my mind. Tanu glanced at me over her shoulder. She felt uneasy as I looked at her. I gathered the newspaper and went to the other end of the room. I could hear her prayers. I had heard them innumerable times because Ma also used to chant them. Is Tanu a Hindu? But the prayer sought only the welfare of the household, nothing about any religion or enemies of that religion!

I did not leave my section the whole of yesterday. When I left office, I used the lift. I felt uncomfortable in my thirty-two-year old workplace. Was someone watching me? This nagging thought was there at the back of my mind. It was the same today.

My section was absolutely normal, as if nothing unpleasant had happened. That day they were talking of cracking a skull open, were they referring to me? Come off it, it was not that easy. Weren't there people around? But that day in the canteen there were many of them. What if they had beaten me up? There must be so many like those boys on the roads, round the corner. No one objected when *pandals* were built on the roads, blocking them for three or more days, merely to sing the praise of some idol or other. Who organised these programmes? Where did the money come from? Mikes blared day and night though everybody knew that playing loudspeakers was restricted to definite hours. Why did no one protest? Were they all afraid? But yesterday we were just discussing things. Then why should they talk of me in such a manner? I had passed fifty-six years without bothering about religion, and no one had fussed about it. Baba and Ma had their own ways of offering prayers. Tanu had her own. There are all kinds of people on this earth: many Hindus do not practise caste distinctions; many Muslims do not have four wives. How can that be a reason for hatred?

That was my problem now. I must hate the people of some other country, some other caste, some other religion, for my own security. But how did one hate? For hating somebody one would have to know the person. I could not think of this 'other' barring Chacha-jan. And how could I hate him? I was trying real hard to recall any face, in my class, in the office, in my neighbourhood that I knew well enough. Just one face that would help me to gather the much-needed hatred. How could I hate an unknown person? Could that be the reason to crack an old man's head? Someone would hate me because I could not find a person to hate? I didn't think Tanu would be of any help in this matter. I felt lonely and anxious.

Translated from the Bangla by **Joya Mitra.**

Border Stories*

SUNANDA BHATTACHARYA

B. D. Singh

The rain pierced the skin like sharp needles. The wind was hard too, and the cold. None of them had the kind of clothes that would have given respite from the elements. When it became very chilly, they lit a fire. They had set fire to an almost worn out tire and sat huddled around it. As the BSF jeep went past with blaring horn, they turned their heads to watch it speed past. Subol said: 'That son of a bitch B. D. Singh again.'

Two years ago, B. D. Singh was posted here. Under his supervision all the trade had come to a standstill: people were in a tight spot. He would enter homes to confiscate bales of cloth, cartons of medicines. He had kept the border tightly closed. When he was transferred, everyone had heaved a sigh of relief.

Was that B. D. Singh in the jeep?

'*Haw*. It was him. B. D. Singh *rey chinumna?* Wouldn't I recognise B.D. Singh?' Subol Biswas would never forget B. D. Singh. For two years that man had haunted him; his appearance was now fixed in Subol's mind.

'His two eyes are like swords....'

---

* Originally published in Bangla as 'Borderer Golpo' in *Pubduari* (Tripura: Book World, 2014).

Those sword-like eyes had pierced Subol's entity to interrogate: '*Kaha becha tumne?* What did you sell?'

At first Subol refused to admit that he had sold the bull. He had, but not alone. It was not possible to do such a big job on his own. It was a job just to capture the animal: 'Had to give that boy two hundred for that alone...*adbans!*'

The boy had been surprised to get the money as advance—he had never seen so much money in his life. And the work was easy; in the dead of the night he had to take the bull Mahadev to the end of the *char* land where a man would wait with a rope. The boy would have to slide the rope gently around Mahadev's neck. The animal was very obedient; he followed the boy everywhere. The boy fed him the leftover vegetables and fruits from the market, and Mahadev understood every word he said.

Mahadev was the community bull who was allowed everywhere and everyone prayed to him. The bull wandered all over but was always to be found in the market, charging towards the stalls of fruits and vegetables, and the shop owners would be busily thwarting him by throwing a banana or a radish at his mouth. Eating all that good stuff instead of fodder, Mahadev had become exceptionally healthy. He was the icon of the town, a well-fed bull with smooth flanks.

For a few days, Mahadev went missing. At first no one paid attention, but soon enough everyone began to talk about it. Where was Mahadev? Where could he have gone?

'What? Has he been smuggled out?'

It was Bakr-Id after a few days. The price of gram-fed mutton would go up; imagine the price of vegetable-fed beef!

'What! They want to slaughter a religious icon! What audacity!'

Things had heated up; there was an imminent danger of a riot. Since the affair smacked of smuggling, B. D. Singh took some proactive steps. At midnight he picked up Subol Biswas for interrogation. Whatever had to be done must be done quickly, before the interference of the local politicians.

It did not take long to break Subol Biswas; after all he was not a hardcore smuggler. Yes, five of them had smuggled the bull.

'How much did you make?'

'*Bisha hajar tyaha...*'

'Twenty thousand rupees?'

Subol had nodded his head. B. D. Singh had taken the name and address of the buyer and let Subol go. He had got what he wanted; there was no reason to keep Subol. It was outside his jurisdiction, and therefore illegal. B. D. Singh had a flag meeting with the BDR. Mahadev was returned and everything was back to normal. Subol-Nitai-Gofur-Haru went underground for a few days. The boy was given a sound beating by the shopkeepers. The incident had ended there. In a place where the main economic activity was smuggling, the excitement of bull smuggling was short-lived. If it was not a *dharmershar*, a religious icon, no one would have bothered. Cows and bulls often went missing here; everyone knew where they had gone. So all the cowsheds here had sturdy doors. At night people used Godrej locks to shut the cow-sheds—like keeping a banana in a locker!

That episode involving Subol Biswas, an *adharma* of the worst kind, was now forgotten. So it was now possible for him to sit around a burning tire with others, keeping warm. Everyone knew who went smuggling in the dead of night across the border. No one gave a hoot about it; after all they never created the border. If there was an epidemic of cholera on the other side, people's lives were saved with the medicines from this side; the *hilsa* fish from that side decorated the dinner plates of people from this side. Many houses here stacked goods, like a carton of medicines or a few sacks of salt or soap or cosmetics: to smuggle out when the coast was clear. The time when onion prices had hit the roof this side of the border, sacks of onions from the other side had made some people very rich. From the time he understood it, Subol had seen this state of affairs. But there had never been a commandant like B. D. Singh. The man had been transferred and Subol had breathed a sigh of relief. Now it seemed he was back again, the son of a bitch!

International Dispute

The rain had stopped. The sun was peeping out in golden rays from behind the clouds. Subol Biswas got up from bed. He started walking towards Haripada Goswami's house. Haripada must be told about the news of the return of B. D. Singh. As he walked he could hear the cries of children: of course a football match was in progress on the char.

If the children played in the disputed territories, the BSF and the BDR looked the other way. They sat relaxed in their bunkers, watching the match. And when there was a goal, they too sat up in excitement.

That excitement was enjoyable, benign, harmless. The excitement that broke out between the two countries about the ownership of the char land sometimes reached the zenith. The char, stretching over a few acres, remained fallow: no one could cultivate it. The river had crept far away to the other side; the char had risen on this side and its soil was very fertile. Bangladesh claimed it was theirs while India claimed the contrary.

According to the 1972 treaty between Indira and Mujib, 'the deepest point of the river is the border.' Then the char belonged to India. But Bangladesh disagreed: argument-counter-argument; bullets; counter-bullets; lots of excitement. When the boys played football on the large swathe of excitement's land, a temporary relief was established. Subol too stood to watch the match. Hey, hey, a missed goal. Arre! The boy at the goalpost looked like Akram Mian's nephew!

Akram Mian's whole clan had a cloth business, on that side of the border. Subol often helped them to carry the bundles of cloth to their shop. During play, the border did not exist: no this side or that side. *Bhala! Khub bhala!* Excellent! Those who quarreled about this side and that side had made Subol's life difficult. If there were no sides, how good it would be! During winter, the char land yielded a bumper crop of potatoes! Three crops easily each year! There would be no need to smuggle goods. But what's the use of talking. *Koiya labh nai!*

One Bullet, One Enemy

Going past the BSF camp, one could easily see the board that said in Hindi, 'Ek Goli, Ek Dushman.' What did it mean? Sujoy said, 'This is to warn the jawans not to be trigger-happy. To fire a bullet means to create an enemy.'

'Don't be absurd. This is meant to urge the soldiers not to waste a bullet. Each one should find its mark.'

They asked the jawan who was showing them around, and he said: 'Don't know *saab*.'

Really! The board was meant for the soldiers, and they did not know what it meant!

The bunker was a series of small rooms underground, with a bit of the ceiling poking over ground. A few bunkers lay scattered all around, with peepholes turned towards the border. If one stood with a binocular and looked out of the peepholes, the movements of people were clearly visible. A peasant with a long beard weeding his potato patch; a young girl wearing green bangles walking her cow. An intrusion on privacy! The peasant or the girl did not know that every movement of theirs was under surveillance. Pinaki jotted down a few points.

Pinaki was a freelance journalist. He had been assigned a piece from *India Today* on the Northeast border areas. He had covered Assam and had come to Tripura. His friend Sujoy lived in Agartala. Both of them had come together to get a first-hand experience of the border.

They went into all the six bunkers. The Muhuri river turned from here; on the other side was Bangladesh. The bend in the river encircled a large char land: it was disputed territory. Boys were playing football there, completely covered in mud. No one could tell them apart, not even people who knew them!

'No one stopped these kids from playing there?'

'Oh no. They are kids after all.'

When they returned to the camp, they came to sit in the recreation room. B. D. Singh asked, 'Tea, coffee or *nimbu pani*?'

Sipping his coffee, Pinaki asked him the meaning of 'one bullet, one enemy.'

'It means save a bullet.'

B. D. Singh and his men worked only with bullets. They sported rifles in their hands, so they needed to have good aim so that not one bullet was wasted. 'We are not a *danda* force like the police or the home guards.' B. D. Singh spoke with pride and contempt, a half-inch smirk on his lips. Pinaki shook his hand and got up to leave. B. D. Singh urged him again to make sure that his photograph was published in *India Today*.

The damn beggar!

Haripada Goswami

Sujoy knew some people in the area. He had given Pinaki the contact of Haripada Goswami. They set off to meet the man late in the evening. Haripada lived in a two-storey brick house. There were very few of these in the town. It was obvious Haripada was well off.

Sujoy said in a low voice: 'You know, this guy is the kingpin of the smuggling racket.'

It was late, almost eight-thirty. The rain had stopped but it was bitterly cold—the wind lashed their skins. That was why Haripada's main door was closed; people never kept their doors closed in these parts except when they were sleeping. Before they could knock, they heard a loud voice: 'You are stepping on my tail now! I have told you, I will get the job done.'

When they knocked loudly, a man opened the door.

Sujoy said: 'Arre Subol! How are you?'

'Bhalo. And you?'

Before Sujoy could reply, the man named Subol turned to another man sitting on the bed, wrapped in a shawl: 'I should be leaving now. Will come tomorrow morning.'

Pinaki understood that Haripada was asking Subol to do some job. Haripada got off the bed and welcomed them in: '*Aiyen, aiyen.*'

When Pinaki put the question to him, Haripada said: 'Smuggling? Oh no...we have very little of that here...nothing worth mentioning that is; a little medicine, a few dried fish. Most goods cross the border with valid papers. They go through the check-post. Haven't India and Bangladesh signed a trade agreement?'

Valid Papers

Pinaki said: 'Can you take me to that man who was talking to Goswami? Haripada didn't spill a bean, that old rogue!'

'Who?'

'The man who left after we went in.'

'Subol Biswas? Don't really know where he lives. It's late today. Let's see if I can track him down tomorrow.'

It was a smallish place, and it didn't take them long to find where Subol lived. It was a house a little away from habitation. The place had a rustic look.

It was evening and Subol was home.

'What did Haripada say? No smuggling? Son of a bitch! Then how did he get so rich, eh? And after he got rich, he is now involved in another business.'

'What is that?'

'He is now a comrade! Smuggling is no longer so profitable, so he is the local party comrade. The contract for making roads, food for work contract, mid-day meal contract, if you want to do a start-up you will have to grease his palms.'

'Why were you upset with him yesterday?'

A bag of *dhakai* saris have come to Akram Mian's shop, and Subol had to go and collect it. Haripada was urging him to do the job quickly. The saris had to reach a top bureaucrat's home; his daughter was getting married, so they were needed as gifts to the in-laws. Smuggling was viable because the goods came cheaper than market rates. The profit margin was however on the wane.

'How will you get the saris in? What about B. D. Singh?'

Subol smiled like a feline. Before he could reply, he heard footsteps past his window and hastily got up to peer outside. 'Who is there? Oh it's you, Master Moshai! I thought it was some gentleman!'

Moloy Master was dressed in fresh clothes; he had been invited to a Saturday pujo and he was taking a shortcut through Subol's patch. Sujoy knew Moloy Roy. He said: 'Arre, Moloyda! How come you are here?'

'Huh! I have been transferred here, going to be two years now. How come you are here?'

'Some work of my friend's.'

Moloy looked at Pinaki and said: 'I live next door. Come home when you are through.'

When Moloy had gone, Subol took up the threads of the conversation.

'*Ki kaitachhilam?* Where was I? If you want, I can show you how I get the saris in.'

The next day at two in the afternoon, Subol took the men to sit under a leafy fig tree. The check-post was clearly visible. After a while, a man carrying two large bags came walking from the Bangladesh side. He entered the BSF camp and took out some papers from an envelope. The guard took them, looking cursorily and stood chatting and laughing with the man with the bags. Then he peered briefly into the bags and the man crossed the check-post with his bags hanging from his hands.

Subol said: 'Did you understand what happened?'

'What happened?'

'The saris were under the valid objects. The guard should have noticed them, but he did not.' Subol laughed low in his throat.

'That is illegal.'

'So is the stomach. When the government official buys the saris at half the price, he does so with full knowledge. He has no thought for where the next meal comes from...' Subol said with a wry expression on his face.

'How much will Goswami pay you?'

'Haripada *pay* me? Don't be absurd.'

'Why will you do it then?'

'I see you are beginning to interrogate me like a lawyer. Let's go. I have loads to do.'

Subol seemed pissed off. It was strange that he was not getting paid. What was Haripada's hold over Subol? Pinaki had to get to the bottom of the mystery.

Moloy Master

When he heard what Pinaki had to say, Moloy Master said: 'It's not so complicated after all. Haripada knows all of Subol's weaknesses. Subol will be in dire straits if they were to come out...just blackmail, pure and simple...'

'Subol's weaknesses?'

'Like for example when he had stolen someone's cow and smuggled it off....There are many like Subol here who are stupid but reckless. Haripada has made a fool of them and become rich. A large part of the twenty thousand that had come with the sale of the bull had gone to Haripada and B. D. Singh....Really! Why do people like Subol remain poor? People like B. D. Singh take advantage whenever they can...one day they catch a thief and the next day they steal along with him....I have been living here for two years now. I have seen right before my eyes how a pillow stuffed with heroin suddenly transforms itself to flour; how three trucks of Phensedyl are passed while the fourth is stopped to make headlines: "Truck with narcotic substance caught at the border..." The common man is happy that the border guards are doing their job. They feel secure. They praise governmental efforts...The Hero cycle agency at Agartala got the prize for record sales twice running. If you take the number of cycles sold in Tripura then you can easily understand the variance in sales and you can easily understand where the rest of the cycles have disappeared. But no one bothers. Everyone gets a cut...and meanwhile, the small fish like Subol gets caught, gets beaten up....he gets it both ways you know...He has no job, no land, no BPL card. How do people like Subol live? Can you write all this in your newspaper? Can you write why he is a smuggler? In Muhuri's char, while harvesting his crop, he was shot in the leg by the border guards and had to stay three months in hospital. When he came out, a cultivator had become a smuggler. Will you write all this?'

Psychology

Moloy Master saw Subol was limping. He said, 'Are you in pain?'

'Haw....my leg aches during the waning moon.'

The bullet in Subol's leg had been extracted in the primary health centre. The wound had taken a long time to heal. It is better now but he walks with a limp and the leg ached when the moon waxed or waned. The doctor had said the pain was psychological.

'Is it full moon today?'

'Haw.'

'Oh that is what I said to myself. What nice moonlight.'

'Why are you waiting? Will you be going to Agartala?'

'Haw. I am waiting for two hours; no space in the jeeps.'

'How will you get a place? Today is market day.'

On market days, if one had to get a place in the jeeps, one had to walk two miles to the motor stand, but Moloy Master did not feel like walking. Subol had come to wait for Tarani's jeep. Nitai will take Tarani's jeep and will keep a seat reserved for Subol. When the jeep arrived, Subol asked Nitai to get off. 'Let the Master travel. We will take the next one.'

Moloy Master was hesitant but Subol urged him to go. The road was flooded with moonlight. Subol felt lighthearted. However Nitai was pissed off. He asked angrily, 'What will happen to the consignment?'

'Gofur can wait.'

In the market, Gofur would wait for the bundle. Their work would get over with the handing over of the 'maal.' In the eastern part of the market, the jungle road was safe for taking the bundle to Bangladesh and then to the real foreign lands. If this gets over,

Subol will earn a fat commission. Palbabu had told them to be careful; it was a big consignment.

The two men started walking; one of them carried a small pillow under his shawl. Subol assured Nitai that they were safe, but Nitai felt uneasy.

Suddenly a pair of powerful headlights lit up the dark road. They saw B. D. Singh get off the car. Subol was caught with the small pillow stuffed with heroin. Nitai said he did not know what Subol had under his shawl. Subol agreed with Nitai. Nitai was let off.

Subol spilled Palbabu's name, but one of the main provisions of the Illicit Drug Trafficking Prevention Acts says personal possession was a criminal act.

Terrorists used the money from drugs to buy arms and RDX. There was an Intelligence report that said that the Billonia soft border was being used for drug smuggling. B. D Singh had got a posting here again because of that report. He knew the terrain like the back of his hand. Within four days of his posting, he had captured such a big consignment of heroin. He was very happy. He sipped some scotch and phoned Pinaki to give him the news.

Haripada raged on at Nitai: 'You are ruining the country. Do you know you are traitors! Traitors!'

Nitai sat quietly listening to Haripada raging. Why did no one explain to him why he thought Bangladesh as his own country too? In that country where the paddy fields looked verdant, the *shol* fish leapt in the *aal* water, in that country where the smell of soil wafted with his memories of eating a full meal and sleeping like the dead? Those rich memories filled his heart and mocked his colourless present where he did not have the money to fill even half his belly. Nitai, countryless, moneyless, vagabond, anxious, walked aimlessly by the side of Muhurir char. Tomorrow, Subol will go up in court. There was no way Nitai could save him. Haripada had washed his hands off the matter. He had also threatened Nitai not to show his face in the area. What could Nitai do? Whom should he turn to? Moloy Master was still in Agartala.

Nitai walked on. On his left was the fertile char made by the shifting river, acre upon acre of lush land, untilled. Whose fault was that?

On Muhurir char, the moonlight came down with the winter fog. In the moonlit breeze over the char, Nitai's laments were carried off to the deepest point of the river that was the Indira-Mujib Treaty.

Translated from the Bangla by **Debjani Sengupta**.

25   Lost and Found*

JHUMUR PANDEY

With sandal paste smeared on her forehead, a *mukut* on her head, a red saree draped around her, Mokkhada is going round the holy fire. Ramchandra Bhattacharya's daughter, Mokkhadasundari Devi. Her sister-in-law, her friends Sulochana and Arundhati stand with flowers in their palms. The man dressed as the groom has a blurry face. Grandmother is making her sip the holy water of the Ganges. Two of her aunts are sweating from head to toe as they make sweetmeats with coconut and flattened rice.

With the golden pot in my arms
I fill water from the Yamuna
Krishna and Radha reside in the waters

Her friends Parulbala, Satyabhama, cousin Charulata and other women are singing.

As she bathes ceremoniously, with the glow of turmeric smeared on her face, Mokkhada smiles discreetly.

Mother! Mother! I'm hungry!

Who is it? Is it my dear son?

No.

My son, oh my son!

No Mashi, it's me!

Who?

Ratan.

* Originally published in Bangla as 'Mokkhodasundorir Haranoprapti' in *Sukh Gachher Golpo* (Hailakandi: Sahityo Prokashoni, 2005).

Not my son?

No, I'm Ratan!

Oh! Mokkhada comes out of her reverie.

Did you doze off?

Yes.

She stretches her hand under the un-sunned pillow and takes out a box of matches. Still panting, she wonders if she has been dreaming. She must have been. Why else would she try to call out to her long-lost son?

Give me the lamp, I'll light it.

It's not very clean. Light the lantern.

After the lantern has been lit, Mokkhada leaves her bed. Over eighty in years, with a greasy saree wrapped around her, she still had glowing, glistening skin.

Here, take your supplies. I'll get you some kerosene later. I'll have to go now.

Won't you sit?

No, I should leave. There's plenty of work to do.

Had you not been around, who knows what would become of me!

No! Why do you say such things?

Be on your way.

There's not even a window in the room so that Mokkhada could take a look at the sky, get a hint of the intentions of the weather. She doesn't remember the last time she saw the Orion, the Morning Star or even the Evening Star. The humidity and the heat have conjured up a sense of claustrophobia. Earlier, one look at the moon and Mokkhada could guess the probability of rainfall.

Mother used to say that nearer the moon, farther the water and farther the moon, nearer the water.

Once again, Mokkhada got up and sat on the bed. Who knows how late it is! Why is she feeling so sleepy tonight? Usually she spends all night wide awake. Ratna's mother is cooking. One room and five families packed in it. In between there's a partition of just one and a half arm's length. Partition. The word itself is enough to break and grind every ounce of bone and flesh in Mokkhada's body.

This one small word was enough to uproot Mokkhada's home, family, existence and environment. Still, all roots cannot be pulled up. Transformed into thorns shaped by pain, so many roots have survived. Trees don't live without roots. Neither did Mokkhada.

Come hurry, we are going to Hindustan.

What did you say?

Come on. There's a riot out there.

But I don't want to go.

Hurry up. You cannot delay any more.

There was a fire raging nearby. She could smell the acrid smoke.

My son is asleep. Wake him up.

Mokkhada opened the trunk and retrieved all her ornaments. The intricate gold necklace given to her by her mother, the choker gifted to her by her mother-in-law, all of that. She stepped out and gazed at the greenery around—star-fruit, mango, tamarind trees. A small pond with water shrubs floating on it. Such love welled up in her! Mokkhada stared into nothingness for a long time with deep love and affection in her eyes.

My parents and siblings?

Worry about yourself now. Come with us if you want to.

For some distance, they sailed on a boat. And then, who knows for how long Mokkhada had to run. Men and women were running in herds. Some people on the way chopped up her husband's body. Just like that. Mokkhada lost consciousness then and there. Who knows how she reached Zakiganj from there. By then her son was not with her anymore. Mokkhada was so shocked that she did not even shed a tear. And who knows how she reached the relief camp in Karimganj. The aunt from Egarasati died of hunger in front of her eyes. Widows couldn't eat in the company of so many people. And then she arrived here at the Meherpur camp with the others. Many of them had left the camp one by one. Many new people arrived. Mokkhada had stayed on. Every month she could claim eleven kilos of rice, one and a half kilos of lentils, three-fifty grams of sugar, some salt and firewood. Mokkhada is alive. Yes, she is still waiting for her son. What if someday he finally arrives, in search of his mother? How old would he be now? If he was around ten then, he would be sixty now. Will Mokkhada even recognise her sixty-year old son? Every year she tries to re-imagine his face in a slightly different light. Yet, all she can conjure up is the child's face.

Mother, can I go to the fair?

With whom?

With Puthi.

Go then. But come back soon.

Nagen Puthi served Mokkhada's family. He could peel a whole coconut with his teeth and break it with his hands. The same Nagen Puthi...

The palanquin is swaying. Mokkhada is travelling from Basudevpur to Akhailkhura as a newlywed bride. There is so much of noise. The women are blessing her with the sound of ululations. Plenty of puffed rice. Her crimson painted feet. Mother-in-law welcoming her ceremoniously into the house.

What are you doing?

Welcoming my son's bride.

What all can she do?

Well she can sing and dance, stitch and sew, cook and clean... my son...

Mokkhada used to prepare small stuffed parcels of betel leaves for her mother-in-law. And suddenly one day, mother-in-law passed away. That day, Mokkhada couldn't stop crying.

Mother, what should I cook?

Cook bitter gourds stuffed with a paste of poppy seeds.

What else?

Make balls of vegetables with jackfruit seeds. And do use mustard paste. Let it be, I'll make it.

Mother-in-law had no peace. She had to send her sixteen-year old widowed daughter to Kashi. She was married off at nine. She came back as a widow by the age of ten. With time, she grew up to become a beautiful young woman. Already cursed as a brahmin's widow, she fell in love with Bhattacharya's son, Sukharanjan. The boy had gone to study at a college in Calcutta, and there he learnt to eat onions. Later, he had planted onions beneath the banana trees in the back garden. As soon as a couple of sprigs were out, his uncle had come to know. The boy had to repent at last. Society would never accept it. Who keeps young widows at home? That too a widow in love! And no fear of isolation too! At last with tears in her eyes, mother-in-law had sent her away to Kashi. Sukharanjan too lived a bachelor all his life. Finally the girl was...

Mother-in-law called out for Mokkhada.

Yes Mother.

Mokkhada is feeling suffocated under the long end of her saree pulled over her head.

What are you cooking?

Frying some *koi* fish.

See, your aunt has come from Satarosati.

Mashi, are you asleep?

Who is it?

It's me, Ratna's mother.

Where is aunt?

Whose aunt?

She had just come...

You were dreaming.

Ratna's mother laughed loudly.

Mokkhada got up and sipped some water. She fanned herself and undid her blouse. Was she dreaming? How did she sleep for so long? But surprisingly, she never saw her husband in these dreams. His face is a blurred memory now. And when can she meet him but after nightfall?

Mokkhada craves for sweet rice cooked with date palm nectar and milk. But there aren't many palm trees in this area. Mokkhada had a row of palm trees bordering the pond in the east. There were coconut trees as well. In the evenings, Nagen Puthi would tie earthen pots to the palm trees. In the mornings, he would retrieve the pots full of nectar. Mother would cook sweet rice with it, fine, like pounded glass. What a wonderful taste it had! Mokkhada was fasting for the month of *Magh*. She was only five. At dawn, she would bathe, wrap a saree and sit on the painted throne on the ground. So many motifs and paintings were scattered across the courtyard. The sun, the moon, the Milky Way, white bangles, sarees, brinjal plants and so much more! She would shiver violently in the cruel cold of the Magh winter.

Aren't you feeling cold?

No. Mokkhada would shake her head.

On the last day of the fast, grandfather would twirl the umbrella. Grandmother would place so many sweetmeats made of puffed rice, flattened rice, coconuts and other things. Children would pick these up in a hurry. Those memories are still so alive! So fresh! The *bokul* tree, and a boy with a blurry face standing beneath its shade. They were picking flowers to sew into a garland. And suddenly at the tender age of twelve, they were made to circumvent the holy fire of matrimony. What a crazy thing! Where did the moon atop the bamboo trees go? So many poems about the moon recited by her childhood friend Parulbala! Where are they now? Parulbala, Arundhati? She didn't even get to meet her parents and siblings. She didn't even get to know when they had died. Water rolled down her cataract infested aged eyes.

Mokkhada is weeping.

Mashi, it's raining. Do you have clothes left outside?

No. Mokkhada wiped her tears.

It was raining heavily. Rainwater sprayed into the house.

No wonder it was so hot, Ratna's mother was saying. What is it Mashi, you seem very quiet today.

Just like that. Not feeling very good.

She had come once to Palaichhara Gardens before the Partition. Then it was known as Surma Valley.

Who's screaming? She asked Ratna's mother.

It's elections again.

Elections?

Yes.

Elections were being held in Kazibazaar. There a lot of tension in the air. Someone was telling Mokkhada, If the tea garden workers had the right to vote, then Sylhet would have been saved. So would Mokkhada and her family. Now the rainwater was spraying the bed wet.

Mokkhada tried to pull the bed aside, but couldn't.

Ratna's Ma!

What is it?

It's the rain. Pull the bed for me please.

Ratna's mother pulled the bed aside and placed a shallow bucket at the spot to collect the rainwater. The water in the bucket is rising. Tup, tup, tup. Mokkhada remembers playing prisoner in the rain. She remembers Bamacharan Bhattacharya's little school. Steamed leaves of *amrul*, the soft flesh inside palm fruits, tall tamarind trees, Karimchacha, the banks of the river Manu, Nehru at Panchabati, Aminabibi, a sweet dish made of taro roots. Some patchy visions and memories assail her. A pang of pain begins to infest her chest. Life is sustained on the basis of desires, hopes. Mokkhada's life is based on memories; on dreams; on pain.

With needles of memories and florets of dreams, Mokkhada threaded many garlands over her lifetime.

Mother!

Who? Is it my son?

Yes Mother, I have come.

Her little boy... the same smiling face. One black beauty spot on his cheek. You've lost so much weight!

Yes. See, Father has come as well!

Mokkhada hurriedly pulls her saree's end over her head.

Where have you been?

Back home.

But the Partition... How did you come?

Can anyone's heart be bound by partitions?

The storm is getting thicker.

Big round drops of rain have drenched Mokkhada.

The shower of memories and dreams are running in rivulets down her shrunken body. Mokkhada spreads her arms out in deep love and longing.

Translated from the Bangla by
Farha Noor *and* **Debjani Sengupta**.

SELINA HOSSAIN

R afeza is just fifteen years and a few months old. Before her mother died she had told the girl her exact age. From then on, she tries to remember carefully how old she is. She has no idea why she does so but she tries. She thinks there's some calculation in remembering, some arithmetic. That arithmetic is her life's story.

Her age is actually fifteen years, two and a half months. There's a pretty big story nestling within these few years of her life. She forgets her age if that story takes over and looms up in her mind. A deep sense of why she forgets, or rather why she loves to forget stirs inside her. The only thing she seems to understand is that if she forgets, a large flower will bloom in that emptiness. Like an umbrella, that flower will spread a shade over her head. There will be fragrance all around. She will see a petal drop like a waterfall, heavy and thick with the sorrow of her story. Everything will wash off, from head to toe. No dust, no mud, no gritty sand will cover her then.

Right now she is sitting on a chair. It is a chair whose colour has chipped away, a chair without an armrest. But she's relaxed enough to lean and rest herself. She knows in a short while she'll be taken to Bangladesh along with a few others. Right now she's on Indian soil, having spent nine years in an Indian jail. She will go to her

* Originally published in Bangla as 'Meyetir Bari Phera' [The Girl's Homecoming] in *Noon-pantaar Goragori* (Dhaka, 2015).

own country Bangladesh in a little while. She watches people move about as she waits in the BSF office. She is unable to understand the language of the people here. Through the window she can see a large open field without a single house. There are trees scattered around the field. She doesn't know their names. She understands one cannot learn the names of trees from inside a jail, particularly, the flowering trees. She knows mango and jackfruit trees. Among fruits, she also recognises the litchi but does not know the tree. In fact, she has trouble recognising a rose. She knows marigold. She wants to giggle loudly and say, I'm a smuggled girl, but I know marigold. You can spend a whole life knowing just one flower. She makes an effort not to giggle. She knows that this office is not meant for laughter.

She doesn't even know how much time has passed.

Perhaps one hour or three? She doesn't know how to keep time. She has never gone to school. Rafeza wants to laugh again. She doesn't even know what a school is. Doesn't know what studies mean. What's the point wondering about anything then?

Rather, she appreciates her new frock. It's a pretty frock. She tells herself, Rafeza, you've never seen such a lovely frock.

Yes, I haven't. How will I, because when I was three, my father who was a freedom fighter died in a rickshaw accident, his head crushed under a truck.

Rafeza covers her face with her palms. Tears well up in her eyes.

Someone comes close to her.

What's the matter?

I want water.

Are you hungry?

No.

You look beautiful in this bright dress.

I've heard such things many times before.

Many times?

Those men were *shaitan*.

I'm not misbehaving with you. I was sent to buy the frock for you. That's why I said what I said.

I love the new frock. It's very pretty.

True?

True, true, true. Three times true!

Her face bright and shining with happiness, Rafeza stands up from the chair.

Oh, sit down. I have to go. Got a lot of work to finish. The bosses are going to go with you to your country.

I don't remember anything about my country. I remember more about the jail where I stayed.

The man leaves. Rafeza now knows that seven years ago she was smuggled from Bangladesh to India. Along with her mother and younger brother. Her mother was at the mercy of a two-man team. She wasn't aware of anything else. Why do such things happen? She has no clue. She cannot remember the meaning of BSF or of BGB. These are big words beyond her comprehension.

At times she's exasperated with herself; why on earth does she want to understand! All she knows is that the story of her life at just fifteen is a fifteen hundred year-old story.

She looks at her pretty frock again. All these years she has spent in jail, she has never seen such a lovely outfit. Children who live inside jails don't get to wear pretty dresses. Her sandals are lovely too. They had straps that went across her ankles. One of the jailhouse inmates has combed her hair into a ponytail and there are a few colourful clips in several places of her groomed head. Mashi had shaken her ponytail and said, You're looking like a princess, Rafeza. Be careful about birds of prey coming after you. You can save yourself, can't you, girl?

Rafeza hadn't replied. She knows she won't be able to save herself. She couldn't twice before. She was picked up, covered in blood, and admitted to the hospital. That memory is a raw wound. Never will it heal in all her lifetime. Trying to feel happy sitting at the BSF office, she thinks, her life is a story of new frocks, a story stuck to solid stones. But now, someone has spread some fragrance on it. Someone from home has sent her the scent of *shiuli* flowers. That fragrance has flown to her and encompassed the frozen stories of her life.

Rafeza starts swinging her legs. She thinks of how good she feels. I am happy about returning home. But whom would she be with once she is back? Who will hold her close? A fear crawled up her spine. Her freedom fighter father used to be a cycle rickshaw puller. For someone who could fight, pulling a cycle rickshaw was an easy task. Then why does such a person meet with an accident? Is driving a cycle rickshaw tougher than fighting? She doesn't understand. No teacher has ever taught her what is tough and what is not. She has never ever seen a teacher.

A swallow comes flying in to sit on the windowsill. It twits on and on. She stares at it. The bird flies away and then flies back to sit at the window. It does this a few times.

Her face lights up with happiness. She says, you're very happy, aren't you bird? A jailhouse Mashi had told me that you're a swallow. She'd told me that seeing one swallow brings bad luck. Seeing two swallows brings good luck. Seeing three swallows brings a letter. Letter? There's no one to write me a letter. I don't need any letter from anyone. Her body suddenly shakes with stifled screams. The two boys had picked her up. Then left her all bloodied. Oh God!

She covers her face with her palms.

Someone comes and stands near her.

What is wrong?

Nothing.

Why are you crying?

I'm remembering my mother.

Ah, right. Your mother died in the jail, didn't she?

Rafeza hangs her head and mumbles, Yes, in the jail.

Everyone will start in a while. Sit quietly over here. I'll get you a few packets of biscuits.

Rafeza tilts her head. Teardrops still shine in her eyes. The man leaves. She wipes her eyes. The dozen stories of her life start melting slowly. Mother used to say, Our home was in Shibpur village in Belgharia of Natorezilla. After your father died I had no support. There was no place I could take you all with me. A village acquaintance told me, Go to Hasina Khatun in India. Work and earn your livelihood. I thought, not a bad idea. Hasina Apa lives in

Delhi and looks after her family. I can too. I'll put both my children in a school. I really had so much hope, but what terrible luck! They say even God doesn't look at you if your fate doesn't speak up. After working for two months I fell ill. Couldn't see a doctor. Couldn't afford medicines. Seeing me in this state Hasina got angry and told me, go back home. Who's going to look after you in this condition? It's better to die in one's own country. At least your grave will be in your own land.

I understood what Hasina said. Even she's come through her contacts with the smugglers. She doesn't want trouble with another trafficked person. I decided, fine, I'll return home. Whatever fate has in store for me I'll accept. If I work as a maidservant I'll at least get to feed my family.

So one day I start off, carrying whatever belongings I have. I'd taken the hill tract by the borders before. I'll return by the same route. My body was aching with fever. My mouth was full of blisters. I could scarcely walk. Even then I held your hands. But my accursed fate struck once again. The police stopped us at Balurghat border. No passport, no visa. I had entered India through the illegal routes. The police send us off to jail. That was the beginning of a new phase in our lives.

Rafeza tells herself, I know all, Ma. You received some medical treatment in the jail, although you may not have received the exact treatment that would have made you better.

One early morning you left us alone. Then it's another story altogether. I've suddenly become very tall and lanky. I've grown up. I'm scared at the way people look at me. When they know I have no one, they misbehave with me. Why didn't I too leave with you, Ma? Why did you leave me behind?

One day a kindhearted man said, Why should this girl stay in the jailhouse? One must send her to her own country. I'll make arrangements.

He made all the arrangements.

He's the boss of this office. Everyone salutes him. When he walks past, his shoes make a crunching noise. That noise scares Rafeza. But then she thinks he's a kind man. Someone who takes the responsibility for lost girls like Rafeza and who makes arrangements for them. Rafeza decides right then that she'll ask him a question. She'll ask as soon as they enter her country across the border. Would he be able to reply?

The man who has promised her biscuits brings her two packets and a water bottle and says, Come have this.

She stretches her hands and accepts the food and the drink. Her little brother loves biscuits. When will he be sent home? They've kept him in Shubhayan Ashram at Balurghat. He's really very small. He doesn't know about their mother. He hasn't even seen his mother's body. How is Masoom, her little brother? Rafeza's eyes fill with tears once more.

What is it again? Why are you crying?

For all of you.

For us?

Yes, because I'm going to leave all of you, that's why. I'm very upset.

How long have you known us?

Well, for fifteen hundred years.

So what do you think of us?

Phew! She wipes her mouth, blows hard and says again, I see all of you as good men. But I have a question for you.

Yes?

I wanted to grow up here, then why aren't you letting me stay?

What did you say?

This is a fifteen hundred year-old question.

Ask our boss.

Your boss is very kind. But you're the one who keeps coming to talk to me.

You don't like me talking to you?

Please don't come near me anymore.

Ah, I can see you're a feisty lion cub! Any more questions before you leave?

But you didn't reply to my question.

Even the boss doesn't know the answer.

Then please leave.

The man is irritated and says, I'll square up with you if we meet again. Then you'll know your limits.

Sure. I won't spare you either.

Too hot-headed, eh, and just fifteen years of age!

The man leaves in a huff. He stops at the end of the verandah just for a second. He is very angry. Rafeza is sitting over there. One can't see her from this end. He feels like going back and standing in front of her again. He feels like kicking her for being a brat, but this is an office. And the entire office likes Rafeza. Nobody can touch that girl here.

Rafeza wants to stop thinking of the man and remember her mother's death. She remembers her mother died rather simply, silently. She fell ill, and wasn't treated. There was no diet for the patient. She never received nursing care. Naturally a person would only die in that state. Rafeza's mother had effortlessly passed into a simple quiet death. How long did she cry? Masoom has not a speck of an idea about all this till now.

After a moment's silence Rafeza thinks that being all bloodied was tougher than just dying. That was a terrible time she had to battle with in order to stay alive. All the while she had thought death was better.

Now a woman comes and stands near her. She looks at her heavily knitted brow and frightened face and says, Are you feeling upset?

Yes, I'm feeling terrible.

Do you want to say something?

I have a question.

What is it?

I wanted to grow up normally as a teenager. Why can't I?

Forget all that. In a while you'll return home, so be happy.

Be happy? That's tougher than death.

Death?

Yes, I've seen my mother die an easy death. She didn't really suffer. Whereas I suffered when I was hurt and bloodied.

Girl, you're just more grown up than you should be. It's not your fault.

Will you come with us, Mashi?

I will; no need to be scared.

At last Rafeza laughs out loudly. Laughs and says, Mashi, I'm no longer scared. Please give me your blessings.

The woman places her hand over her head.

Arrangements for the return are complete. The vehicle is ready. Rafeza is sitting inside. She is in tears. She has spent a long time in this land even before she understood anything of her childhood or teenage years. And now she has to return just as she has begun to understand a few things. The place of understanding is a brutal one. An older girl in the jailhouse had taught her to write her own name and to read a bit. Almost eight years have passed. That memory is unforgettable. Whether she'll ever see her mother's grave again she doesn't know. The thought of her mother makes her heart heavy. The tears begin to fall in a gushing flood. She controls herself with much difficulty. Mashi keeps her hand over her head and comforts her.

I have such a huge amount of tears that they won't dry up till I die.

Shall I get you some *pani*?

Yes. I'm thirsty.

The woman gets her a bottle of water. Rafeza keeps it in her handbag after taking a gulp. Now she thinks about Masoom. She didn't get to meet Masoom before she left. He'd be so grown up when they would meet next. Perhaps he would not even recognise her.

The vehicle rushes towards the Bangladesh border.

Rafeza doesn't know that there will be a border meeting under the aegis of BSF-BGB at the director's level. Rafeza will be handed over to the BGB. The initiative has been launched by the boss, Mr. Sharma, who's looking after her. He has told her, Humanism is a great truth for us. That's the reason we want Rafeza to go home. She'll live with her own family. The young cannot grow up as fine human beings if they don't live with their own family.

Rafeza asks herself, What does this growing up as fine human beings mean? She'll ask this question to the kind boss. Suddenly she stops. But she has only one question to ask really. She'll ask that question before they cross the border. Then the very next moment she thinks there's no need for me to ask any question. Instead, she'll ask for punishment for those boys who raped her.

Suddenly she calls out, Mashi!

What is it, child?

Criminals don't get punished.

Of course they get punished.

Then those two boys, they'll be punished, right?

If they're caught, they will be punished.

And what if they don't get caught?

The police will try to catch them.

Some day they'll be caught, right?

Of course they will be. They have to be punished for the crime they have committed.

Rafeza firmly holds on to Mashi's hand and then pushes it away. She looks outside. The fast-moving landscape outside the window changes in a frantic run. Rafeza is feeling sad. She will have no family once back home. No father, no mother, even her brother isn't there though he's alive. Where is her family then? She'll have to figure out ways to fend for herself. Her body turns ice cold.

The vehicle stops at a designated spot. Rafeza will be handed over to the BGB office across the border post. It will be done by the Special DG of the BSF. He is the one who looked after her when her mother died. He took all responsibility and paid for her upkeep. His dream was to see her grow up in her own country where she will lead a normal life. And then the girl puts this question to him, Sir, why could I not grow up here?

I'm sorry, dear. I won't ever be able to compensate for this loss of yours.

Rafeza's eyes well up. Large teardrops keep falling. She doesn't wipe them.

Come.

Rafeza holds the boss' extended hand. They cross the border. She has stepped into her own country. Suddenly it seems the breeze, the soil, trees and people, everything is so familiar. And these people who have accompanied her till this place are also her own. What can she do now? She starts remembering her father the most. The memory of her father's crushed head is concealed in her heart. Her head is held high when she remembers her father telling her stories about the war. He told her about the enemies he had destroyed. And how tough it was to stay in the *muktijoddha* camps. She feels dazed to be back in her own country after such a long time. It's the same country for whose independence her father had fought. Then a group of people had smuggled them to the other side. She walks as though she's carrying the flag of an independent country, followed by a group of people from both countries.

Rafeza is handed over. The director of BGB presents her with a large bouquet. From now on we're responsible for you, my dear, he says.

What can she say?

Her voice is choked. Tears, only tears come out of her eyes. She remembers her mother. Her mother had wanted to work and live. Oh mother! She has left her mother behind. How friendless she is!

The vehicle speeds towards Natore.

In a while she says, Sir, I have a question.

You want to ask something?

Yes, sir.

Tell me, my dear. You won't face any problem. We'll keep you in a safe home. Educate you. We'll also see that once you grow up, you can find work.

Sir, I have a question.

Someone addresses her in a sweet tone but she hardly hears anything. The churning of the question in her heart has restrained her so far. She feels she's still not in her own country. As though she's a country-less person: a woman who has changed hands constantly.

You said you have a question. Tell me, dear child, what do you want to know?

She looks at the kind man. He is speaking to her ever so gently. She lets the air escape from her lungs in a rush. My father was a freedom fighter, she says.

That's right; it is because people like your father fought that this country is free today.

She shifts in her seat and now raises her voice. Then why was I, a freedom fighter's daughter, illegally taken across the borders from this free country?

It's hot and still inside the car. She repeats her question a few times. But only silence greets her.

Translated from the Bangla by
Nabina Das *and* **Debjani Sengupta.**

POETRY

Birendra Chattopadhyay
Sankha Ghosh
Sahir Ludhianvi
Javed Akhtar
Kaiser Haq
Sukrita Paul Kumar
Tarun K. Saint

27   After Death: Twenty Years*

BIRENDRA CHATTOPADHYAY

All the terrible catastrophes
Escaped your eyes
You did not burn in the tortuous fire of '46
The famine and the epidemic
That came through the blood
The land where sons killed each other
The flesh of mothers
Fueled a living hell.
You did not have to see
The '47 Partition that was
Worse than madness in Lumbini.[1]
Contrary to these experiences,
A light of humanity had filled your life, Poet.[2]
We too had learnt to dream from you.
These past twenty years
A history of sewage afloat,
Thirst, a bath, life, all inhuman.
Worse than the old hag
Who runs the brothels at Shonagachi.

* Originally published in Bangla as 'Mrityur Por: Kuri Bochhor' in
   Shreshtho Kobita (Kolkata: Dey's Publishing, 1998).

Ministers, leaders, teachers, writers, students,
Dogs on heat,
This independent land joins all together.
All our dreams are like drunken jokes
Played on the reeds of an oft-used harmonium.
Even in your nightmares
You had not thought such calamity
Would befall this free country
You had thus remained true
To your dreams of humanity.

Translated by **Debjani Sengupta.**

Notes and References

1. Lumbini Park is a mental asylum in Kolkata.
2. Poet Rabindranath Tagore.

Rehabilitation*

SANKHA GHOSH

Whatever I had around me
Grass and pebbles
Reptiles
Broken temples
Whatever was around me
Exile
Folklores
Solitary sunset
Whatever was around me
Landslides
Arrows and spears
A homestead
All shiver with their faces turned west.
Memories are like a serpentine crowd
Under the mango trees, broken boxes
One step denying another
And suddenly all are homeless.

Whatever is around me
Sealdah station
High noon
Pockmarked walls
Whatever is around me

* Originally published in Bangla as 'Punorbashon' in *Shreshtho Kobita*
(Kolkata: Dey's Publishing, 1970).

Blind alleys
Slogans
The Monument
Whatever is around me
The bed of arrows
Lamp-posts
The Ganges flowing red
The bones and the darkness within
Surround them all
Inside a tune plays on
The Howrah Bridge is holding up high
The void
Under my feet drifts Time.

Whatever is fountain around me
Flying hair
Naked path
The stormy torch
Whatever is transparent around me
The sound of the dawn
The body after a bath
The Shiva of the cremation ground
Whatever is death around me
Each day
A thousand days
A birthday
All return in the palms of memory
As the beggar who sits in the fading dusk
What was and what remains,
Two flintstones that scrape each other
And ignite my daily rehabilitation.

Translated from the Bangla by
Sankha Ghosh *and* **Debjani Sengupta.**

29 Twenty-sixth January*

SAHIR LUDHIANVI

Come, let us ponder on this question
What happened to all those beautiful dreams we had dreamt?

When wealth increased why did poverty also increase in the country?
What happened to the means of increasing the prosperity of the people?

Those who walked beside us on the street of the gallows
What happened to those friends and comrades and fellow travellers?

What is the price being set for the blood of martyrs?
What happened to the punishable ones for whom we were ready to lay down our lives?

The helpless cannot even afford a shroud to cover their nakedness
What happened to those promises of silks and brocades?

Cherisher of democracy, friend of humanity, wisher of peace
What happened to all those titles we had conferred upon ourselves?

Why is the malady of religion still without a cure?
What happened to those rare and precious prescriptions?

Every street is a field of flames, every city a slaughterhouse
What happened to the principles of the oneness of life?

---

* Originally published in Urdu as 'Chhabbees Janwary' in *Aao Ke Koi Khwaab Buney* (New Delhi: Punjabi Pustak Bhandar, 1971).

Life wanders aimlessly in the wilderness of gloom
What happened to the moons that had risen on the horizon?

If I am the culprit, you are no less a sinner
O leaders of the nation you are guilty too

Translated from the Urdu by **Rakhshanda Jalil.**

30   After the Riot*

JAVED AKHTAR

The silence is deep
Rising silently from some houses
A dense black smoke
Carrying filth in its heart
Is spreading far in all directions
The silence is deep

The road is lifeless like a corpse
A broken cart
Lies upside down
Its wheels up in the air
Looking upon the sky in amazement
As though it has still not fully comprehended
Whatever has happened
The silence is deep

A wasted shop
Like a mouth opened to scream
Remains open, agape
From its broken doors
It looks with longing eyes
At the shards of broken bangles

---

* Originally published in Urdu as 'Fasaad ke Baad' in *Tarkash* (New Delhi: Star Publications, 2008).

Scattered far and wide
For, till yesterday
These bits of glass were
Teeth of a hundred colours
In a toothless mouth
The silence is deep

The deep silence speaks to the scene around it:
Listen, O wasted shop
O smouldering house
O broken cart
You are not alone here
There are others here too
Who have been destroyed
We will mourn them too
But first let us cry over those
Who had come to loot
But were themselves looted
What were they robbed of
They themselves don't know
For they are weak
These poor things have no idea
Of their centuries-old civilisation

Translated from the Urdu by **Rakhshanda Jalil.**

31 Six Shared Seasons*
(for Rubana, a true Southasian)

KAISER HAQ

Since we are
    our worst enemies,
        is it any surprise
that barbed wire,
    watchtower and searchlight
        keep neighbours apart,
border guards suddenly
    slug it out
        for no apparent reason,
families picnic
    willy-nilly, as they wait
        in visa queues,
and poor people are
    rounded up—undesirables
        or aliens or both—
we're almost as bad
    as Europe was
        till the other day.

* Originally published as 'Grishma, Barsha' in *Published in the Streets of Dhaka: Collected Poems* (Dhaka: The University Press Limited, 2012).

All the time
    the year keeps rolling
        to its celestial schedule.
Grishma's furnace heat,
    barsha's monsoon floods,
        sarat's mellow skies,
hemanta's fresh harvest,
    mist over the fields,
        dew underfoot,
warmth of embroidered quilts,
    winter bonfires, snow on the mountains,
        fog on the plains,
then every girl a beauty
    in *basanta's* vibrant amber,
        and flowers with humid lips
kissing the passionate bee.
    Six seasons to everyone else's
        four—from the Himalayas
to Serendip, and the Indus plains
    to the delta
        of the Ganges and Brahmaputra—
hold the whole
    of Southasia* together,
        six shared seasons
making nought
    of borders and barbed wire.
        Nature as usual is
prodigal with gifts and lessons—
    and as usual, alas,
        we take one and ignore the other.

---

  * Writing 'Southasia' instead of 'South Asia' is a charming orthographic
    innovation that indicates the region's civilisational unity; it is used by
    Himal, the weekly published from Kathmandu, and the Southasian
    TV Channel, of which Rubana was CEO for some years.

Cold Storage*

SUKRITA PAUL KUMAR

The letter...
postmarked,
stamped and
delivered
half a day late
or a decade later
it matters not

It reached when
all was over

History had raised its hood
flapping its forked tongue

The letter...
words
languishing on
yellowing paper,
corners rusted brown

crackling folds and
moaning lines
blotched
by Vaddi ma's tears,

* Originally published in *Without Margins* (New Delhi: Bibliophile South Asia, with Promilla & Co. Publishers, 2005).

warm and starry then,
now shadowy tips
of icebergs

'*Kaké*, my own,
take me back to my *Bhatindé*
to my Rano
the *bachhda* is due
and Rano needs me...
cows get difficult
with so many months gone...'

Between the writing
and its reading
Time cracked

Dipped in Jinnah's sweat
the pen
sliced the land of five rivers
giving birth to the sixth...

the bloody stream
flowing from Vaddi ma's heart;

Kammo and Chhoti
Mauled and dumped,

Rano's squeals
ripped the clouds
over the aborted calf

Postmarked and stamped
the letter was delivered

with time rolling back
into bewildered clocks...

33 Cyril's Map*

TARUN K. SAINT

I placed a map over a plot of land.
    Furrows of soil tamed anew,
as map shadow looms over root and seed.

    Map contours move, boundaries alter.
Below map shadow, shapes shift; seedlings
    once planted shrivel without sunshine.

I thought I had mastered the parched earth.
    As seasons fled in turn, dust rose.
Plants writhed, photosynthesis stilled.

    Map levitates, extends branches beneath,
like a banyan tree in flight. Map
    moment of stillness; veins open below.

I placed a map on a plot of land
    cultivated once for crops, dark loam
interspersed by map stems now taking hold.

    Map becomes mapmaker, makes cracked earth
a mirror in which new maps appear.
    Myriad map images: go forth and multiply.

---

* Cyril Radcliffe was assigned the task of drawing the boundaries of
the newly formed states at the time of the Partition of India in 1947.

DRAMA

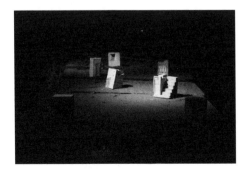

Asghar Wajahat

Overleaf photograph: Unum Babar

Those Who Haven't Seen Lahore Haven't Lived*

A Play about the Partition of India

ASGHAR WAJAHAT

Scene 1

(*The stage is dimly lit. A procession of people shouting slogans can be heard in the background. As the demonstrators come closer, the slogans become louder and clearer.*)

Nara-i-takbir...
Allah-ho-Akbar

Ley ke rahenge...
Pakistan, Pakistan...

(*The demonstrators appear on stage shouting slogans.*)

Pakistan, Pakistan...
We shall win Pakistan...
Muslim League, Muslim League...
Zindabad Muslim League...

(*One group of demonstrators shouts*)

Kick him hard without a hitch...

* Originally published in Hindi as *Jis Lahore Nai Dekhya O Jamyai Nai* (New Delhi: Vani Prakashan, 2006).

(*The other group replies*)

Khizar is a son-of-a-bitch...

(*The entire procession repeats*)

Khizar is a son-of-a-bitch...

(*As they shout slogans some begin to dance wildly chanting over and over again*)

Son-of-a-bitch...Son-of-a-bitch...

(*One group shouts*)

Khizar is...

(*The other group replies*)

A son-of-a-bitch...Son-of-a-bitch...

(*Suddenly, a member of the Muslim League comes running on to the stage.*)

MUSLIM LEAGUER: Oye Fayyaz...stop...Stop...!

(*People stop shouting slogans. There is silence. The Muslim Leaguer takes Fayyaz to one side.*)

MUSLIM LEAGUER: Oye Fayyaz...Don't shout that slogan...

FAYYAZ: Why, what's happened?

MUSLIM LEAGUER: Don't you know...Khizar's joined the Muslim League!

FAYYAZ: Oh, no!

MUSLIM LEAGUER: What do you mean? We just heard the good news! Isn't it great?

FAYYAZ: It's a miracle.

MUSLIM LEAGUER: Of course...Now Pakistan will surely be formed.

FAYYAZ: Khizar has at last proved that he's a Muslim...

MUSLIM LEAGUER: Oye Fayyaz, there's courage in Muslim blood. Go, carry on with the demonstration.

(*Fayyaz walks up to the demonstrators, whispers the news to a few and the group shouts enthusiastically.*)

1st Group: (*shouting*) Have you heard the latest news...

2nd Group: (*completing the sentence*) Khizar is our brother!

(*They repeat this slogan a few times. The demonstrators become even more enthusiastic.*)

1st Group: Pakistan! Pakistan...!

2nd Group: We shall win Pakistan...!

(*Slowly the light changes on stage to indicate that some time has passed. The procession leaves from one side of the stage and enters again from the opposite side. The slogan 'Pakistan! Pakistan...!' is repeated again and again. Suddenly, the member of the Muslim League returns and, grabbing Fayyaz by his arm, drags him to one corner of the stage.*)

MUSLIM LEAGUER: Fayyaz, the news is wrong!

FAYYAZ: What news?

MUSLIM LEAGUER: Khizar hasn't joined the Muslim League!

FAYYAZ: Oye, what the hell?

MUSLIM LEAGUER: I'm telling you the truth, Fayyaz...the truth...carry on...

(*Fayyaz goes back and whispers to a group of demonstrators. Everyone falls silent. Suddenly one group shouts...*)

1st Group: Kick him hard without a hitch...

2nd Group: Khizar is a son-of-a-bitch...

(*Mad with rage, the entire procession repeats 'Khizar is a son-of-a-bitch...son-of-a-bitch' and begins to dance. This goes on for sometime. The lights begin to dim and the slogans fade. The stage becomes dark. After a brief pause a faint light reveals a caravan of tired and sad* refugees. *As they walk across the stage the following song can be heard in the background.*)

And the result was
    India was divided.
This earth was divided
    This sky was divided.
The language we wrote was divided.
    The language we spoke was divided.

Flowering trees were divided.
    Our homes were divided.

The dreams we had dreamt were different
The Punjab we see now is different.

Scene 2

(*Sikander Mirza, Javed, Hamida Begum and Tanno enter carrying luggage. They look around at the haveli allotted to them by the Custodian of Migrant Properties. Their faces light up with delight and satisfaction. Sikander Mirza, Javed and the two women put down the luggage they are carrying in their hands.*)

BEGUM: (*Looking around at the haveli*) Ya Khuda, we are grateful to you. A thousand, thousand times grateful.

MIRZA: The Custodian officer wasn't wrong. It is a haveli, an entire haveli.

TANNO: Abbajan, how many rooms does it have?

MIRZA: Twenty-two.

BEGUM: Look at the condition of the courtyard...it's so desolate. It's scary.

MIRZA: What else did you expect? No one has lived here for months.

BEGUM: I must first offer my prayers in gratitude...I had made a wow...At least we are out of that wretched camp.

(*Hamida Begum spreads a mat and stands on it to say her prayers.*)

JAVED: Abbajan, who owns this house?

MIRZA: Son, now we do.

JAVED: I meant who owned it earlier?

MIRZA: What have we got to do with that...We left our property behind in Lucknow. This haveli has been allotted to us in exchange.

TANNO: This haveli is much larger than our house.

MIRZA: No son...There is no comparison with our house. There is no *raat ki rani* in the courtyard, is there? The veranda is also not as broad. If it rains our cots will be soaked.

TANNO: But it's elegantly built.

JAVED: Must have belonged to a rich Hindu.

MIRZA: Someone said it belonged to a famous jeweller.

JAVED: Let's unlock the doors. Maybe we'll find some stuff.

MIRZA: Alright son, go ahead...I'm going to sit...Now that this haveli has been allotted it seems as if a weight has been lifted off my head.

JAVED: Can I see the entire haveli?

TANNO: Can I also come with you?

MIRZA: No, you go to the kitchen...How long can we eat meat and rotis from the hotel? Mashallah, if possible make soft parathas and scrambled eggs...And Javed, switch on the lights and see if they work...Check the water tap also...We'll have to make a list of things that don't work and tell the Custodian's office...

(*Hamida Begum returns after reading her namaz.*)

BEGUM: I don't know...I'm afraid...

MIRZA: Afraid?

BEGUM: Who knows to whom it belonged...What dreams, what hopes are built into this haveli?

MIRZA: Don't talk nonsense, Begum...Some migrant must have occupied our ancestral home today...The times are such... Shame, concern or fear will not get us anywhere. If not for ourselves, at least for the sake of Javed and Tanvir Begum, we'll have to find our own feet...We left Lucknow and found Lahore—at least both begin with 'L'. Stop being afraid and make this your home...Bismillah... After the Isha prayer tonight, I shall read the Quran...

(*Tanno comes running in. She seems scared and out of breath.*)

BEGUM: What's the matter?

TANNO: There is someone in the haveli, Amma.

MIRZA: Someone? What do you mean?

TANNO: When I climbed the stairs, I saw...

MIRZA: Don't talk rubbish.

TANNO: I'm telling the truth.

BEGUM: She's scared... I'll go and see...

(*Begum exits to the right. She calls from there.*)

BEGUM: There is no one here...Where did you go?

TANNO: Toward the stairs. Someone...

(*Begum goes toward the stairs. Tanno and Mirza move to the right where the door with an iron grill is locked. Suddenly they hear Begum shriek.*)

BEGUM: There is someone...Someone's coming down the stairs.

(*Mirza runs towards the right. By then an old woman, dressed in white, comes and stands by the door.*)

MIRZA: Who are you?

RATAN'S MOTHER: Who am I! You are asking me! You tell me, who are you? How dare you break into my house without permission?

MIRZA: Break into...We didn't break into your house. It's been allotted to us by the Custodian...

RATAN'S MOTHER: Forget allot-plott...This is my house...

MIRZA: How's that possible?

RATAN'S MOTHER: You ask anyone...This is the haveli of Ratanlal, the jeweller, and I'm his mother.

MIRZA: Where is Ratanlal the jeweller?

RATAN'S MOTHER: He went out to search for a Hindu driver before the riots began...You see, our driver was a Muslim and wasn't willing to leave Lahore...(*with tears*) Since that day... (*starts crying*).

MIRZA: (*Nervous and upset*) We're very sorry to hear about what happened...But as you know, Pakistan has been created...Lahore is now in Pakistan...There is no place for people like you here...We can take you to the refugee camp...People there will take you to India...

RATAN'S MOTHER: I'll not go anywhere.

MIRZA: What are you saying...you mean...this house...?

RATAN'S MOTHER: This is my house.

MIRZA: See, we have legal papers...

RATAN'S MOTHER: I, too, have legal papers...

MIRZA: Please try to understand the situation...no Hindu can live in Pakistan...

RATAN'S MOTHER: I'll live here...Till Ratan comes back...

MIRZA: Ratan...

RATAN'S MOTHER: Yes, my son, Ratanlal, the jeweller...

MIRZA: Please listen, we respect your feelings. But the truth is that your son, Ratanlal, will never come back...

RATAN'S MOTHER: Are you God? How can you predict everything?

MIRZA: Sister...there's been a massacre...Hundreds and thousands of people have been killed...

RATAN'S MOTHER: But hundreds and thousands have also survived...

MIRZA: Please listen...the simple fact is that you have to vacate this house...It's been allotted to us...by the government...

RATAN'S MOTHER: I'll not leave this place.

MIRZA: (angrily) Excuse me...you are older than me...but if you continue to be obstinate, then I may...

RATAN'S MOTHER: Yes, yes, kill me and throw my body in the Ravi...and then grab this haveli...Well, I won't let you as long as I am alive!

MIRZA: Ya Khuda! This is impossible!

BEGUM: Days of decency have gone...If you get the Custodian officer...now...then...

RATAN'S MOTHER: Beta, you can get whomsoever you want... He can't take anything more than my life...Even you can't...

MIRZA: Ya Khuda, what should I do?

BEGUM: Ajee, go at once to the Custodian's office...Why did they allot us a house which is not vacant?

MIRZA: (To Javed) Fetch my sherwani...and Tanno, give me a glass of water.

RATAN'S MOTHER: There's water in the tap...the water supply was restored only last week...Beti, get water from the tap.

MIRZA: (*wearing his sherwani*) Please understand...if the police mistreat you we'll feel bad.

RATAN'S MOTHER: Son, a great tragedy has fallen upon me... There can't be a greater tragedy than that...My young son is dead... jewellery worth lakhs was looted...my relatives were killed...

BEGUM: So Bua, come to your senses now...Go to India...live with your own people...

RATAN'S MOTHER: My blessed son is dead...where can I go now?

(*Mirza drinks water and gets up.*)

MIRZA: So, Begum, I'll go then.

JAVED: Should I come with you?

MIRZA: No, you stay at home...Maybe this old woman has hidden some others in the house...

RATAN'S MOTHER: I swear by God...there is no one else.

MIRZA: No son, you better stay.

(*Mirza begins to leave.*)

BEGUM: Khuda Hafiz.

(*Begum, Javed and Tanno move away from the right of the stage.*)

MIRZA: Khuda Hafiz.

BEGUM: Tanno, have you seen the kitchen?

TANNO: Yes.

BEGUM: We have pots and pans...Go and cook something quickly...It'll be nice if food is ready by the time your Abba returns.

TANNO: Ammijan, in the kitchen there is no wood or coal...How can I cook?

BEGUM: No wood or coal!

TANNO: Not a single piece of wood.

BEGUM: Then how will you cook?

RATAN'S MOTHER: Beti, the small room on the left of the veranda is full of wood...get some...

(*Surprised, Begum and Tanno look at each other with joy.*)

Song

There is a surge of pain in my heart now
A fresh breeze has begun to blow now.

A noise resonates deep in the heart
As if a wall has collapsed just now.

Disenchanted with this world of plenty
Who knows what I long for even now?

Good days shall also come, O Nasir
Don't grieve, there is life ahead even now.

Translated from the Hindi by
Alok Bhalla *and* **Nishat Zaidi.**

INTERVIEW

Intizar Husain
in conversation with
Nasir Kazmi

INTIZAR HUSAIN in conversation with
NASIR KAZMI

Pakistan Television had arranged for this interview to be recorded about three or three-and-a-half weeks before Nasir Kazmi passed away. The task of conducting this interview was assigned to me. Putting formal questions to Nasir was difficult for me as Nasir was not one for carrying out formal conversations even as a joke. So beginning this interview was a difficult task for both of us, but people coming in between the conversation made this easier for us. This interview was carried out in the room at the Mayo Hospital where Nasir was admitted and where he breathed his last. We had started talking when the doctor came in to examine his patient. After he had left, we resumed the conversation but then another doctor entered the room and after a while the nurse came in with a thermometer in her hand and after she had left, Nasir Kazmi's wife came in. So in this entire process all the discipline the TV authorities were trying to teach us vanished, and then Nasir's unique style of speaking asserted itself.

During this conversation, I never suspected that Nasir was not recording an interview, but putting together all his scattered things. He had to collect all this, hand it over to us and then go his way. During conversation when he asked me to convey his salaam to the coffeehouses and trees of the city, I did not realise that this was Nasir's last salaam to the world of birds and trees. I do not know if Nasir himself realised this or not. In any case, after the interview was recorded he asked me several times when it would be telecast.

Once he got upset and asked me if the TV authorities were waiting for him to die. I tried to make up an excuse that actually they had to postpone the telecast because of the special programmes during Muharram and that they have fixed some date after Muharram. A few days after Muharram, that unfortunate date did come. This interview was telecast among the condolence programmes for Nasir which the TV channel aired, but only to the extent of an excerpt. Later, other excerpts from this interview were also included in subsequent programmes, but they do not give a sense of the entire conversation.

The entire conversation lasted fifty-five minutes of recording time. What follows here is an excerpt.

INTIZAR HUSAIN: This is Room number 27 in the Albert Victor Hospital. Nasir Kazmi is under treatment here. I keep thinking that the person whom I had always seen walking, going around the city, sometimes in the deep shade of trees, on hot afternoons, late evenings, the dark moments of the monsoons, on autumn evenings as leaves begin to fall from the trees and sometimes late at night, today that same person lies sick in his bed. I considered these few odd moments to be sufficient and thought that I should make use of this free time and take a walk down memory lane along with Nasir Kazmi. At this instant I am standing next to the headrest of his hospital bed (and as the poet said)

Speak softly when you are next to where Mir rests his head

But Nasir Kazmi is awake and I ...

Nasir Kazmi, those were the last few days of 1947 when I first saw you and since then I have been looking at you. But before that, where were you and what were you doing, I don't have a clear idea about that. But I have heard what you have been saying about your earlier days, the artists and the horses. So tell us something about those days.

NASIR KAZMI: Actually, I apparently do not move about physically because I have not been well for some time, but my mind, my eyes and my memories keep wandering around just as before, along with you in the lanes of Lahore and through the trees. But this matter of the past which you have asked about is really a long story. So the matter is that when Pakistan came into being, there was a town called Ambala.

Ambala was a town. They say it survives to this day.

I am the light of that plundered city.

So I migrated from over there. I had been born there. My father was in the army. It was a small town with a small community. Our home was a community of birds, memories, children, flowers, trees and interconnected lanes. All the rich and poor lived there in great harmony and peace. There were great men of learning there, too. But the wonderful thing in that community was that the seemingly poor and tiny people who lived there commanded the same respect as the big shots, perhaps even more than them. A pensioner had the same respect there that perhaps even a minister or a very rich man would not. There was a small school there, the Muslim High School—that is where I received my education. There were some highly memorable teachers, the likes of whom you will not find today.

My father was in the army. So I went to Peshawar, Nowshera, Dakshai, Shimla, Dehradun. I travelled a lot and it was my great wish to join the army. I did go into the army but left it soon. And the pastimes I had in my childhood were the same: horse-riding, hunting, wandering about in the villages, exploring rivers and hillocks. I learnt to love nature and appreciate poetry from that young age. So this was my childhood. I completed my tenth class from there... We used to hear then about Lahore, that it was a big city. I was fond of studies so I came here to study and I wrote this couplet, perhaps about the feeling this city evoked in me.

Lahore, may the hustle-bustle in your streets remain forever
The air of your lanes drew me towards you!

When Pakistan came into being, we moved here in a small caravan along with friends and relatives. When we crossed the Wagah border, my father saw the green flag with the crescent and said,

'Congratulations, my son! You have attained Pakistan.' I said to my father, 'Congratulations to you, too.' My father replied, 'I am offering my congratulations to you as you are the inheritor of this land and have to live longer here. I am but the waning sun and I walk only with my hands taking support from the walls.'

So when we arrived in Pakistan, there were no pens, no ink, nor any stationery in the offices. We did not have anything to call our own. You would remember this. You were among the first people I met. Hassan Askari, Manto and other friends—Nadeem Qasimi, Qateel Shifai, Faiz Sahib, Hafeez Hoshiarpuri, I met them all afterwards. Shops were closed in the markets. Some houses had open doors gaping wide, others were closed. Some windows were open. In some places the fans were working; in others, heaps of garbage had piled up. All these tall buildings reaching out to the sky which you see on the Mall these days, this WAPDA House, there was nothing like this. There were only a few trees which held hands and danced in the wind. It seemed that the trees danced all night in the moonlit spaces and we roamed around. Those nights were coloured green. But there was something about this condition of not having any possessions and it was this great will to live, as if we were the inheritors of this new country. And then there was this strange thing. I am almost afraid to say this but I am one of those small, unworthy people who once shook hands with the Quaid-e-Azam Mohammad Ali Jinnah, and I have since then not used this hand to greet anyone else. So on coming to Pakistan I saw that I have entered *dar-ul-amaan*, a place of safety and peace. Doctor Alamgir, Salam alaikum!

DR ALAMGIR: Salam alaikum!

NASIR KAZMI: Come in, please!

DR ALAMGIR: How are you feeling?

NASIR KAZMI: Much better, thanks to your kind attention. There was some heaviness at night, but I feel that with your attention and your affection, I will now go on living.

DR ALAMGIR: Inshaallah!

NASIR KAZMI: And I am getting better.

DR ALAMGIR: Take a deep breath.

NASIR KAZMI: Doctor Sahib, can I smoke or not?

DR ALAMGIR: Yes ... a little.

NASIR KAZMI: Can I smoke three or four cigarettes?

DR ALAMGIR: Three or four—you should try and not smoke at all. But if you can't remain without it, then ...

NASIR KAZMI: What about food? You know I relish good food.

DR ALAMGIR: You should eat. No problems. You can eat.

NASIR KAZMI: What special items should I include in my diet?

DR ALAMGIR: Nothing special. Eat what you like but reduce water and salt. It will be good if you can eat meat. Eat chicken.

NASIR KAZMI: Very kind of you. Salam alaikum ... So Intizar Sahib, what I was saying was that my childhood—and I did give some background of it to you—after coming to Pakistan, I kept remembering my childhood, but you know that memories can come back in the minutest of details. Memory selects. Some events come back to haunt me again and again and halt me in my path, they come alive. And,

> So the distant voice comes from close by

There are some very small and tiny memories of my childhood which make me turn towards poetry. Intizar Sahib, you were saying something ...

Translated from the Urdu by **Asif Aslam Farrukhi.**

Bibliography

Agamben, Giorgio. 1988. *Homo Sacer: Sovereign Power and Bare Life*. 88–100. Stanford: Stanford University Press.

Ahmad, Aijaz. 1997. "'Tryst with Destiny"—Free but Divided.' *The Hindu*, Independence Day Supplement. 22–23. 15 August.

Ahmed, Nihal. 2005. *A History of Radio Pakistan*. Karachi: Oxford University Press.

Ahmed, Tajuddin. 2000. *Tajuddin Ahmed's Diary*. Vol. 2. Dhaka: Pratibhash.

Akbarabadi, Makhmoor. 2003. 'Introduction.' In *Rooh-e Nazir*, ed. Makhmoor Akbarabadi. Lucknow: Uttar Pradesh Urdu Akademi.

Ali, Anwar. 1998. *Gwacchiyyan Gallan*. Pakistan Punjabi Adabi Board.

Amin, Shahid. 1989. 'Will Recognition of Urdu Slow Down Hindi's Progress?' *The Times of India*. 19 October.

Auden, W. H. 1966. 'Partition.' http://www.poemhunter.com/poem/partition-2/ Accessed 4 July 2017.

Azmi, Faheem. 2009. 'Art ka Pul.' Trans. from the Urdu to Hindi by Shambhu Yadav. In *Vibhajan: Bharatiya Bhashaon ki Kahaniyan, Khand-II*, ed. Narendra Mohan. 214–218. New Delhi: Bharatiya Gyanpeeth.

Bandyopadhyay, Sekhar. 2011. 'The Minorities in Post-Partition West Bengal: The Riots of 1950.' In *Minorities and the State: Changing Social and Political Landscape of Bengal*, eds. Abhijit Dasgupta, Masahiko Togawa, and Abul Barkat. 3–17. New Delhi: Sage Publications.

Bandyopadhyay, Sekhar, and Anasua Basu Ray Chaudhury. 2014. 'In Search of Space: The Scheduled Castes Movement in West

Bengal after Partition.' *Policies and Practices* 59: 10. Kolkata: Mahanirban Calcutta Research Group. February.

Banerjee, Sarnath. 2004. *Corridor*. New Delhi: Penguin Books.

Barnow, Eric, and S. Krishnaswamy. 1963. *Indian Film*. New Delhi: Orient Longman.

Benjamin, Walter. 1969. *Illuminations*. New York: Schocken Books.

Bhalla, Alok. ed. 1994. *Stories about the Partition of India*. Vols. 1–3. New Delhi: Indus.

_____. ed. 2012. *Stories about the Partition of India*. Vol. 4. New Delhi: Manohar.

Bhaskar, Ira, and Richard Allen. 2009. *Islamicate Cultures of Bombay Cinema*. New Delhi: Tulika Books.

Bhattacharya, Gayatri. 1988. *Refugee Rehabilitation and Its Impact on Tripura's Economy*. New Delhi: Omsons.

Bhattacharya, Sunanda. 2014. 'Borderer Golpo.' In *Pubduari*. Tripura: Book World.

Brenton, Howard. 2013. *Drawing the Line*. London: Nick Hern Books.

Butalia, Urvashi. 1993. 'Community, State and Gender: On Women's Agency during Partition.' *Economic and Political Weekly* 28(17): WS12–WS24. 24 April. http://jstor.org/stable/4399641 Accessed 4 July 2017.

_____. 1998. *The Other Side of Silence*. New Delhi: Penguin.

_____. 2002. 'The Nowhere People.' *Seminar*. http://www.india-seminar.com/2002/510/510%20urvashi%20butalia.htm Accessed 6 July 2017.

_____. ed. 2015. *Partition: The Long Shadow*. New Delhi: Zubaan.

Byapari, Manoranjan. 2011. 'Ananta Ratrir Chandal.' In *Deshbhag: Binash O Binirman*, ed. Madhumoy Pal. 212–213. Kolkata: Gangchil.

Chatterji, Joya. 2007. *The Spoils of Partition: Bengal and India 1947–67*. Cambridge: Cambridge University Press.

Chatterjee, P. C. 1987. *Broadcasting in India*. New Delhi: Sage.

Chaudhury, Anasua Basu Ray. 2012. 'Remembering the Communal Violence of 1950 in Hooghly.' *Journal of Borderland Studies* 27(1): 45–59.

Cilano, Cairo N. 2013. *Contemporary Pakistani Fiction in English: Idea, Nation, State.* London: Routledge.

Coppola, Carlo, ed. 1974. *Marxist Influences and South Asian Literature.* East Lansing: Michigan State University.

Cowasjee, Saros, and K. S. Duggal, eds. 1995. *Orphans of the Storm.* New Delhi: UBS.

Daiya, Kavita. 2008. *Violent Belongings: Partition, Gender, and National Culture in Postcolonial India.* Philadelphia: Temple University Press.

Das, Veena. 1995. *Critical Events.* New Delhi: Oxford University Press.

———. 2006. *Life and Words: Violence and the Descent into the Ordinary.* New Delhi: Oxford University Press.

Das, Veena, and Deborah Poole, eds. 2004. *Anthropology in the Margins of the State.* Santa Fe: School for American Research Press.

Datta, Nonica. 2005. 'Partition and Many Nationalisms.' *Economic and Political Weekly* 40(28): 3000–3002. July. http://www.jstor.org/stable/4416866 Accessed 4 July 2017.

Devji, Faisal. 2012. *The Impossible Indian: Gandhi and the Temptation of Violence.* 169–171. Cambridge, MA: Harvard University Press.

Dhulipala, Venkat. 2015. *Creating A New Medina: State Power, Islam, and the Quest for Pakistan in Late Colonial North India.* Cambridge: Cambridge University Press.

Didur, Jill. 2006. *Unsettling Partition: Literature, Gender, Memory.* Toronto: University of Toronto Press.

Doraiswamy, Rashmi. 2009. 'The Panoramic Vision and the Descent of Darkness.' In *Narratives of Indian Cinema,* ed. Manju Jain. New Delhi: Primus Books.

Faruqi, Shamsur Rahman. 2002. 'The Power Politics of Culture: Akbar Ilahabadi and the Changing Order of Things.' Fourteenth Zakir Husain Memorial Lecture, Zakir Husain College, New Delhi. January.

Gazdar, Mustaq. 1997. *Pakistan Cinema: 1947–1997.* Karachi: Oxford University Press.

Ghosh, Papiya. 2008. *Community and Nation: Essays on Identity and Politics in Eastern India.* New Delhi: Oxford University Press.

———. 2014. *Partition and the South Asian Diaspora: Extending the Subcontinent.* 214–216. London: Routledge.

Ghosh, Vishwajyoti. 2010. *Delhi Calm.* New Delhi: HarperCollins.

———. 2013. *This Side That Side: Restorying Partition.* New Delhi: Yoda Press.

Gopal, S., ed. 1982. *Selected Works of Jawaharlal Nehru.* First Series. Vol. 15. 177. New Delhi: Orient Longman.

Government of India. 1981. *Collected Works of Mahatma Gandhi (CWMG).* Vol. 84. New Delhi: Government of India, Publications Division.

Groensteen, Thierry. 2013. *Comics and Narration.* 114–115. University Press of Mississippi.

Gujral, Satish. 2000. *Satish Gujral: Selected Works 1947–2000.* New Delhi: Lalit Kala Akademi.

Gupta, Saibal Kumar. 1994. *Kichhu Smriti, Kichhu Kotha.* Calcutta: M. C. Sarkar and Sons.

Gwyer, Maurice, and A. Appadorai. 1957. *Speeches and Documents on the Indian Constitution, 1921–47,* Vol. 2. Bombay: Oxford University Press.

Hajari, Nisid. 2016. 'Nehru Was as Much to Blame for Partition as Jinnah.' Interviewed by Vaihayasi Pande Daniel. *Rediff.com.* 28 January. http://m.rediff.com/news/interview/nehru-was-as-much-to-blame-as-jinnah-for-partition/20150813.htm Accessed 6 July 2017.

Haldar, Dilip. 2008. *Atrocities on Dalits since the Partition of Bengal: A Human Right Question.* 19–20. New Delhi: Mittal Publications.

Hasan, Mushirul, ed. 1995. *India Partitioned: The Other Face of Freedom.* 2 Vols. New Delhi: Roli Books.

Hirsch, Marianne. 1997. *Family Frames: Photography, Narrative and Postmemory.* Cambridge, MA: Harvard University Press.

_____. 2012. *The Generation of Postmemory: Writing and Visual Culture After the Holocaust*. New York: Columbia University Press.

Hossain, Selina. 2010. *Bhumi O Kusum*. Dhaka: Ityadi Grantha Prakash.

Husain, Intizar. 2015. *Story is a Vagabond*, eds. Frank Stewart, Alok Bhalla, Asif Farrukhi, and Nishat Zaidi. 1–24. Karachi: Oxford University Press.

_____. 2015. *The Sea Lies Ahead*, trans. Rakhshanda Jalil. New Delhi: Harper Collins India.

Jaffrelot, Christophe. 2012. *India since 1950: Society, Politics, Economy and Culture*. New Delhi: Yatra.

Jain, Manju. 2009. *Narratives of Indian Cinema*. New Delhi: Primus Books.

Jalal, Ayesha. 1985. *The Sole Spokesman: Jinnah, The Muslim League and the Demand for Pakistan*. Cambridge: Cambridge University Press.

_____. 2013. *The Pity of Partition: Manto's Life, Times and Work across the India-Pakistan Divide*. New Delhi: HarperCollins.

Jalil, Rakhshanda. 2013. 'Reflections of 1857 in Contemporary Urdu Poetry.' In *Mutiny at the Margins: New Perspectives on the Indian Uprising of 1857*, ed. Crispin Bates. New Delhi: Sage.

_____. 2014. *Liking Progress, Loving Change: History of the Progressive Writers' Movement in Urdu*. New Delhi: Oxford University Press.

Jassal, Smita Tewari, and Eyal Ben-Ari, eds. 2007. *The Partition Motif in Contemporary Conflicts*. New Delhi: Sage.

Jawad Zaidi, Ali. 1993. *A History of Urdu Literature*. New Delhi: Sahitya Akademi.

Jinnah, Quaid-i-Azam Mohammad Ali. 1989. *Speeches and Statements as Governor General of Pakistan 1947–48*. Islamabad: Ministry of Information and Broadcasting, Government of Pakistan.

Kabir, M. G. 1980. *Minority Politics in Bangladesh*. New Delhi: Vikash Publishing House.

Katin, Miriam. 2006. *We Are On Our Own*. Montreal: Drawn & Quarterly.

Kaul, Suvir. 2001. 'Introduction.' In *The Partitions of Memory: The Afterlife of the Division of India*, ed., Suvir Kaul. New Delhi: Permanent Black.

Kisantal, Tamás. 2009. *Túlélő Történetek, Ábrázolásmód és Történetiség a Holokauszt űvészetében* [Survival Stories, Artistic Method and History in the Art of the Holocaust]. 35–71. Budapest: Kijárat.

Kothari, Rita. 2007. *The Burden of Refuge: The Sindhi Hindus of Gujarat*. New Delhi: Orient Longman.

———. 2013. *Memories and Movements: Borders and Communities in Banni, Kutch, Gujarat*. New Delhi: Orient BlackSwan.

Kothari, Smitu, and Zia Mian, eds. 2010. *Bridging Partition: People's Initiatives for Peace between India and Pakistan*. 87–95. New Delhi: Orient BlackSwan.

Köves, Margit. 1997. 'Telling Stories of Partition and War: Saadat Hasan Manto and István Örkény.' *Economic and Political Weekly* 32(33–34): 16–23. August.

Lelyveld, David. 2003. 'Talking the National Language: Hindi/Urdu/Hindustani in Indian Broadcasting and Cinema.' In *Thinking Social Science in India: Essays in Honour of Alice Thorner*, eds., Sujata Patel, Jasodhara Bagchi and Krishna Raj. New Delhi: Sage.

Mahajan, Manohar. 2010. *Yaadein Radio Ceylon Ki*. Jaipur: Vangmaya Prakashan.

Mandal, Jagadish Chandra, ed. 2004. *Mahapran Jogendra Nath*. Vol. 4. Kolkata: Chaturthho Dunia.

Mandal, Jogendra Nath. 1950. 'Resignation Letter to Liaqat Ali Khan.' 8 October. http://bengalvoice.blogspot.in/2008/05/appendix-1-jogendra-nath-mandals.html Accessed 6 July 2017.

Mansergh, Nicholas, and E. W. R. Lumby. 1970–1983. *The Transfer of Power, 1942–7*. London: H. M. S. O.

Manto, Saadat Hasan. 1988. 'Kal Savere Jo Meri Aankh Khuli.' In *Manto Ki Rajneetik Kahaniyan*, ed. Devendra Issar. New Delhi: Indraprasth Prakashan.

———. 2001. *Black Margins: Stories*, ed. M. U. Memon. New Delhi: Katha.

———. 2014. 'Pakistani Film.' Introduced, translated and annotated by Ali Nobil Ahmad. *BioScope* 5(2): 163–166.

Mashhadi, Zakia. 2002. 'Sada-e Bazgasht.' In *Sada-e Bazgasht*. New Delhi: Educational Publishing House.

Mathur, Ramesh, and M. Kulasrestha, eds. 1976. *Writings on India's Partition*. Calcutta: Simant.

Memon, M. U. 1980. 'Partition Literature: A Study of Intizar Husain.' *Modern Asian Studies* 14(3): 377–410.

Memon, Muhammad Umar, ed. 1998. *An Epic Unwritten: The Penguin Book of Partition Stories from Urdu*. New Delhi: Penguin.

Menon, Ritu, and Kamla Bhasin. 1998. *Borders and Boundaries*. New Delhi: Kali for Women.

Mitra, Joya. 1990/'91. 'Ghrinar Samasya.' In *Kal Porshur Dharabahik*. Calcutta: Karuna Prakashani.

Musafir, Gurmukh Singh. 1955. 'Allah Wale.' In *Aalney de Bote*. Delhi: Sikh Publishing House.

Nandy, Ashis. 2011. 'The Days of the Hyaena: A Foreword.' In *Mapmaking: Partition Stories from Two Bengals*, ed. Debjani Sengupta. New Delhi: Amaryllis.

Narang, Gopichand. 2007. 'Tehreek-e Azadi aur Urdu Shairi' [The Movement for Independence and Urdu Poetry]. In *Jang-e Azadi ke Awaalin Mujahideen aur Bahadur Shah Zafar*, ed. Vidya Sagar Anand. New Delhi: Modern Publishing House.

Nauriya, Anil. 1999. 'Some Portrayals of Jinnah: A Critique.' In *Minority Identities and the Nation-State*, eds. D. L. Sheth and Gurpreet Mahajan. 73–112. New Delhi: Oxford University Press.

———. 2011. 'Soundings in Kindred Struggles: The Egyptian Voice in Gandhi.' *Identity, Culture and Politics* 12(2): 43–66. December.

Nayar, Kuldip. 2006. *Scoop! Inside Stories from the Partition to the Present*. New Delhi: HarperCollins.

Nazli, Amena. 1969. 'Allah-ho Akbar.' In *Bare Feet*. Karachi: Ismat Book Depot.

Nehru, Jawaharlal. 1962/1975. *Glimpses of World History*. 761–775. Bombay: Asia Publishing House.

Pandey, Gyanendra. 1994. 'The Prose of Otherness.' In *Subaltern Studies VII*, eds. David Arnold and David Hardiman. New Delhi: Oxford University Press.

———. 2004. *Remembering Partition: Violence, Nationalism and History in India*. Cambridge: Cambridge University Press.

———. 2010. *Subaltern Citizens and Their Histories: Investigations from India and America*. London: Routledge.

Pirzada, Syed Sharifuddin, ed. 1970. *Foundations of Pakistan: All India Muslim League Documents: 1906–1947*, Vol. 2. 371–372. Karachi: National Publishing House.

———. 1977. *Quaid-e-Azam Jinnah's Correspondence*. 124. Karachi: East and West Publishing Company.

Prakash, Gyan. 2016. 'Karan Johar Controversy Mirrors Rising Populist Politics.' *The Indian Express*, 4 November.

Pritchett, Frances. 1994. *Nets of Awareness: Urdu Poetry and its Critics*. Berkeley and Los Angeles: University of California Press.

Rai, Alok. 1984. 'The Trauma of Independence: Some Aspects of Partition Literature, 1945–47.' *Journal of Arts & Ideas* 6: 19–35. January–March.

Rashid, Salman, and Mohit Suneja. 2013. *I Too Have Seen Lahore*. In *This Side That Side: Restorying Partition*, curated by Vishwajyoti Ghosh. New Delhi: Yoda Press.

Ravikant. 2016. *Media ki Bhasha-leela*. New Delhi: Vani Prakashan.

Ravikant, and Tarun Saint. 2001. 'The Dog of Tetwal in Context.' In *Translating Partition*, eds. Ravikant and Tarun Saint. New Delhi: Katha.

Roy, Anjali Gera. 2016. *Cinema of Enchantment: Perso-Arabic Genealogies of the Hindi Masala Film*. New Delhi: Orient BlackSwan.

Russell, Ralph. 1995. *Hidden in the Lute: An Anthology of Two Centuries of Urdu Literature*. New Delhi: Viking.

Sadiq, M. 1984. *A History of Urdu Literature*. New Delhi: Oxford University Press.

Saeed, Yousuf. 2008. 'Fled is That Music.' *India International Centre Quarterly* 35(3/4): 238–249. http://www.jstor.org/stable/23006263 Accessed 4 July 2017.

Sahni, Bhisham. 1980. *Apni Baat*. New Delhi: Rajkamal Prakashan.

———. 2004. *Aaj Ke Ateet*. New Delhi: Rajkamal Prakashan.

———. 2015. *Today's Pasts: A Memoir*, trans. Snehal Shingavi. Gurgaon: Penguin.

Saint, Tarun K. 2010. *Witnessing Partition: Memory, History, Fiction*. New Delhi: Routledge.

Samaddar, Ranabir. 2003. 'The Last Hurrah that Continues.' In *Divided Countries, Separated Cities: The Modern Legacy of Partition*, eds. Ghislaine Glasson Deschaumes and Rada Ivekovic. New Delhi: Oxford University Press.

Sarkar, Bhaskar. 2010. *Mourning the Nation: Indian Cinema in the Wake of Partition*. 200–239. New Delhi: Orient BlackSwan.

Sarwar, Beena. 2013. *Milne Do*. In *This Side That Side: Restorying Partition*, curated by Vishwajyoti Ghosh. New Delhi: Yoda Press.

Seervai, H. M. 1991. *Constitutional Law of India*, Vol. 1, 4th edition. Bombay: N. M. Tripathi.

Sen, Dwaipayan. 2012. 'No Matter How Jogendra Nath had to be Defeated: The Scheduled Castes Federation and the Making of Partition in Bengal 1945–47.' *Indian Economic and Social History Review* 49(3): 321–364.

———. 2012a. 'The Emergence and Decline of Dalit Politics in Bengal: Jogendranath Mandal, the Scheduled Castes Federation and Partition, 1932–1968.' Unpublished PhD Dissertation. University of Chicago.

Sengupta, Anwesha. 2012. '"Preserving" an Identity: Schedule Caste Politics in East Pakistan 1947–1952.' Paper presented at the International Students Conference, Centre for Historical Studies, Jawaharlal Nehru University. April.

_____. 2016. 'Breaking Up Bengal: Land, People and Things, 1947–1952.' Unpublished PhD Dissertation. Centre for Historical Studies, Jawaharlal Nehru University.

Schendel, Willem van. 2005. *The Bengal Borderland: Beyond State and Nation in South Asia.* 80, n54. London: Anthem Press.

Shackle, Christopher, and Javed Majeed, eds. 1997. *Hali's Musaddas: The Ebb and Flow of Islam.* New Delhi: Oxford University Press.

Siddiqi, Abdul Rahman. 2008. *Partition and the Making of the Mohajir Mindset.* 106–118. Karachi: Oxford University Press.

Sidhwa, Bapsi. 2002. 'The Way It Was: The Television Boycott.' *Daily Times,* Lahore. 23 July. Reproduced on *Sarai Reader* Mail List: http://mail.sarai.net/pipermail/reader-list_mail.sarai.net/2002-July.txt Accessed 4 July 2017.

Sikri, Meera. 2009. 'Saccho Sach.' In *Vibhajan: Bharatiya Bhashaon ki Kahaniyan,* Vol. 1, ed. Narendra Mohan. 298–303. New Delhi: Bharatiya Jnanpith.

Singh, Amritjit, Nalini Iyer, and Rahul Gairola, eds. 2016. *Revisiting India's Partition: New Essays on Memory, Culture and Politics.* Lanham: Lexington Books.

Singh, Jaswant. 2009. Quoted in 'Search for the Real Villain of Partition Divides India Again,' Andrew Buncombe. *Independent,* UK. 17 August. http://www.independent.co.uk/news/world/asia/search-for-the-real-villain-of-partition-divides-india-again-1773486.html Accessed 4 July 2017.

Sontag, Susan. 2003. *Regarding the Pain of Others.* New York: Picador.

Speigelman, Art. 1986. *Maus: A Survivor's Tale.* New York: Pantheon Books.

Steiner, George. 1967. 'K.' In *Language and Silence, Essays on Language, Literature and the Inhuman.* New York: Atheneum.

Sur, Malini. 2014. 'Divided Bodies: Crossing the India-Bangladesh Border.' *Economic and Political Weekly* 49(13): 31. March.

Talbot, Ian, and Gurharpal Singh. 2009. *The Partition of India.* 79–80. New Delhi: Cambridge University Press.

Talbot, Ian, ed. 2013. *The Independence of India and Pakistan: New Approaches and Reflections*. Pakistan: Oxford University Press.

Taunsvi, Fikr. 1988. 'Chhata Dariya: Taqseem-i-Hind ke Mauqe par Fasadat se Mut'aliq Roznamcha' (1948). In *Fikr Taunsvi: Hayat aur Karname*, ed. Shama Afroz Zaidi. 232–270. New Delhi: Biswi Sadi Publications.

Vasudevan, Ravi S. 2015. 'Film Genres, the Muslim Social, and Discourses of Modernity C. 1935–1945.' *BioScope* 6(1).

Virilio, Paul. 2005. 'The Politics of Disappearance.' In *Negative Horizons: An Essay in Dromoscopy*. London: Continuum.

Wajahat, Asghar. 2006. *Jis Lahore Nai Dekhya O Jamyai Nai*. New Delhi: Vani Prakashan.

Wavell, Archibald. 1973. *The Viceroy's Journal*. Delhi: Oxford University Press.

Zamindar, Vazira Fazila-Yacoobali. 2007. *The Long Partition and the Making of Modern South Asia: Refugees, Boundaries, Histories*. New York: Columbia University Press.

Select Filmography

Barsaat ki Raat (P. L. Santoshi, 1960)
Chacha Zindabad (Om Prakash, 1959)
Khayal Darpan: A Mirror of Imagination (Yousuf Saeed, 2006)
Komal Gandhar (Ritwik Ghatak, 1961)
Jukti, Takko aar Gappo (Ritwik Ghatak, 1974)
Meghe Dhaka Tara (Ritwik Ghatak, 1960)
Milange Baba Ratan De Mele Te (Ajay Bhardwaj, 2012).
Mousiqar (Qadeer Ghori, 1962)
Pakeezah (Kamal Amrohi, 1972)
Rabba Hun Ki Kariye (Ajay Bhardwaj, 2007).
Subarnarekha (Ritwik Ghatak, 1962)
Sur (Tanuja Chandra, 2002)
Tamas (Govind Nihalini, 1988)
Titash Ekti Nadir Naam (Ritwik Ghatak, 1973)

Notes on Contributors

JAVED AKHTAR is a scriptwriter, film lyricist and poet. He is the son of renowned Urdu poet Jan Nisar Akhtar and the writer Safiya Akhtar and the recipient of the Padma Shri (1999), Padma Bhushan (2007) and the Sahitya Akademi Award (2015).

ANWAR ALI (1922–2004), creator of the character Nanna, was the first cartoonist to be associated with *The Pakistan Times* from 1947 to 1977. He also worked for *Dawn* and *The Civil Military Gazette*. *Kaalian Ittan, Kaale Ror* and *Noori* are his collections of short stories.

SYED MUHAMMAD ASHRAF is Chief Commissioner of Income Tax, Kolkata. His work includes two collections of short stories *1994 Daar Se Bichchre* (1994) and *Baad-e Saba Ka Intizar* (2000), which won the Sahitya Akademi Award. His two novels are *Number Dar ka Neela* (1997) and *Akhri Sawariyan* (2016).

UNUM BABAR is a Pakistani artist, Fulbright Scholar, and Assistant Professor at Beaconhouse National University, School of Visual Arts and Design, Lahore.

ALOK BHALLA retired as Professor of English from English and Foreign Languages University, Hyderabad. His published works include *Stories About the Partition of India* (four volumes), and *Story is a Vagabond: Fiction, Essays and Drama by Intizar Husain* (co-edited with Asif Aslam Farrukhi and Nishat Zaidi, 2015).

SUNANDA BHATTACHARYA was born in Tripura. *Chanchtalay Rode* (2003) and *Borderer Golpo* (2014) are two of her short story collections. She lives and works in Delhi.

MAAZ BIN BILAL is a writer, poet, translator, and Assistant Professor at Jindal School of Liberal Arts and Humanities, O. P. Jindal Global University, Sonepat.

BIRENDRA CHATTOPADHYAY is a Bangla poet of the post-Tagorean era. *Sabha Bhengey Gelo* (1964) and *Mahadeber Duwar* (1967) are two of his poetry collections. He received the Rabindra Purashkar in 1982.

JULIEN COLUMEAU writes contemporary Urdu fiction and has published two prose collections, *Teen Novilette* and *Zahid Aur Do Kahaaniyaan*. *Zain Te Doojiyaan Kahaaniyaan*, a collection of his first stories in Punjabi, is forthcoming.

NABINA DAS, a writer and poet, teaches creative writing at the University of Hyderabad as a guest faculty. She has published a novel *Footprints in the Bajra* (2010), two books of poems, and a short story collection *The House of Twining Roses: Stories of the Mapped and the Unmapped* (2014).

ASIF ASLAM FARRUKHI, writer, scholar and translator, is the Director of the Arzu Centre for Regional Languages and Humanities and Dean, School of Arts and Humanities, Habib University, Karachi.

SANKHA GHOSH is a Bangla poet whose major collections of poetry include *Deenguli Raatguli* (1956), *Baborer Prarthona* (1976) and *Gandharba Kobitaguccho* (1994). He received the Padma Bhushan in 2011 and the Gyanpith in 2017.

VISHWAJYOTI GHOSH is a graphic novelist and author of *Delhi Calm* (2010). He is the curator of the anthology *This Side That Side: Restorying Partition* (2013).

SAIBAL KUMAR GUPTA (1902–1989) was an ICS officer who had served in many parts of undivided India. After 1947, he worked under the West Bengal government in the areas of Sports and Urban Planning.

KAISER HAQ, a Bangladeshi poet, essayist and translator, is Professor of English, University of Dhaka. His recent works include *Pariah and Other Poems* (2013), and *The Triumph of the Snake Goddess* (2015). He won the Bangla Academy Award in 2014.

SALIMA HASHMI is a Pakistani painter, art historian, curator and former Professor at the National College of Arts, Lahore. She is the eldest daughter of the renowned poet Faiz Ahmad Faiz and his British-born wife Alys Faiz.

ZARINA HASHMI is an Indian artist based in New York. Her work has been exhibited internationally and won numerous awards.

SELINA HOSSAIN is a novelist from Bangladesh who has authored several works, of which *Purno Chhobir Mognota* (2008) and *Japita Jiban* (1981) have received critical attention. She received the Ekushey Padak in 2009 and her works have been translated in many languages.

INTIZAR HUSAIN (1923–2016) was a legendary Pakistani writer and columnist. *Basti* (1979), *A Chronicle of the Peacocks* (2002), *Justujoo Kya Hai* (2012), and *Apni Danist Mein* (2014) are a few of his significant works. He was shortlisted for the Man Booker Award in 2013.

ASMAT JAHAN is Assistant Professor of English, Jamia Milia Islamia, New Delhi, and is interested in Translation Studies, Indian Literature and Eighteenth Century British Literature.

RAKHSHANDA JALIL is a writer, critic, translator and literary historian. She has published over twenty books, including *Release and Other Stories* (2011), *Invisible City: The Hidden Monument of Delhi* (revised reprint 2013), *New Urdu Writings: From India and Pakistan* (2013), and *Liking Progress, Loving Change* (2014).

NASIR KAZMI (1925–1972) was a Pakistani poet and one of the founders of the modern ghazal. He wrote extensively on the sufferings of Partition.

Margit Köves teaches Hungarian in the Department of Slavonic and Finno-Ugrian Studies, University of Delhi, and translates Hungarian prose into Hindi. Her works include *Resistible Rise: A Fascism Reader* (co-edited with S. Mazumdar, 2005), and *Gezababua* by János Háy (co-translated with Girdhar Rathi, 2008).

Sukrita Paul Kumar, a poet and critic, holds the Aruna Asaf Ali Chair, University of Delhi. Her published works include *Without Margins* (2005), *Speaking for Herself: An Anthology of Asian Women's Writings* (co-edited with Malashri Lal, 2009), and *Dream Catcher* (2016).

Sahir Ludhianvi (1921–1980) is the pen name of the poet and film lyricist Abdul Hayee. His first collection of poetry *Talkhiyan* [Bitterness], published in 1945, established him as a major voice in the Progressive Writers' Movement. He received the Padma Shri in 1971.

Aanchal Malhotra is a multidisciplinary artist, writer, oral historian, and was Assistant Curator at Chitrashala, the Museum of Indian Graphic Art in Kumaon, India. Her dissertation 'Remnants of a Separation' is a study of material memory of the 1947 Partition of India, archiving objects that refugees from both sides took with them when they migrated across the border.

Zakia Mashhadi has published five collections of short stories in Urdu and translated several books from English and Hindi into Urdu, and vice versa. A new collection of short stories, *Ankhan Dekhi*, and a novelette, *Parsa Bibi Ka Baghar*, are forthcoming.

Maya Mirchandani worked at NDTV for several years and has been reporting for television since 1994, making her amongst the first generation of Indian broadcast journalists.

Joya Mitra is a writer and activist based in Asansol, West Bengal. Her autobiographical work *Na Hanyaman* has been translated into English as *Killing Days: Prison Memoirs* (2004).

GURMUKH SINGH MUSAFIR (1899–1976) was born in Adhval, Campbellpur (now in Pakistan). His published works include nine collections of poems, eight anthologies of short stories, including *Vakkhri Duniya, Satai Janvari, Allah Wale*, and *Sasta Tamasha*. His book of short stories, *Urwar Par*, won the Sahitya Akademi Award posthumously.

HINA NANDRAJOG is Associate Professor, Department of English, currently serving as Officiating Principal, Vivekananda College, University of Delhi. She translates from Punjabi and Hindi into English, and won the Katha Prize for Translation (1999 and 2001).

ANIL NAURIYA is counsel at the Supreme Court of India and High Court of Delhi. His published works include *The African Element in Gandhi* (2006), and *Non-violent Action and Socialist Radicalism: Narendra Deva in India's Freedom Movement* (2015).

AMENA NAZLI (1914–1996) wrote short plays in Urdu for the radio and edited the journal *Ismat*. Her published works include *Doshala* (1945), a collection of short plays and *Hum Aur Tum* (1947), a collection of short stories.

FARHA NOOR is pursuing a PhD in Modern South Asian Studies at the University of Heidelberg, Germany. A native Bengali, she translates from Urdu, Hindi and Bengali.

JHUMUR PANDEY lives and works in Assam. *Jol Khaben Bonodurga* (2013) and *Sukh Gachher Golpo* (2005) are her short story anthologies and *Kichhu Bolar Chhilo*, a book of poems.

VIDYA RAO is a performer of thumri-dadra and ghazal, and disciple of the late Naina Devi, Shanti Hiranand and Girija Devi. The author of *Heart to Heart: Remembering Nainaji* (2011), she is an editorial consultant with Orient BlackSwan.

RAVIKANT, a bilingual historian, writer and translator, is Associate Professor, Centre for the Study of Developing Societies, New Delhi. He has authored *Media ki Bhasha-Leela* (2016), and *Translating Partition* (with Tarun Saint, 2001).

MANAS RAY is Professor, Centre for Studies in Social Sciences, Kolkata. He is the author of *Growing Up Refugee* (2002), and works in the field of Cultural Studies.

TARUN K. SAINT is an independent scholar who taught English literature at Hindu College until recently. His published works include *Witnessing Partition* (2010), *Bruised Memories: Communal Violence and the Writer* (ed., 2002), and *Translating Partition* (co-edited with Ravikant, 2001).

ANWESHA SENGUPTA is Assistant Professor, Institute of Development Studies, Kolkata. She completed her doctoral research from the Centre for Historical Studies, Jawaharlal Nehru University.

DEBJANI SENGUPTA teaches at Indraprastha College for Women, Delhi University. She has authored *The Partition of Bengal: Fragile Borders and Unstable Identities* (2016) and edited *Mapmaking: Partition Stories from Two Bengals* (2003, 2011). Her translations have been published in *Oxford Anthology of Bengali Literature* (Vol. 2) and *Essential Tagore*.

MEERA SIKRI was born in 1941 in Gujranwala (now in Pakistan). She won the Hindi Akademi's Kriti Samman (2002–03) for her short story collection *Balatkar aur Anya Kahaniyan*, and the Lekhika Ratna Samman (2007–09) for her novel *Anupasthit*.

FIKR TAUNSVI (1918–1987) was the pen name of Ram Lal Bhatia born in Taunsa Sharif, now in Pakistan. An Urdu poet, critic and writer, he wrote the satirical column 'Pyaaz ke Chhilke' [Onion Skins] for the Urdu daily *Milap*.

KAJAL TEHRI is Assistant Professor, University of Delhi, whose areas of interest include Partition Studies, Indian Writing in English and British Romantic Literature.

SAMEER ABRAHAM THOMAS is an MA student of English at Shiv Nadar University, New Delhi.

ASGHAR WAJAHAT retired as Professor of Hindi from Jamia Millia Islamia, New Delhi. His published works include *Dilli Pahunchna Hai* (1981), *Mai Hindu Hoon* (2006), *Jis Lahore Nai Dekhya O Jamyai Nai* (1991), and *Godse@Gandhi.com* (2012).

NISHAT ZAIDI is Professor of English, Jamia Millia Islamia, New Delhi. Her publications include *Story is a Vagabond: Fiction, Essays and Drama* by Intizar Husain (co-edited with Alok Bhalla and Asif Farrukhi, 2015), *Makers of Indian Literature: Agha Shahid Ali* (2014), *and Pencil and Other Poems* (2014).

Index